Radiant Days

Radiant Days

Writings by Enos Mills

Edited by John Dotson

Foreword by Bill McKibben

University of Utah Press
Salt Lake City

Enos Mills selections © 1994 by Enda Mills Kiley; photographs © 1994 by Elizabeth M. Mills; introduction © 1994 by John Dotson
All rights reserved

♾ Printed on acid-free paper

Frontispiece: Enos Mills at Longs Peak Inn, 1920s; photographer unknown.

LIBRARY OF CONGRESS CATALOGING-IN-PUBLICATION DATA

Mills, Enos Abijah, 1870–1922.
    Radiant days : writings / by Enos Mills ; edited by John Dotson ; foreword by Bill McKibben.
        p.   cm.
    Includes bibliographical references.
    1. Natural history—West (U.S.) 2. Natural history—Outdoor books. 3. Natural history—Rocky Mountains. 4. Rocky Mountains—Description and travel. 5. Mills, Enos Abijah, 1870–1922.
    I. Dotson, John, 1950– . II. Title.
QH104.5.W4M54   1994
508.78—dc20   94-27590

Book design by Richard Firmage

Contents

Foreword		vii
Introduction		ix
1.	Camping on the Plains	3
2.	A Nose for News	17
3.	Tramp Days of Grizzly Cubs	29
4.	Trailing without a Gun	36
5.	The Story of a Thousand-Year Pine	47
6.	A Coyote Den by the River	58
7.	Summer Travels of a Beaver	66
8.	The Ruined Colony	75
9.	The Forest Fire	87
10.	The Love Song of Little Blue	104
11.	A Mountain Pony	122
12.	Trailing Utah's Shore Lines	131
13.	Ups and Downs of the Grand Cañon	143
14.	Trees at Timberline	155
15.	Wild Mountain Sheep	165
16.	Winter Mountaineering	178
17.	Wind-Rapids on the Heights	190

18. Snow-Blinded on the Summit	200
19. Racing an Avalanche	213
Enos Mills Chronology	221
Selected Bibliography	223

Foreword

ENOS MILLS WAS A LUCKY MAN. He was independent enough to set off at the age of fourteen for the West, where he landed at the foot of Longs Peak, as sweet a spot as you can find. He was eventually strong and healthy enough to climb and snowshoe most of that part of the state of Colorado that lies above tree line. He was sensible and sensitive enough to realize that animals were more than dinner encased in fur, Engelmann spruce more than timber in the raw, the Rockies more than a hiding place for minerals—and so he had the great joy of countless hours lying still and just watching. Most of all, perhaps, he was fortunate enough to meet John Muir in San Francisco. As a result of that encounter his life took on new purpose—protecting America's wild lands by showing them to all he could, by writing about them in his infectious, enthusiastic essays, and by forcing the politicians to rope them off from commerce.

Would that each of your meetings with Mills prove as important, though in reverse. We have lots of environmentalists now, but too few naturalists. He calls us not just to action, but to the woods. He would like us to establish more national parks, but he would like us, too, to sit very still on a fallen tree and watch the woodpecker at work, the bear in transit. "Irresistible is nature's call to play," he writes. Irresistible too is Mills's call to nature.

—Bill McKibben

Longs Peak, across Tahosa Valley, Colorado

Introduction

Enos Mills of Colorado Nature-lover and Interpreter

More than ten thousand climbers set out to reach the summit of Longs Peak in Rocky Mountain National Park each year. The majority succeed, but as an old saying has it, the peak does not stay conquered.

Longs is roughly equidistant from Chicago and San Francisco and just over forty miles north of Denver. At 14,255 feet, the peak exceeds the elevation of all peaks to the north of it in the Rocky Mountains. Prominently visible for fifty miles from the plains, Longs Peak and adjoining Mount Meeker appeared to the Arapaho as Nesotaieux, the Two Guides. French-speaking trappers took their bearings from Les Deux Oreilles, the Two Ears. The Great Peak mentioned by Zebulon Pike in 1806 may have been Longs, but the peak's official name came in 1829 when members of an army expedition so memorialized their leader, Major Stephen Long. Longs was a landmark for John C. Frémont in 1842, and Kit Carson likely trapped in the vicinity in the 1840s.

By 1866, the renown of the peak was such that science-fiction author Jules Verne placed on its flat summit an observatory for tracking space travelers in his novel, *From Earth to the Moon*. In 1868, the first non–Native Americans on record as achieving the summit were led by John Wesley Powell who journeyed on to make his historic explorations of the

Colorado River and Grand Canyon the following summer. William Henry Jackson photographed Longs in 1873, and that same year, English journalist Isabella L. Bird, author of *A Lady's Life in the Rocky Mountains*, reached the summit. Albert Bierstadt accepted a commission to paint Longs in 1876.

Perhaps no individual has known Longs Peak better or been more deeply influenced by it than Enos Abijah Mills, Jr. He made it to "the top of the world," three hundred times, forty times solo. He reached the top at every hour of day and night, in all months and seasons, the first to do so in winter, and the first to do so by way of the precipitous north face.

Features near Longs Peak bear names he gave them—Battle Mountain, Storm Peak, and Sandbeach Lake. Later, Mills Lake, Mills Glacier, Mills Moraine, and the Mills Route on the Diamond facet of the north face carry his name. Rocky Mountain National Park, centered on Longs Peak, carries his dream.

East of Longs Peak, in Tahosa Valley, the homestead cabin that Mills built as a teenager in 1885 is still maintained by the Mills family as a National Historic Landmark open to visitors. A monument placed by the Daughters of the American Revolution reads

Enos A. Mills
Father of the Rocky Mountain National Park,
Internationally known naturalist,
author, lecturer and nature guide,
homesteaded on this site
1885

On a hand-lettered wooden shingle beside the cabin door appear Mills's words: "This is a beautiful world and all who go out under the open sky will feel the gentle influences of nature."

A writing desk beneath the single window allows the guest

Introduction

Homestead cabin with Twin Sisters in background

to experience the westward vision of this place that Mills felt he belonged to—more than it belonged to him.

Under glass are several labeled photographs: "The Birthplace of Enos A. Mills near Fort Scott, Kansas"—a sturdy and ample plains farmhouse. "Parents of Enos Mills, Pleasanton, Kansas"—Ann Mills a scant, pioneer woman in a black, Quaker-style dress with bloused sleeves; Enos, Senior, seated, in a three piece suit with watch-chain, well-worn shoes. "Enos Mills of the Rockies, First Trip Up Longs, 1885"—

climbing up the Homestretch, young Enos twists to face the camera. "Enos Mills and His Mother at Longs Peak Inn"—she much as described above, her accomplished son at her side. "Enos and Esther Mills"—in front of the inn, Enos and his wife, both wearing pants and high-laced mountain boots.

Nearby bookshelves display Mills's gold pan, a photograph of Mills among nearly fifty other young miners at the Anaconda copper mine in Montana, a call slip from the Butte Free Public Library. Double-thick winter socks and hobnail boots, crampons and binoculars surround a placard with a Mills maxim:

> Go light! Take camera, binoculars, hatchet, matches, raisins, notebook, raincoat.

Mills considered raisins to be the ideal energy food for mountain climbing, and it was at his suggestion that a national manufacturer marketed raisins in individual serving size boxes.

On a rough-hewn table rests a glass case holding the Kodak reflex camera with which Mills exposed over twenty thousand negatives.

Above the case hangs a framed letter with expansive handwriting:

> Martinez, Aug 2: 1907
>
> Dear Mr. Mills:
> When you come to California come to my home. Every forest lover is welcome & I'll be glad to see you. Congratulations in your fine work.
>
> I am faithfully yours,
> John Muir.

Against the table leans a large, heavy-framed official document with highly embellished, antique calligraphy—Resolutions of Respect from The State Historical and Natural History Society of Colorado. It is dated two months after Mills's death and pronounces that the directors do

Introduction

...most heartily commend the staunch western spirit of this loyal mountaineer... his dispositions to familiarize himself with the works of nature about him, the plants, birds and beasts of the majestic mountains among which he spent his best days and did his immortal work; his willingness to defy danger and death in order to disclose the secrets of rock, stream and forest; and finally his toil and patience in recording the knowledge thus obtained, and bestowing it as a priceless heritage upon his approving countrymen.

Enos Mills and His Times

Born April 22, 1870, Enos Mills was the third youngest of eleven children. Eager, in the Quaker tradition, for westward migration, Mills's parents had trekked from Indiana to Iowa to southeast Kansas where they settled on a farm in Linn County, five miles south of Pleasanton.

Ill-suited for farm work by a digestive problem—diagnosed by his father as a "stubborn streak" but more likely an allergic reaction to wheat, of all things—Mills followed his mother's urgings to set out for Colorado. Ann Lamb Mills, "a dreamer and a story-teller," seems to have roused her son's imagination and nurtured his independence. She held memories of the Rockies from traveling there with her husband at the time of the Breckenridge gold rush in 1859.

In the summer of 1884, at age fourteen, Enos Mills headed for Kansas City. He earned sufficient wages as a baker's helper to purchase a railroad ticket to "beautiful and progressive" Denver City. On the recommendation of his sister Naomi, Mills traveled on to Estes Park, a resort area since Joel Estes had first raised a cabin there in 1860.

South of Estes Park, Longs Peak Valley (Tahosa Valley) was the home of the Reverend Elkanah Lamb to whom Mills was related through both parents. Lamb had cut the first road into the valley, and, in 1875, he had built the cabin that would later become Longs Peak House. Mills found a summer job at Elkhorn Lodge in Estes Park, then he hitched on as a ranch hand in the eastern part of the state for the winter. Returning to the high country to work for Lamb in the summer of 1885, Mills was soon guided by Lamb's son, Carlyle, to the summit of Longs Peak for the first time. That season, Mills staked his claim, and although it was tentative until his twenty-first birthday, he began raising his own homestead cabin. He left it unfinished and occupied himself for another winter ranching on the plains. The next summer he again worked with Carlyle and constructed the Longs Peak hiking trail. He also topped off his cabin.

In the summer of 1887, Mills climbed Longs Peak solo for the first time. At the end of the season he journeyed to Butte Hill in Montana territory, the Richest Hill on Earth, and apprenticed as a tool boy at the Anaconda mine. For the next sixteen winters he advanced through the ranks from nipper, miner, machine-driller, and compressor-man, to licensed stationary engineer.

Butte boasted the best library in the West. Mills directed his own reading of Shakespeare, Burns, Byron, Walter Scott, Dickens, and Robert Louis Stevenson. Studies of Darwin, Huxley, and Spencer brought him up to date with the prevailing scientific and social theories of his day. In the American literary lineage, Mills read Washington Irving, Emerson, Thoreau, Whitman, and Burroughs.

Finding Thomas Paine to be a particular hero, Mills's own free-thinking and at times eccentric attitude would combine with sufficient outbursts of ego and Scottish blood to overshadow many relationships—including some with family members—and to make real enemies of bureaucrats, cow grazers, timber cutters, prospectors, and hunters.

In the summer of 1889, Mills guided his first expedition to the summit of Longs Peak. That autumn, when a fire closed the mine at Butte, Mills set out for the Pacific coast. There he happened upon John Muir at age fifty-one and still three years away from founding the Sierra Club.

Muir was guiding a small group that had stopped to exam-

Introduction

ine a specimen of yerba buena on the beach near the Cliff House in San Francisco when Mills approached him. Their conversation extended for four miles through the area where Golden Gate Park was taking shape and resulted in an invitation for Mills to visit Muir at home. The two later hiked Mount Tamalpais.

Muir suggested that Mills put his knowledge in order and learn to write and speak publicly. Until his death in 1914, Muir remained a source of vivid inspiration and encouraged Mills especially in the fight to establish Rocky Mountain National Park.

After exploring the national wonders of California, Mills enrolled at Heald's Business College in San Francisco and obtained business skills he would later apply at Longs Peak Inn.

Mills continued his mining career into his twenties, visited Yellowstone, and worked with a geological survey party. He visited Alaska twice, the second time hiking alone more than two hundred miles on his return to Juneau. He traveled to Chicago for the Columbian Exposition in 1893 and was impressed with the human ingenuity exhibited as well as with the beauty of Lake Michigan.

On a later expedition, he traced the Missouri River from its source in Montana to its confluence with the Mississippi in St. Louis and onward to the Gulf of Mexico. At age twenty-five, in Kansas City, he delivered his first address on forestry. Soon after he took an assignment to report news of Estes Park to Denver newspapers.

Mills marked his thirtieth birthday and the turn of the century by joining Elkanah Lamb for a five-week European tour that included Stratford-on-Avon, Burns's birthplace, the Paris Exposition, the Swiss Alps, and Mount Vesuvius—which he climbed.

Mills published his first major article in *Outdoor Life* in 1902 in an era of a virtual awakening concerning threats to America's natural resources and the urgency of conservation. Mills quickly finished off his mining career, sufficiently well-off to purchase the Lamb acreage. Soon after, he acquired Longs Peak House, which he renamed Longs Peak Inn.

Longs Peak Inn was a unique and highly successful enterprise. Mills urged his guests to "go out under the open sky with confidence" that "unaltered nature" would "recharge" and "recreate" them. The rituals of the inn were intended to bond guests with one another, with the community of forest and mountain creatures, and with the whole environment.

Mornings began with Mills's legendary query, "Glad you're living?" Through the day, he would approach his guests to ask, "What's up?" He kept no piano, discouraged card games and "talk of movies," allowed no drinking and no firearms. He delivered nature talks after dinner, would usher guests outside alone and particularly into the rain.

Famous guests at Longs Peak Inn included novelist and playwright Edna Ferber, after whom Mills's daughter was named; labor leader Eugene V. Debs, a close friend; novelist Gene Stratton Porter; lawyer, lecturer, and author Clarence Darrow; jurist Charles Evans Hughes; social activist and writer Jane Addams, recipient of the Nobel peace prize in 1931; biologist and educator David Starr Jordan; and actor Douglas Fairbanks, Sr.

In a rather exotic arrangement, Mills was contracted for two winters as snowman for the state, that is, the first official snow observer for the Colorado State Irrigation Department. This experimental work involved hiking the upper slopes of the Rockies through the winter and sending information as promptly as possible to Denver so that projections could be made of the summer water supply for the lowlands. On one exploit, Mills hiked 120 miles in six days. Subsequently, he hiked along the Great Divide the full length of the state of Colorado—from Wyoming to New Mexico—in the dead of winter.

In 1903, he made the first recorded winter climb of Longs Peak. Two years later, at age thirty-five, he published his first book, *The Story of Estes Park and a Guide Book,* and presented eighty lectures on a tour of eastern cities. In the sum-

Introduction

mer of 1906, his last as a guide, Mills led at least seventy-five parties to Longs Peak, thirty-two ascents in the month of August alone. On an autumn lecture tour in the east, Mills formed an acquaintance with John Burroughs.

Early in 1907, President Theodore Roosevelt invited Mills to become Government Lecturer on Forestry, a position that enhanced and expanded Mills's already growing reputation throughout the country. He resigned after two years when his first nationally distributed book, *Wild Life on the Rockies,* was published by Houghton-Mifflin of Boston. This house also published Muir and Burroughs, both of whom Mills routinely outsold. Like Muir, Mills also published articles in *Atlantic, Collier's, Harper's, Sunset, Country Life, American Boy,* and *Youth's Companion.* He supplied more than fifty pieces to the *Saturday Evening Post.*

Having addressed more than two thousand audiences on forestry topics, speaking "at least twice in every state and territory in the Union," and continuing to publish widely and frequently, Mills had become a nationally recognized figure by his fortieth birthday. He travelled continually, often to Washington, D.C.

Less than a year after Muir's death, Mills realized what he considered to be his great life achievement—the creation of Rocky Mountain National Park. President Woodrow Wilson signed the bill establishing America's thirteenth national park on January 26, 1915. Enos Mills stood as master of ceremonies at the park dedication on September 4.

In 1916, Congress approved the Organic Act incorporating contributions of both Muir and Mills in founding the National Park Service. At home, Mills determined that the success of the inn warranted its expansion. He also met the youthful Esther Burnell who quickly became his secretary and protégé.

In 1917, Mills published his triumphant volume, *Your National Parks,* though public attention was soon diverted from conservationist causes by America's entry in the First World War. In the summer of 1918, as Mills turned forty-eight, Esther Burnell, twenty years younger, became his wife in a ceremony in the homestead cabin.

Mills continued to take initiatives, developing a trail school both for training nature guides and for conducting summer programs. He commissioned his well-credentialed sister-in-law, Elizabeth Burnell, as director. He himself watched over the thriving inn operations and prepared numerous manuscripts for publication while becoming mired, ironically and inextricably, in conflicts with the National Park Service he had helped institute.

The mission of the Park Service had been stated to "conserve the scenery and the natural and historic objects and wildlife therein and to provide for the enjoyment of same in such manner and by such means as will leave them unimpaired for the enjoyment of future generations." Details were left to the director of the service and to park superintendents with full confidence that a progressive, rational bureaucracy would carry through.

The first director, Stephen Mather, seemed to bring imagination and foresight to his commission. Mather recognized that adept nature interpretation was needed to prepare visitors for appropriate wilderness experiences and to teach principles of preservation. Since Enos Mills had pioneered the art and science of interpretation as a full profession and had been the first to establish a school to train interpreters, his advice to Mather contributed much to the evolution of ranger naturalists. Only later did the role devolve to one of protecting people from the parks and protecting parks from people.

The great conflict that came about between Mills and Mather centered on the issues of concessioners and jurisdiction over roads. Most visitors in the early days arrived by train and coach and needed suitable accommodations and transportation. Reacting to abuses by gougers, Mather favored concessioner monopolies in the belief they could be strictly regulated. Thinking in stark terms of right and wrong, Mills's extended conflict hinged on legal nuances that were

Introduction

exceedingly complex but caused such painful confusion that he felt personally persecuted.

In 1919, the year his daughter Enda was born, Mills sued Mather. The struggle kept Mills on the lecture circuit throughout the country. But the war had brought rapid economic and social change. Race riots erupted in twenty-six cities. Twenty-two million persons died in a worldwide outbreak of influenza, the worst pandemic since the Black Death. Audiences lost interest in Mills's entrepreneurial battle with the Park Service.

Domestic travel after the war was on the increase and prospects for the inn were bright, but in the judgement of Enos Mills of the Rockies, many people had become "pleasure bent" and "money mad."

In January, 1922, Mills suffered injuries from a subway collision in New York City. Emotionally depleted, he succumbed to a tooth infection that developed into septicemia. Mills died on September 22, autumnal equinox.

The funeral was conducted in the lobby of Longs Peak Inn by his close friend, Judge Ben Lindsey of Denver, who eulogized that while "men like Zebulon Pike discovered the bodies of our mountains . . . Mills discovered their souls."

Sunrays pierced the notch in Longs Peak as the service concluded with Keats's trenchant lines read in epitaph,

"Beauty is truth, truth beauty,"—that is all
Ye know on earth, and all ye need to know.

Across the Atlantic, novelist Thomas Hardy wrote, "It is as if a mountain peak had sunk below the horizon."

Later, Esther Mills had her husband's body exhumed and cremated, with ashes scattered by airplane over the Longs Peak region.

The Writings

These selections of the writings of Enos Mills have been made on the basis of quality and their suggestion of the variety of Mills's work. They are arranged to present a diverse

Enos Mills on Cricket with Scotch

and balanced sequence of themes—wilderness environments, experiences with animals, contemplations of primal discoveries, and journeys of high adventure.

Overall, the selections move from the simplicity and lower elevation of the first story detailing one of Mills's earliest outings, "Camping on the Plains," to the peak experiences of Mills's maturity portrayed in the final story, "Snow-blinded on the Summit."

Introduction

That silent waiting could be high adventure in the manner of Enos Mills would strike most individuals today as an alien concept, but wait he did: "In Alaska, Canada, Mexico, and in every state in the Union I have sat by a camp-fire all alone." He mentions waits of hours, days, weeks. In "Camping on the Plains" (from *Waiting in the Wilderness*, 1921), Mills re-creates a place with "not a person within fifteen miles, perhaps not for twice as far" where he hikes for days without seeing a house or a fence. Developing powers of visualization, Mills learns to center himself. On hands and knees, he integrates instinct and intellect in a practice he terms simply "woodcraft."

In "A Nose for News" (from *Wild Animal Homesteads*, 1923), Mills explains a way of gaining information vital to animals and virtually lost to civilized humankind. Mills counsels that when the continuity of body-sense and environment is intact, life is lived more abundantly. Human beings, in Mills's view, have projected onto wild creatures something of the Darwinian notion that wilderness is a bloody battleground of unceasing hostilities, yet he proposes that those who wait patiently will discern "the greater wilderness of coöperation."

Nature writer Barry Lopez speaks of the observation of animals as the study of cultures "developing in parallel to human culture." Enos Mills possibly gathered more firsthand knowledge of the culture of grizzlies than has any other human being. In "Tramp Days of Grizzly Cubs" (from *Waiting in the Wilderness*, 1921), Mills observes grizzlies early in their life cycle. As he often does, he writes with special sensitivity for young creatures and the truths he learns from them, particularly regarding the play instinct. "Trailing without a Gun" (from *The Grizzly, Our Greatest Wild Animal*, 1919) portrays a dramatic episode in the lives of two cunning adults, one human, one bear. Strongly vouching for the intelligence of his trail companion, Mills also celebrates Old Timberline's "sheer joy" in the snow. The last grizzly in Rocky Mountain National Park was lost during Mills's lifetime.

The veteran ponderosa in "The Story of a Thousand-Year-Pine" (from *Wild Life on the Rockies,* 1909) was cut down in 1903. Mills's reading of its rings preceded the development of modern dendrochronology by nearly a decade. The science is, however, secondary to the contemplation. This story, Mills's most popular and most frequently told, was a vehicle for lifting his audiences out of their daily lives into the larger cycle of tree time that concludes in a poetic vision.

In "A Coyote Den by the River" (from *Wild Animal Homesteads*), Mills berates the mayhem and disruption caused by firearms and indicates the clear advantages of venturing unarmed. While this tale ends unhappily, the account is straightforward with an application that death is integral to the organic wholeness of life.

After birds, Mills holds more affection for the beaver than for any other creatures. This affection is recounted with a full display of Mills's animated curiosity in "Summer Travels of a Beaver" (from *Wild Animal Homesteads,* 1923). The events in "The Ruined Colony" (from *In Beaver World,* 1913) occur when Mills is seventeen. As elsewhere, he profiles human destructiveness by illuminating the dignity of the animals he watches. Distinctions of human and animal are not sharp for Mills. When he regards beaver as "engineers," he is using that term in its original reference to clever inventors with innate mental powers to engender useful designs. When he refers to beaver "industry," the word is not yet tainted. Mills tells much that we can learn from beaver culture about the continuity of the life process—birth, growth, maturity, parenthood, death. The beaver provide salient lessons not only in their tenacity but also in their playfulness and enjoyment of life despite ruination and upheaval. Mills recorded observations of the Moraine Colony of beaver on Roaring Fork Creek for thirty-six years.

While many may know the joy of heading out on a high-altitude trail at dawn, few have the opportunity or inclination to embrace the expanse of possibility Enos Mills avows: "All

Introduction xxiii

autumn was to be mine . . . upon this alpine skyline." In "The Forest Fire" (from *The Spell of the Rockies*, 1911), Mills accepts the mystery of life as personal, organic, cosmic reality. The fire's "eloquent death song" is followed by fierce explosions, an ominous, elemental silence, and a stark feast.

In "The Love Song of Little Blue" (from *Bird Memories of the Rockies*, 1931), Mills describes the "barbaric sport" of a boy who later brags to "proud parents" about his destructiveness. Mills feels the loss as a deep personal tragedy. Still, out of it comes new awareness and renewed exuberance. For Mills, to know the humblest of creatures as individuals and to have companionship with them affords insights of a higher moral and spiritual order. To honor the human in animals is to some extent to respect the animal in the human and to know life on earth as a balanced partnership.

"A Mountain Pony" (from *Rocky Mountain Wonderland*, 1915) is a death-defying horse story of the first order. The flavor of a Colorado mining town is poignant here also. The protagonist is Cricket, a return horse. As Mills explains, a return horse is "one that will go home at once when set free by the rider, even though the way be through miles of trailless mountains," rendering a peculiar service to those not wishing to climb up a slope though willing to climb down it. Cricket became Mills's permanent mount and lived past age thirty.

Mills is dismayed in "Trailing Utah's Shore Lines" (from *Romance of Geology*, 1926) that teachers in the Utah schools he visits do not share his belief that their students would be bettered by knowing the geology of their home place. "I assumed that everyone in Utah knew the wonderful story of old Lake Bonneville." For Mills, knowledge of nature stimulates active imagination, alters perception of time, and enlivens curiosity and eagerness: "Several times I wished there had been children with me to enjoy the romance of it, for none of the older people along the way caught the story."

"Ups and Downs of the Grand Cañon" (from *Romance of Geology*, 1926), exemplifies the acute writing Mills accomplishes by joining direct personal experience with "solid information." The source of the Colorado River is La Poudre Pass on the Continental Divide in Rocky Mountain National Park, west of Enos Mills's cabin.

In "Trees at Timberline" (from *The Adventures of a Nature Guide,* 1920), Mills conveys his sensation of leaving behind the polarities and oppositions of the human condition at lower altitudes. Having hiked hundreds of miles at timberline, he attests that those who follow the high trails with open hearts can discover nature's wisdom symbolically and in plain view. "Trees have tongues." A campfire can transform onlookers into time travelers. Frequently presenting elevation as distance "above the sea" and "above the tides," Mills expresses his knowledge of the complete water cycle: mountain snows and rushing streams, rivers and plains, sea and sky, sky and snow. Mills was among the first popular writers to bring to public consciousness the interconnectedness of such functions as that of beaver dams in preventing floods on the plains below.

By Mills's time, the animals described in "Wild Mountain Sheep" (from *Rocky Mountain Wonderland,* 1915) had already been endangered by the intrusion and disease of domestic flocks. Their habitat he describes as "wildly royal and romantic," the quintessence of the "richness and nobility" to be found in the national parks. Mills's description of the ram slain on barbed wire in reacting to human movements has the semblance of a religious image. Although mountain sheep were gone from the lower elevations in Rocky Mountain National Park by mid-twentieth century, recent corrective actions have allowed Colorado's animal symbol to survive and to thrive.

"Winter Mountaineering" (from *The Adventures of a Nature Guide,* 1920) expresses Mills's willingness to be vulnerable to elemental powers; peril and injury are simply part of the wilderness process. He celebrates the sublime breakthrough in lifting his head above the upper threshold of a blowing snowstorm, penetrating the veil between ground be-

Introduction

The Narrows on Longs Peak with climbers

low and sky above. The experience only heightens when he discovers that a surprise guest has preceded him.

The landmarks of "Wind-Rapids on the Heights" (from *The Adventures of a Nature Guide*, 1920) will be familiar to those who have followed Mills's path over Granite Pass, through the Keyhole and along the Narrows toward the summit of Longs Peak. All those who have done so will appreciate the interpersonal character of Mills's relationship with the winds. His language strains here, yearning for the poetry to express these phenomenal interactions.

> We simply cannot tell what nature will have of us, or where next. But from near and far, ever calls her eloquent voice . . . It was seriously splendid to play with these wild winds. There is no greater joy than wrestling naked handed with the elements.

In "Snow-Blinded on the Summit" (from *The Adventures of a Nature Guide,* 1920), stripped of his snow glasses, forced into life and death choices on the Continental Divide, Mills is for once, "thoroughly, briefly, frightened." His body-senses are heightened, his faculties "intensely awake." Imagination becomes his "guiding faculty." In this ultimate test, a successful descent is contingent on his intimate knowledge of the environment. He contemplates the unity of life and death while transferring heat from the carcass of a mountain sheep into his own body. Journeying in blindness, he comes down from the mountain to encounter a little girl with a curious welcome.

The final text of this collection, "Racing an Avalanche" (from *The Spell of the Rockies,* 1911), illuminates Mills's exuberant eagerness to explore the transpersonal forces of nature by entering the flow of chaotic conditions with the full force of his own physical and intellectual powers. The story is a fine example of Mills's vigorous confidence that the fulfillment of the human occurs in active engagement with larger life-processes that continuously form the context of all our experience.

Readers at the close of the twentieth century may at times find Enos Mills's prose to be cutely sentimental, quaintly embellished, inhibited. Mills does not speak to the dark side of things not only because of his Victorian sensibilities but also because of his explicit outlook that the benign and cooperative side of nature predominates.

Introduction xxvii

His familiar reference to animals as "folks," addressing them as "Mr. and Mrs. Coyote" and so forth, may jar at first and remind some readers of the nature faker phenomenon of the early 1900s when some popular writers transformed animals into anthropomorphic heroes. Mills writes after those controversies had subsided, but he remains a storyteller first, then scientist and rhetorician. His language was comfortable to his readership, most of whom commonly had contacts with animals in daily life.

Enos Mills finds his literary voice in the Progressive Era, the Gilded Age. He expresses genuine concern for the public welfare in accord with democratic tenets of the national park movement. Admiring of children, Mills often wrote for the youth who encountered his articles in classrooms across the country, and he conscientiously stood as an exemplar. His earnest tone blends a laborious perfectionism with outspoken, righteous zeal.

Mills's philosophical and humanitarian standpoints harmonize with the precepts of a Quaker heritage that opposes war, advocates equality of races and sexes, and supports quality education; institutional religious forms are to be avoided. In this tradition, every creature and every particle of creation has a place in the total cosmic order. Individuals may gain access to the ever-present inner light through silent waiting.

Such religious imagination had shaped Mills's insights that the individual "who feels the spell of the wild, the rhythmic melody of falling water, the echoes among the crags, the birdsongs, the wind in the pines, and the endless beat of wave upon the shore, is in tune with the universe."

Assuming the majority of his readership to acknowledge some form of transcendent deity and to be familiar with the philosophies of Emerson and Thoreau, Mills speaks in his own manner of divine immanence and pastoral myth. Using upper case frequently, he refers to wilderness in one sentence as "No Man's Land, the Undiscovered Country, the Mysterious Old West, the Land of Romance and Adventure." He evokes feelings for the Great Mother.

> If you are dulled and dazed with the fever and the fret, or weary and worn, — tottering under burdens too heavy to bear — go back to the old outdoor home. Here Nature will care for you as a mother for a child. In the mellow-lighted forest aisles . . . amid the silence of the centuries, you will come into your own.

In the starkly patriarchal West, Enos Mills — pure idealist, fiercely independent conservationist, quirky eccentric — exudes his eagerness to converse with bluebirds, to nurture their wounded young, to observe animal families and communities for hours and days at a time, to defend wildflowers. For Mills, the Rocky Mountain wilderness is not opaque, dark or menacing but rather infused with radiance. Instead of a rifle, he carries a camera.

Although the first-person narrator is ever central, the tenor of Mills's narratives remains somehow self-effacing, his exploits a celebration of spunk, curiosity, and self-reliance more than personal heroics. Mills motivates readers who perceive wilderness either as threat or as bonanza to find out for themselves the sensation of direct discovery.

"Go out into the wilderness and meet yourself," he advises. Be receptive to new perceptions of what is real and what is possible beyond the scale of an isolated human life.

> Stirring and wild, wonderful scenes are encountered during storms on mountain-tops, by the lakeshore, and in cañons. The dangers in such times and places are fewer than in cities. Discomforts? Scarcely. To some persons life must be hardly worth living. If any normal person under fifty cannot enjoy being in a storm in the wilds, he ought to reform at once.

Mills's enduring theme is that Nature provides her own timeless wisdom in bringing health to body and to soul. The cycle of human life and all life includes insuring the young opportunity to survive, helping the mature to thrive, and allowing the old to die with integrity.

Introduction

He continually insists that the spell of the high country can transform human nature through a consciousness of freedom so immediate and profound as to become childlike play. Novelist Wallace Stegner described the Rocky Mountain region as "the native home of hope." Enos Mills once dreamed that Colorado's entire front range might be set apart as a "playground for the nation."

Through these writings, Mills still serves as nature guide and interpreter. He proposes that any one of us may fill the role of guide and interpreter, qualified first of all by the devotion and immediate experience of being a nature lover. Were he alive today, he would surely be quick to point out that while some national park trails are worn out by popularity, the use of many others is actually declining.

The writings of Enos Mills form a vital component of American nature writing, and the voice of Enos Mills still suggests, "Why don't you start something?"

—John Dotson

Radiant Days

Big Thompson Road with Longs Peak in the background

1.
Camping on the Plains

I WALKED OUT OF CHEYENNE early one morning thirty-odd years ago with a camp outfit and a week's provisions. It was late May. One mile out and I was on the fenceless, trackless plains. The prairie was green with low-growing buffalo grass and brilliant with dashes of red, yellow, and blue wild flowers on short stems. Meadow larks were singing and prairie dogs barking merrily. The sun shone hot from a clear blue sky all day.

A little before sundown I dropped my heavy pack by an old buffalo wallow near the Wyoming-Nebraska line. I could see miles across level plains toward every point of the compass; not a house, a fence, or a tree within the horizon. I was alone. I judged there was not a person within fifteen miles, perhaps not for twice as far. Although I travelled about for days I did not see a house or a fence.

For months I had planned to have a camping trip out on the Great Plains to see what wild life lived on the prairie and how it lived. I felt that I was well prepared. I had learned to identify numbers of trees, birds, and wild flowers. I was certain I knew how to camp and especially that my camp equipment was correct. In fire starting I could have taken a prize. But I found myself embarrassed with green grass and old "cow-chips," by a treeless, rockless water hole.

At last I had a fire glowing in the darkness out in the lone wide prairie. The water hole by which I camped was a shallow buffalo wallow about fifty feet long and half as wide. Ten years before thousands of buffalo had ranged these scenes.

Water is scarce on the plains, and these wallows once served both the antelope and the buffalo as drinking places. The crowding stars seemed only a stone's throw above the wide, flat prairie, and the merry coyotes were having fun all around me when I lay down to sleep.

I wasted a lot of time the next morning in trying to find something among my too numerous pieces of camp outfit. Just as I had things scattered over the prairie two cowboys came riding up. They were from a cow outfit that was drifting northward and had seen me from afar. They were grazing two thousand head of cattle and had a six-horse cook wagon and seventy saddle ponies.

"What's this, a general merchandise store?" one of them called, pleasantly, as he viewed my equipment scattered around the water hole.

"The kid has more kitchenware than the cook at our cow camp," said the other kindly but merrily as they rode off.

The prairie dogs were yapping and scampering about and I threw my belongings into a heap and went toward the nearest dog town. They were excited over my presence: sat up and barked and chattered, and I am certain used bad language because I did not move on. When I approached nearer than twenty feet they ducked into their holes. They looked and acted more like fat woodchucks than dogs.

In a shallow ravine near camp I came close to a mother antelope and her two kids. She made the youngsters lie down the instant she saw me and then edged off, plainly with the hope of leading me to follow. But I wanted a closer view of the kids.

When I reached the spot where I supposed them lying I could not see them. A young antelope blends with the plains, plants, and soil so that it is well hidden when it flattens down. I stumbled over one of the youngsters. He leaped up and then I spied the second. But not until I had touched it with my hand did it quit playing dead and rush off with the other toward the mother.

They went only a short distance when they reentered the

Camping on the Plains

ravine. I slipped down this, crawled over a ridge, and came within a hundred feet of them. The youngsters were busy suckling. One was kneeling on each side, occasionally urging mother to speed the milk by butting her. When they started across the prairie I went far around and came in behind a low ridge, planning to get close to them or to another mother with one kid whom I saw in the distance. After a number of trials and much travelling I was again close to the mother and two kids. But she scented me and ran far away.

It was time to start for camp. I looked around to figure out where it was. Out on the plains where most of the time one can see miles in every direction I had not thought of using a compass.

I had known the points of the compass all day. There was the sun a little above the horizon and I knew that beneath it was a little to the south of west. But knowing the directions did not tell me the all-important thing—the direction to camp. I did not know whether camp was miles south or miles west.

I walked a short distance to the top of a ridge. I could not see a single landmark that I recognized. Landmarks had been forgotten in the watching of antelope. The sun was setting red in the west. This was a landmark, and as I had wandered eastward from camp I thought and also felt that my buffalo wallow camp must be somewhere off in the west.

I headed at the sun and walked rapidly until dark. I still was uncertain where camp was and stopped and made a fire. A compass will not do a fellow any good, nor will knowing points of the compass, unless he constantly uses his head and keeps the position of camp in mind. I should have looked back occasionally during the day and made mental pictures of the few landmarks. But I spent the night on the prairie without supper or bedding.

Daylight came grandly at four o'clock and I at once started off to back-track myself to camp. A number of antelope stood for a time on a ridge between me and the red rising sun. I headed eastward. I had walked due west after leaving the mother antelope the night before and easily back-tracked this straight line.

Back-tracking myself over the course where I had crawled, curved, and doubled in following the antelope was a task. Occasionally I got down on hands and knees to find the dim trail, or to determine which way I should follow it. This was the best of trailing experience.

Finally I arrived at the place where I had first seen the mother antelope and kids. Then, certain of the way, I gave up trailing and started on a short cut to camp. I met a vigorous whirlwind spinning across the plains and taking with it tinware and other non-essentials from camp. "Go it," I called, and let it go. On the way I must have picked up fifty-seven varieties of my camp stuff. Then I walked upon the ashes of a camp-fire that appeared familiar. The tracks were my own. Here within five hundred feet of Buffalo Camp I had spent last night.

This experience showed me that the supreme camping test for an outdoor fellow is finding the way back to camp. He cannot do this with a compass alone unless he turn surveyor and make notes every little while. I have known many a man with a compass to become hopelessly lost. One who makes a mental log of his movements, who knows where he is every minute, will be able to return to camp without a compass or even without landmarks.

In back-tracking myself I discovered a number of Nature's points of the compass, pointers that I had not before noticed. They were plentiful enough and I was surprised not to have seen them earlier. These were made by the prevailing westerly winds. Piles of tumbleweeds against the westerly sides of sagebrush clumps. On the eastern leeward side of these clumps were sand drifts. These formed east and west lines here and there that showed long distances. Here were home-grown compasses that would not get out of order, or become lost or broken.

I was eager to see the country off in the north beyond the North Platte River. Leaving most of my things at Buffalo

Camping on the Plains

Camp I started northward one morning, travelling light. I would return to this camp in three or four days. I did not stop often or long, but headed northeast and at noon came to the river. Following downstream along its low bank I saw a number of logs on a sand bar. With willows I lashed two of these logs together and after a delay of only an hour pushed off into the water with a pole. Annual high water had not yet arrived and in a few minutes my two-log raft was on the sandy, shallow farther water edge. I tied the raft, thinking I might come that way again, and went on. When evening came I was a long distance from Buffalo Camp and the river with an empty canteen. I had not seen any water since crossing the river, about twenty miles back. A map that I carried indicated a small stream a little more than twenty miles off to the north. As I was northward bound I concluded to travel on through the night.

It was a perfect evening and off I walked across the lonely prairie, heading for the North Star. Clouds came floating across the sky and in watching closely for the star I walked off a bank. It seemed as though I had stepped into a cañon. But it was only a gully about five feet wide and about as deep. Uninjured, I climbed out and went on, but I added gullies to my plains woodcraft.

In a little while all stars were shut out by clouds. I went on more slowly so as not to stumble or step overboard again. I might be going too far to the right or to the left. If I was I might walk all night and still be as far from water as when I started.

Suddenly something leaped to its feet and dashed through the sagebrush on my left. It sounded like an elephant. I turned to see what this was and took a header over a bunch of sage, landing in a pile of tumbleweed. This reminded me. Here were guides—weeds drifted against the sage by prevailing westerly winds and sand in shelter to the leeward. From these I easily faced north and went on across the plains.

At intervals far off in the north I saw a dim light, perhaps a camp-fire. It strangely appeared to be as distant as a star. It disappeared and reappeared as my viewpoint changed a number of times. As it was straight into the north I had begun to use it as a guide when it grew dim and then faded. From time to time I came upon sage clumps. I checked directions and, being confident that I was right, went on to water, which I found at a little past two in the morning.

After sunup I tried to locate the source of the fire that I had seen during the night. With glasses I discovered the cook wagon of a cow camp miles away in the north. I started across the prairie toward it, planning to spend the night there.

On the way I stopped twice to watch prairie dogs and to examine their "towns." In one town a mob of its inhabitants was trying to kill a rattler or to drive him out of the city limits. He finally ran into a prairie-dog hole. Two or three dogs, all excited, looked into the hole while the others all together kept up a yapping and yelping. I planned to return to the plains sometime and have several days getting acquainted with the life of these fat, brown little people who live in towns on the prairie.

The two cowboys who had called at my camp were the first men I saw as I approached the camp wagon. They asked if I was still running a dry goods and hardware store. I laughed and told them I thought to add a grocery department. I bought supplies enough for several days. I did not tell the cowboys that when I left Buffalo Camp the whole prairie-dog village was yapping at the pile of non-essential camp stuff that I had left behind. I did not need it and never went back for it. From that time I planned to "go light."

The cow-camp foreman told me of a rough sand-hill region about twenty miles off to the northeast where I could see a beaver colony. There were other things of interest, too, but beavers out in the plains were enough. Again I travelled.

A long day's journey landed me in the northwestern corner of Nebraska, perhaps somewhere in what now is Box Butte County. A flood of some years before had made a long, narrow island in a little stream and on it were a number of old cottonwood trees. One of these stood on a ten-foot bank.

Camping on the Plains

Beneath its flat, spider-web roots a badger and perhaps later coyotes had had a den. As the roots held the earth and would make a good roof I cleared out the loose sand and enlarged this den into a cave. Then I cut a number of sods from the bank near by and closed up part of the opening. In less than a half day I had a shelter that would have made any bandit happy.

I called the place Kingfisher Camp as a kingfisher had a nest hole in the bank close to my cave. Here I had shelter, wood to burn, and running water. The first night in this camp was rainy—the only rain I had while on this trip. My equipment now consisted of a haversack, one blanket, one waterproof canvas, a large and a small tin cup, tin pan, canteen, hatchet, pocketknife, and a field glass. This seemed to be enough. I did not have any kind of a gun. Later I often carried still less equipment. I have found a sleeping bag the most satisfactory bed, but I sometimes went without bedding.

Many of the cottonwoods along this stream had fire scars on the westerly side of the trunk. The bark on a number was burned off on one side nearly as high as my head. I puzzled for two or three days why this was all on the westerly side. Against the westerly side of other clumps of cottonwoods I saw quantities of windblown trash, leaves, grass, and tumbleweeds. Then, of course, I knew the burning of west-side trash piles would make fire scars on the westerly side of tree trunks. Every few years the plains are swept by prairie fires. These fire-made tree blazes were a new point in woodcraft.

To watch the ways of antelope I one morning climbed to the top of a hill, waved my hat, then looked through my glass at the antelope on a hill miles off. A number saw me and flashed or opened their white rump patches. This flashing was seen by antelope still farther off on the horizon; for I saw their rumps suddenly show white flags. By watching and signalling each flock becomes a sentinel for all other flocks. I imagine that an alarm flash may be relayed to the third or fourth flock in the distance.

The antelope is the animal of the plains. He is adjusted

to treeless, flat, level distances. Most animals aim to escape enemies by running out of sight. But the antelope often cannot get out of sight on the level, treeless plains. He escapes by having the right kind of eyes, legs, and signals. He probably is the swiftest of long-distance animal runners. His eyes are large and almost telescopic.

The third day that I was in Kingfisher Camp I started to follow up to the source of the stream that passed my cave. About two miles up I came to the beaver dam, probably built the year before. There was not the sign of a house. I smelled something very like beaver and, looking down, saw a hole where an antelope had thrust its foot through the top of a beaver den that had been built under the bank. A tunnel whose entrance was concealed more than a foot under water reached the den from the pond.

Several miles up I left the channel to make a long half circle through a hilly, rough country and try to find my way back to camp. I wanted to get the habit of taking my reckoning, so that I could be certain that I could do so all the time without thinking about it, and do it right. I had good experience. Camp was where a camp usually is—where one leaves it.

In Kingfisher Camp again I sat down and traced my route in a notebook. I was surprised that I remembered the turns and the objects passed. In making this tracing my memory insisted on recalling a number of objects I had not remembered passing. It recalled a tree with an old axe mark on it. I could not remember seeing this; in fact, I could not believe that I had seen it. The following morning I was by this tree before sunrise. It did have an old axe mark on it; one, so the annual rings said, that had been there for twenty-four years. I must have been watching the way closely, as well as other things even more interesting, but I saw this landmark.

In Alaska, Canada, Mexico, and in every state in the Union I have sat by a camp-fire all alone. And the most useful resource that I had in all these hundreds of camping experiences in all sorts of places and in all kinds of weather was in ever having my reckoning without stopping to take it.

Camping on the Plains

A captain must often take reckonings; wind and tide drift the ship out of its course. The man at the wheel must have a compass, but this alone cannot navigate the ship; the compass shows the north, it does not show where in the ocean the ship is, or the direction to port desired. These must be determined by mathematical reckonings.

The captain, pilot, scout surveyor, timber cruiser—each is doing a work somewhat akin to the work of the others; and the explorer must be a combination of all these and something more. A boy out camping in a region new to him is an explorer even though he does not wear buckskin and have a beard—or go far from home.

One morning two coyotes came near camp. I followed them nearly all day. "Will I be able to find my way back to camp?" I asked myself. I had looked back at landmarks, noticed turns, planned to remember ravines, hills, prickly-pear beds, and distances from one turn or landmark to another.

The coyotes made loops, turns, went off over a confusion of sand hills, travelled toward every point on the horizon, and kept me hustling to keep up. For a time both coyotes were together. One then turned aside and dug out mice and the other appeared to be leaping into the air after grasshoppers. They tried to slip up on prairie dogs. One hid while the other made a dash into the dog town. It failed to catch any and went on for a short distance and sat down. While the dogs were interested in watching him the other coyote slipped up close and made a dash after one farthest from the hole, but the fat dog won by half a length.

While the coyotes were together on a ridge another coyote passed near. They watched him, but he went by pretending not to see them. They hunted on. One turned to right of a sand hill and the other to the left. I watched the one on the right slip up and peep over into a ravine. He then descended slowly as though waiting for the other coyote to start something. It started a jack rabbit. This was overhauled before it could get out of the rough ravine.

Here, as in the mountains and forests, I constantly tried to get close to animals. I would crawl to the top of a hill or ridge and peep over before showing myself. I would peep out on the plains before climbing out of a ravine. Often this manner of stalking brought me close to a coyote or an antelope, and frequently I lay for a long time watching them without frightening them by showing myself.

As the afternoon was well along and as I had travelled twenty miles or farther in a roundabout way, the thing now was to go directly to camp. I felt it would not be more than five miles away, across the confusion of sand hills. To be certain of my reckoning I sat down by a smooth patch of sand and marked the crooked line in it which showed my kinked, looped, and tangled trail since leaving camp.

To keep in mind just where camp was at all times I hit upon this plan, which I have since used hundreds of times. I imagined myself attached to camp with a line and reel which promptly pulled in slack and also kept a steady pull on myself. At all times I knew where camp was and where I was. This plan kept before me a map picture of the locality and mentally showed me camp. I could estimate the distance.

Off I started down the sand hill for camp. It was dark before I had gone a mile. I had to travel slowly for these hills were cut with deep gullies. Twice I had to go around a long, deep gully. If ever I could get down on the level plain I could go straight to camp, even though blindfolded, I thought. There was no fear in my mind of getting lost. And I did not. Out into the level prairie I walked at last, and made my way easily to Kingfisher Camp. By blazing cottonwood camp-fire I marked my day's trail, its loops, reverse loops, circles, zigzags, and twists upon a whitened buffalo skull. Then I drew it in my notebook. It had been my most eventful day in the realm of woodcraft. I could now ramble over the roughest of country and at any instant, without consulting compass, point my finger at camp.

I knew only a few of the plants and animals on the plains. The yucca, a green, bristling, plant-porcupine, was one of these. I carried home with me a few pressed plants which I wanted to know about. After each of the camping trips that I made later I went to a library as soon as I could and also talked with people who might give me information about some of the new plants or birds seen on a recent trip.

Often I could not find what I wanted to know. Sometimes both books and people gave misinformation. By and by I learned that there were many points concerning outdoor life that I would have to find out for myself. I had no end of fun and camping in exploring for what I wanted to know. Beavers, bears, and mountain sheep gave me many a day in the wild places between camp-fires. The greatest fun connected with camping is tracking, trailing, and at last discovering another chapter of a real unwritten nature story.

I carried a notebook but I used it sparingly. Sometimes I measured something and wanted the exact figures. Or I put down the unusual, or made a note of things I wanted to find out. Here are a few of the things written while out in the plains:

"Sage is the only thing antelope ate while I was watching them. Queer if this bitter stuff is all that is eaten."

"In a lone cottonwood there were nests of bluebirds, woodpeckers, wrens, and robins. Pretty thick, yet peaceable as far as I saw. I had thought that each pair claimed at least four trees."

"Prairie dogs act more like chipmunks than dogs and look more like pigs than dogs. Who could have named them dogs?"

"Find out about that story that owls, prairie dogs, and rattlers live in the same hole."

"Coyotes seem to have more fun than any other animal on the plains. They are hollering around thick all night. Last night it sounded like several thousand, but this morning there were only two in sight."

"I cannot hear anything mournful in the barking and howling of coyotes. Sounds more like a gang having a time. At times last night they were signalling. One near camp started a song and stopped; then another about two miles off tried the same song; when he quit a third who sounded a million miles away tried his voice."

"The meadow lark seems sometimes to say, 'By the Great Gewhittaker.' He is the best singer I have heard on the plains."

"To-day saw a prairie-dog town that was a quarter of a mile across. Thousands of holes close together. Each had an opening that the top of my hat just plugged. Each hole had a dam of dirt around it that looked like a little crater. I stepped off ninety feet square, size of a baseball diamond, and inside this there were forty-six holes."

Most camping trips were made alone and without a pack horse. During each trip I watched for new animals. The ones I had known always gave new performances. Often I sat for two hours watching a mother bird feed her young, or sometimes it was a lesson in flying. Frequently I came upon a battle between ant colonies. The last day on the plains, while two colonies were fighting around and all over a big ant hill, two flickers came along and ate hundreds of the fighters.

When vacation ended I returned to the cow camp and one of the cowboys took me to the nearest railroad station and I went home to my log cabin in the mountains at Longs Peak.

Of all the useless hardware which I carried around during my earlier camping trips a big compass was the most unnecessary.

A compass will get out of order or lost or jammed. And magnetic iron in some places influences it so strongly that its needle goes round and round like lost geese. The needle is unable to calm down and point at anything definite. And then it is sometimes sufficiently influenced to point wrong without one suspecting it. A man with whom I was camping was uncertain as to direction and climbed on a quartz outcrop that carried iron and read his compass. The needle pointed east and not north. He arrived in camp in time for breakfast instead of supper.

Everywhere outdoors Nature has compasses, guideposts, landmarks—markers and pointers. East, west, north, and

Camping on the Plains

south are shown. Frost, fire, ice, water, trees, and plants; these in designs, symbols, signs, and showy colours are as thick as flags, banners, and bunting on Celebration Day.

In deserts, most vegetation is on steep, northerly slopes and north facing cañon walls.

In arid territory, most grass is on northerly slopes.

More moss and lichen are on northerly sides of trees, cliffs, and boulders that are found in the open.

In Canada and Northern states, rocks are marked with north and south scratches from southerly glacier flow. If these vary from north and south the local point will be uniform.

Prevailing direction of wind near seashore in many localities is pointed by limbs of trees.

At timberline in most mountains many of the trees are flaglike, all limbs stream leeward.

During years of camping I have used all these signs and many others.

I once said that if carried blindfolded into the Rocky Mountains I could examine a few trees with my hands and tell the points of the compass, the altitude, and the season of the year. And also that in determining these trees I could name the plants and the kinds of insects, birds, and animals most likely to be found near these trees. Afterward I became snow-blinded on the summit of the mountains when I was alone. I started down off these high, snowy mountains with their icy slopes and precipitous cañons believing that I could find my way without eyes. Once down to timberline I determined directions by feeling of trees. Finding Englemann spruce and limber pine and knowing on what slopes these grew, I used these guides and compasses. By using these and other reckoners I managed to get down off the mountains, a journey of perhaps twenty miles, without breaking my neck and with little suffering.

In each state in the Union there are wild places in which one would be allowed to camp, and in which one would have fun camping. The camper who is a real explorer makes the most of each outing, will receive from these experiences the best possible preparation for camping in the wildest places on earth.

Most men and women, boys and girls, go camping, just to go camping. They have a fair time. Others go camping chiefly because it gives them the opportunity to fish or hunt or take pictures. These campers are certain to have a good time. As I think of it now, after hundreds of camping trips, I went camping chiefly because I enjoyed watching the ways of birds and the habits of animals. The rocks, the trees, and the flowers caused me to look at them again and again. So, too, did the mountain tops, the cañons, and the lakes. I enjoyed winter camping as well as summer camping and camping on deserts, plains, and in the forested mountains. I was ever excited to know *how a plant or animal came to be what it is and where it is.*

2.
A Nose for News

A FLOCK OF BIGHORN SHEEP were lying on the steep mountain side among the scattered boulders and the stunted trees at timberline. Two ram sentries stood guard on scene-commanding boulders. The other sheep were at rest and all seemed secure. I was watching them from the top of a nearby cliff. I was out of sight, made no sound, and was up where my scent did not reach them.

In the distance a mountain lion came leisurely out of the woods and started across an opening. Suddenly he crouched to look and to listen. A breeze down the slope had given his nose the scent news—the near location of the sheep. With head up, shoulders prominent above the sagging, low-held body, and with long nervous tail sweeping out behind, he moved cautiously up the slope.

Nearly every condition was in his favour. He made no sound, and the scattered boulders and the steep, uneven slope concealed his slowly creeping body. The flock had just lain down and were not likely to move. The breeze was blowing down the slope. The lion evidently was trying by detour to crawl up beneath and immediately behind one of the proud, big-horned sentries.

He paused in his creeping. Immediately in front and above him on a boulder the sentry stood like a statue. He was an old, wary ram whose experience included successful and unsuccessful secret lion raids upon the flock. He was alertly vigilant but none of his senses had registered a suggestion of danger. The lion had concealed everything from the ram's

Clouds and sun above Cabin Rock

watchful eyes and listening ears. He was now within leaping distance—close enough, it seemed, for the ram to touch or taste him. But the ram's other sense—the sense of smell—was also on guard.

If the breeze would waver only for a fraction of a second, as sometimes happens, the silent, invisible scent message would reach the ram's sentinel nose. Suddenly it did. The ram's nose instantly gave his brain a lion-scented message—and the lion failed.

A Nose for News

Each animal is steadily giving off scent. This radiated scent odour is received by the noses of surrounding animals as news. It gives information concerning food, friends, and foes. Each animal thus knows that other animals are about him, knows who they are and where they are—approximately the distance and the direction he is from them.

This to me is a remarkable and most useful development of the nose. It is of utmost importance for a bear or any animal to be able to determine just where the enemy is, otherwise he would be all fussed up with no safe place to run.

Imagine, for instance, a day without wind, a grizzly standing in the forest. In this forest are a number of other animals—say a man, a wolf, a black bear, two herds of deer, and the carcass of an elk. These the grizzly cannot see and he has not heard them. But scent from each individual informs the grizzly where it is and the peculiar scent of each tells him the species. If the grizzly, like an Indian, could draw an animated map in the sand, he would sketch each animal in the scene correctly placed both as to distance and direction.

Scent is irrepressible. It steams from an animal standing in concealment and reveals him to noses within range. If he be moving it is a shadowless scent cloud. An animal may thus move without a sound and also keep out of sight, yet his scent, silent as a shadow and invisible as an echo, signals his position like a carried bell.

Thus, wireless scent and the receiving nose determine and direct most of the repose and the movements of wild life. The eyes and the ears take second place much of the time in the constant vigilance and scouting of the animal.

One July morning in the mountains I glimpsed a lion stalking a deer that he had scented afar. The deer had two fawns. There being no wind, the scents of both the lion and the deer were radiated in all directions. The deer on scenting the lion stood alert to learn if the lion had discovered her. His freshening scent told her that he was approaching.

On the final stretch the lion crawled low through a willowy swamp. The deer used deceiving strategy. Hurrying toward the lion for a distance she stopped and trampled about—threw off scent—then hurried back to her fawns. As the lion neared the place where she had trampled about he hesitated and raised his head to look around. Her ruse delayed him. While he was trying to discover her at this place, she and the fawns ran off up the mountain side. He half circled the place before he appeared to realize that she was not there. Then he slipped along her trail nearly to the point where she had been when he first scented her, but without finding her.

She had gone above the swamp—her usual safe retreat, with the fawns. As she went up the mountain there was a slight ascending current which carried the lion scent up the mountain side to her, but did not allow her scent to descend to him.

The lion did not know where the deer now was, as her scent no longer directly reached him. But her trail led away up the mountain side. This was as plain to his nose as a roadway to our eyes. It led to her whenever she might be. Along this deer-scented trail he hurried in pursuit.

An animal makes a tracked trail as he travels, if he is not swimming and if the surface beneath his feet is sufficiently soft. But his scent musk is ever sifting beneath him. The earth, trees, rocks, or any object with which he comes in contact absorbs it. From these the scent is slowly radiated and a slow, fading record of a passing traveller is given out.

Commonly a lion captures his prey by stealth. If he misses in leaping, or if his approach is discovered and the prey retreats, rarely does he pursue. But in this instance, the deer had two fawns and perhaps the lion felt that one of them might be secured in another attempt.

When some distance from the swamp the deer again used strategy to confuse and delay the lion. She ran in a small circle, then went a short distance down the mountain near the trail by which she had come but parallel to it. Here she and her children stood waiting in silence. A stronger wave of scent told her when the lion was passing on her old trail coming up. After he was safely by she slipped down the trail and retreated to the swamp. For a time the lion stalked about the freshly scented circle. On discovering that the deer had vanished he turned off, perhaps to seek something that had not scented him.

Two beavers were dragging a small tree down a slope when it jammed between a stump and a boulder. It was daylight and I was watching through a field glass. Closely I looked to see if they would call or signal for help. But there was no voice, no wig-wag.

However, a few seconds later two other beavers, that were at work out of their sight on the dam, paused, raised their heads, and then started along the dam and came up to help the loggers. Had these loggers called for help with a wireless scent message?

The castor gland of the beaver is a complex structure. It probably generates and gives off a variety of scents—a language—a means of communication between all beavers, strangers as well as home folks.

The beaver has long been known as an animal most susceptible to the scents of his species. Each individual scent given off appears to be a special signal or announcement—a particular bit of news. To all beaver noses within range it is a message and all other beavers in the colony will know who and where the sender is.

Among the given-off scents, understood perhaps by their own kind only, are those that warn of danger, that ask for help, that suggest keep away, that solicit a companion, or that plead for love. And still others give out personal uncensored news that reveal youth, age, sex, health, or sickness.

Many times in earlier years I had the good fortune to see beavers at close range at work and at play during daytime. Often I have seen them start in a definite direction, plainly in response to a scent message. Slowly, quickly, eagerly, and in alarm was their response, and many a time their attitude and actions revealed the very character of the message.

One day a number of beavers from a far-off colony came upstream. As they made a portage around a bouldery rapids they were seen or scented or perhaps both by a local beaver. With scent message he revealed their presence to the other local beavers. This news was received with hurrah and numbers of local folks hurried eagerly to the visitors. On the dam and in the pond all proceeded to have a play.

One afternoon a beaver was killed by a tree that he had just felled. The news of this accident was probably radiated by the scent of the beaver that was working with the one killed. I was standing by the pond and had heard the tree fall. A few seconds later, so it seemed to me, a number of beavers were on their way toward the scene of the accident.

A lone young beaver that I was once watching was playing listlessly. Suddenly he eagerly rose up on hind feet like a bear cub, sniffed, then hurried off to where another young beaver had come out of the water. Evidently he recognized the difference between the scent of an old and a young beaver, for the other youngster came out of the water by an old one that had been there for some time.

Three beavers one day were at work on the opposite side of a pond and I was trying to watch them. They were up a steep slope perhaps eighty or ninety feet above the water's edge. Each was gnawing on a green aspen four or five inches in diameter.

Out of sight of the workers a short distance upstream was a single beaver either loafing or doing sentinel duty. At any rate, on detecting danger he signalled a warning with scent. In alarm he leaped up on hind legs, stood for several seconds, then ran for the pond.

At the same instant the three workers made a dash for the pond. Each as he dived hit the water a resounding whack with his tail. A few minutes later two wolves appeared at the place where the three had been at work.

As I get it, this is a plain case of signalling danger with scent. The beaver that signalled had wolf scent for information as the wolves were out of sight in the woods. A roaring rapids would have prevented any sound from the sentinel reaching the workers, even though he had sounded. The workers were completely out of his sight. I am certain that any one who has the time to watch beaver movements will discover that they appear to be almost constantly signalling and generally with scent.

In the beaver the castor gland appears to be the main source of scent. Does the beaver consciously control it, or do the scents come in response to his joy, fear, or anger change and ever reflect the mental attitude he is in? I do not know. But a number of the scents given off by beavers do each give to other beavers a message of distinct meaning.

While I was watching a wild-life trail-crossing in the woods, a deer came along and saw me without scenting me. He paused and stared, full of curiosity. While he thus stared and stamped, a lion that probably had been stalking him came in sight and drew himself up for a spring. As I watched the lion through my glasses in the few seconds that he waited before leaping, he had an expression of, "Here is where I eat." But he missed. The deer detected him just in time.

Two or three hours later a lone mountain sheep came along and, like the deer, caught sight of me without scenting me. Slowly, full of curiosity, he continued along his way with head to one side, wondering what I might be. While thus preoccupied he walked into the deeply lion-scented spot. As he leaped to escape, his action and expression said, "Here is where I am eaten."

The scent of an animal, like delicate pollen, rides merrily away with the wind but it advances little against the wind. When there is a dead calm, it radiates rapidly to long distances. Once, within perhaps ten minutes, I realized that something had stirred up a skunk. I was at a point more than two miles from the stirring.

Animals understand the extraordinary advantage of travelling with faces in the breeze. They appear clearly to comprehend that thus their scent will not reach any point until they reach it; while they themselves will have advance information concerning the inhabitants of a locality before they enter it. They will know if they be coming to food, friend, or foe.

However, a deer that has been travelling into the wind will about-face if he stops to lie down. The wind will continue to bring him scout news from the windward, but if a hunter or other enemy be following him, he must see him or hear him.

Young animals probably are taught by their parents or learn from their associates to flee from man scent. They may flee a thousand times without seeing a man. Many a wild animal may live its normal life and not see this man whose scent has so often caused it to flee.

The first sight that an animal has of man, if it has not scented him, is likely to cause it to stand still in astonishment or even advance for a close-up look.

A Utah pioneer told me his experience with a deer. The deer, it seems, ranged near his cabin and was a giant. One day he had a good look at it without himself being seen. Now and then he went out hoping for a shot at it.

But the giant was wary, and occasionally the hunter came upon the freshest of signs which showed that the deer had detected his approach and escaped. Three or four years went by and still not a shot. During those years, judging from what finally followed, the giant probably had not even a glimpse of him.

One day the man peeped out of the woods into a sunny opening and there, near-by, saw the giant in the sunshine. Instead of shooting, he stood to admire. The deer saw him. Keeping wondering eyes upon the hunter it slowly arose, curious and puzzled over this dark, two-legged thing.

One day, in stalking a grizzly, I leaned against a stump to change kodak films. This stump retained a quantity of my scent. Two or three minutes later I was almost ready for a close-up snap when the grizzly detected me—with eyes, nose, or ears, I know not—and fled down the wind toward this stump. He caught my lingering scent just as he neared the stump, and stopped as suddenly as though he had collided with it.

Scent thus serves by waiting—reveals by lingering—as well as by speeding through the wireless air.

When an animal travels he leaves behind, whether he will or not, an invisible trail. But to the nose this odorous trail is obvious, and hide where he will, friend or foe can follow him to his hiding-place.

This trail of scent sometimes endures for days and retains its individuality to the last. That is, to the last it reveals the species, and to one of its species it may even tell to the trailer the fellow of his acquaintance who must have left it.

As an animal travels, a half-dozen other animals follow him for a time or cross and involve his scent trail with theirs. But an animal with a good nose, that is following a particular one of these trails, will not get his trail scents and signals crossed, but will continue following to the end the particular trail he started to follow. The other scent trails that mingled with it cause no confusion.

Many species of animals and birds have protective or concealing coloration. But these colours do not suppress the scent of animal or bird of hamper the nose seeking them.

Hunting dogs point to the exact spot where invisible birds—perhaps invisible to both dog and hunter—are clustered.

Nose skill appears the most fitting factor of the present generation in the survival of the wolf. His amazingly keen nose generally reveals to him exactly where the buried trap is concealed. Or the faintest man scent upon a fragment of meat whispers to his brain, "Skull and Cross-bones—poison."

With large rewards for his scalp, with heavy bounties, the wolf has survived. In Wyoming for a period of twelve years or longer the wolves actually multiplied under maximum bounties. Wolf risk was made still more risky by numerous wolfers on the monthly pay roll, together with the numerous cowboys and settlers all of whom were eager and ready for a shot or a chase whenever a wolf showed. The wolf with amazing keenness avoided contact with anything and everything that carried man scent or the scent of steel. He safely crossed entanglements of buried steel traps.

Meat, fresh and stale, was skillfully poisoned, and scattered near wolf trails. If it carried the faintest touch of man scent the wolf would have none of it.

Along with this delicately responsive nose the wolf must have a brain of sustained alertness ever to detect this revealing tang. And again and again, when hungry, to walk by without touching tempting chunks and carcasses of meat some of which he was in doubt as to whether they were poisoned or not, is high self-control.

Many an animal gives off as a danger signal an odour that is recognized only by its species. The sight or the scent of a man or a lion will frighten a deer and instantly the tang of the scent given off is changed. If this change be due to fright, if it be done automatically and unconsciously, or if it be done consciously, we do not know. But the result of such scent on reaching another deer, has all the effect of the words, "look out," or "danger."

The wireless and universal air radiates the scents of all species impartially and without censorship, and thus speeds everybody's business, exacts alertness, and is an evolutionary, advancing factor.

Throughout the wilderness scent is a remarkable means of communication and intercommunication between wild animals.

The scent glands of animals are variously placed. The musky goat has a number of these in his neck. Many species have scent glands in the neck, at the root of the tail, between the toes, and at other spots. I know not if in the same animal each of these glands gives off a scent differing in odour and meaning from the other glands.

That most obnoxious maker of scent, the skunk, makes different use of it. He has concentrated and intensified scent into an efficient weapon of defense. Incidentally, it is a warning and a threat.

The antelope has long-range, high-power eyes and depends chiefly upon his eyes. This probably is the result of living for ages upon treeless plains and plateaus. On these magnificent and unobstructed distances the eye would outrange the nose.

During the night I suppose the nose is at the peak of ser-

A Nose for News

vice. The light has failed and animals can no longer maintain an outpost. But through the black of night the nose is steadfastly vigilant. Like a telescopic eye, it knows the happenings in the distance and thus, through the darkness, steadily gives the brain the up-to-the-instant reports of changes around the outposts.

For uncountable ages scent has been the means of communication between flowers and insects. It has interlocked plants and insects and made them inter-dependent; has made them coöperators. Probably there is no stranger or more fascinating story in evolution than that played by the flowers and the beetles, moths, butterflies, and bees.

The brilliant colours of flowers, their pleasing perfumes, and their unwelcome odours are the result of plant and insect fighting, the battle of life largely being coöperating instead of fighting.

Often I have stood still in amazement, thinking of nose, odour, and perfume; of the infinite intricacies by which perfume and nose have played their parts and are still playing them all about me.

The Wilderness Arena, and the greater wilderness of coöperation is the realm of scent news and the nose. Every successful wild animal must have a nose for news. Pursuer and pursued ever use the nose. Mutual aiders and coöperators—team workers—ever use the sense of smell.

A wilderness fellow who is of the vast majority of pursuers and pursued must have good eyes and good ears; and an efficient nose is a necessity. Fortunate the wild fellow that has an extra good nose.

A stranger from the lowlands was crossing the mountains with a burro outfit packed with supplies. He had an extra burro, and as I was camping near, he wandered over to sell it to me. The burro was commended as one easy to catch. But this ease of approach and ease of catch—this lack of depravity on the part of the burro—caused me to ask the stranger to explain it. He frankly accounted for it, "Because the burro can't smell a thing." No scent made any impression on him.

That night this burro was through feeding early and lay down alone. Finally he rose, but stood while the other burrows fed away from him. While he thus dreamed a mountain lion came up unannounced, and he and the burro lay down together.

3.

Tramp Days of Grizzly Cubs

A GRIZZLY BEAR CUB has wilderness adventures that would delight the soul of any real boy—mountain climbing, swimming, exploring—no end of excitement and fun. He is a merry explorer of the wilderness. Prepared and preparing for what comes, he has a variety of experiences. In the period between separation from its mother and the selection of its home the cub is a fun-loving rover and has a jolly tramphood of about two years.

The tramp life of the cub is all the more lively and exciting where there are two or three cubs—brothers and sisters—to rove the wilds together. One of them becomes the leader. Both in fun and fighting the cubs are united, they are loyal to one another even unto death. They have two full summers and one or two winters together. Usually they separate during the third summer. Each then goes forth to select his own exclusive territory, and settles down to serious life alone.

Three grizzly cubs whom I saw a number of times in the Saw Tooth Mountains of Idaho certainly had a lively, varied cubhood, one full of fun and adventure. A prospector had also watched them and told me some of their experiences. A hunter had killed the mother, wounded one cub slightly in a foreleg, and shot a toe off a second cub, the third cub being uninjured. The cubs made their escape. This was in September just after they were weaned. After being weaned, cubs usually run with the mother the remainder of the autumn and den up with her that winter. They leave her and go off together some time the next summer. Through the death of their mother, these cubs were left to look out for themselves earlier in life than is usual.

The cub who was wounded in the leg became the leader of the three. Whether he decided all their movements I cannot say, but whatever he did the others instantly fell in with. Adventure after adventure had this loyal band. They were inseparable playmates and united comrades in face of danger. Wherever they went the cub with the slight limp was invariably in the lead.

During wanderings this autumn they discovered the prospect hole in which my prospector friend was working. When he came up for lunch one day he saw the cubs in the edge of the woods near by, apparently looking, all attention, at the windlass, or perhaps they were both looking and listening. On his appearance they stared for a few seconds and then ran off. The prospector occasionally ran a small suction air machine to help ventilate the tunnel and shaft. This caused a peculiar humming, rattling sound, and it may have been the sound made by it that attracted the attention of the cubs.

There was snow on the ground. On his way to his cabin the prospector saw the cubs' tracks. They had been travelling single file when they became interested in his place of work. All had risen up on hind feet and stood abreast, facing the place, evidently looking, smelling, and listening. Apparently while doing this they had taken alarm. After running back a short distance down their trail they stopped and again stood up. Tracks in the snow showed that they had waited some minutes trying to make up their minds what the excitement was about, and as to the next move they would make. Again advancing single file up the trail, they went beyond the place where they had first stopped and approached much closer to the prospect. But on reaching the edge of the woods they had evidently taken alarm again and retreated single file in their former tracks. They had proceeded once more to the edge of the woods when the prospector appeared.

Tramp Days of Grizzly Cubs

Curiosity seems to be the most striking trait in grizzly bear nature. A grizzly is ever alert for anything unusual, anything that is new. New scents, new sounds, new figures, or even unusual or peculiar actions on the part of wild life, never fail to interest him. Ofttimes this extreme curiosity causes him to approach close to the interesting object in order that it may be seen to better advantage or its peculiarities comprehended. Every cub is full of curiosity.

The prospector was not a hunter. He saw the cubs three or four times that autumn and occasionally crossed their tracks. Once he came upon all three in the woods where they were digging, perhaps for some mice. Another time he saw all three on a rocky mountain side busily engaged eating the red, ripened fruit of the wild rose. A third time he saw them cross, single file, an opening by a beaver pond, cubs two and three carefully stepping in the tracks of the lame leader. Late that November, while returning from an examination of a mineral outcrop some miles from his cabin, he encountered their tracks, trailed them in the newly fallen snow a short distance, and found where they had all entered a den of their own digging. In this den the youngsters spent the winter.

Later when I visited this den it was simply a hole in the gravelly mountain side about six feet deep. In this the cubs had evidently curled up together on the barren gravel. They did not use this den the second winter.

During the second autumn of their lives I saw these aggressive youngsters on the mountains at least twenty miles from the prospector's cabin. They were having a swim in a beaver pond, and no three swimming boys ever had more fun. They splashed water, they wrestled, and occasionally they boxed. I watched their pranks for more than an hour. For a week I followed them and had a number of peeps into their life. Just where they spent most nights I could not discover. But one night they lay close together under the edge of a willow clump at the foot of a steep forested mountain, with a thicket of willows in front of them and a cliff behind.

Another time I watched the cubs with field glasses while

they were catching fish in a little stream that flowed into Red Fish Lake. While thus absorbed a deer came rustling through the willows near them. Evidently the cubs had not scented it. Though in no wise alarmed, they instantly endeavoured to see what it was. The leader happened to be standing near a much-branched tree that lay on the ground. He reared up, put forepaws against it, and peered intently ahead. The other two clubs, unable to get a view either side of him, also reared up; the second cub put forepaws on the back of the leader and the one in the rear likewise upon the back of the second. In this position they looked intently, pointing noses slightly to right and to left as they looked, until the deer came out into the opening. Then, instantly they relaxed, and promptly single filed off upstream.

Although the cubs had been fishing, they had, apparently, between times been eating grass. One of them, as he stood up, presented a strange appearance with a few dozen long blades of grass projecting from between his tightly closed jaws.

One day I saw the cubs chasing and capturing grasshoppers in the edge of the woods. With fat bodies, they made a comical movie show as they slipped up on an alighted grasshopper or leaped into the air and struck after one that flew away. While I was watching the cubs an old grizzly came out of the woods and passed close to them without stopping, showing no objection to their presence. A grizzly will promptly drive off another old bear who prowls in his territory; but prowling cubs appear free to go anywhere. The cubs stood still and watched the old one out of sight, but showed no concern over his appearance.

I hoped to be fortunate enough sometime to see these cubs meet other roaming cubs of their own age, but never did. Just what cubs do on such eventful occasions, just what the wilderness etiquette is for such meetings, I hope sometime to discover.

The day the cubs were catching grasshoppers their colour

came out clearly as they moved about in the sunlight. The colour of each was grayish brown. Often grizzly cubs have coats unlike in colour. The cubs were plump and clean, nearly of a size, the leader being a trifle the largest of the three. He probably weighed one hundred and fifty pounds.

A month after I left this region two hunters came upon the cubs in a partly willow-filled opening by a stream in the woods. Only one cub was seen. Both hunters fired at short range. The cub was knocked down and apparently severely wounded. He set up a terrible bawling and wailing as he thrashed about in the willows. The hunters hurried to right and to left to get another shot at him.

The other two cubs at once charged the hunters. One of the men, seeing a cub coming, all bristled up and snarling, and only a few jumps off, dropped his rifle, leaped up, and caught a limb and swung himself into a tree. He lost a legging from the stroke of the cub and barely escaped the terrific blow of the cub's paw. The other cub—the lame leader—was upon the second hunter before the latter saw him. With a right forepaw the cub knocked him headlong among the willows and cracked two ribs. Then he seized the man, shook him repeatedly, and bit him in the shoulder and in the thigh.

Meantime, the wounded cub had gotten on his feet. The lame one ceased mauling the hunter and began licking the injured cub's wounds. They were joined a minute later by the cub who had been watching the treed hunter, and all three vanished among the willows. A grizzly bear, young or old, will not attack a man unless first attacked, or unless he feels that he is cornered, or in defence of one of his number.

Dropping out of the tree the hunter hurriedly took his wounded comrade to camp and summoned help. From his graphic account of the fury of these charging cubs one could readily believe that a full-grown grizzly when stirred to fight, might, as Governor Clinton said a century ago, "defy the attacks of an entire tribe of Indians," armed as the Indians were with only bows and spears. The formidable manner in which grizzlies fight when driven to it, and not because of ferocity, was the chief reason why they were named *Ursus horribilis* and *Ursus horribilis imperator.*

The loyalty of a grizzly cub to his accompanying comrade or comrades is probably not excelled in the world of animal life. Like the three Swiss on the mountain heights, they stand all for each other and each for all. In every emergency they appear to think only for the common good. The intense devotion which the mother shows for the cubs is in turn shown by each cub to the others.

There are numerous accounts in which grizzly pets have shown all that intense loyalty to man which we have ascribed only to the dog. Grizzlies have dared to die for their masters. Loyalty is a distinguishing trait of the grizzly bear.

Evidently the wounded cub speedily recovered. Less than a month after this shooting the cubs stampeded a trapper's pack horse and put the trapper unceremoniously up a tree. He had set a bear trap, using stale meat for bait. Inside of forty-eight hours the cubs came near. They had caught the scent some distance off, turned, so their tracks showed, and come cautiously toward the trap. They had circled it and evidently paid more attention to the curious trap than to the bait. One of the cubs had reached out a paw, evidently to feel of the trap, and in so doing had sprung it, catching just two toes of his paw; but he was held fast.

The next day the trapper was moving his supplies to a permanent camp on his pack horse. He was close to the trap before the horse became alarmed at bear scent and refused to go on. The trapper dismounted and tied the horse to a small pine, planning to advance with his rifle. The two cubs, loyal to their trapped comrade, had remained near. They charged the hunter and horse. The horse, excited, pulled violently, uprooted the pine, and fell over backward; then he stampeded wildly through the woods and willows. His pack was left partly in the willows and partly adhering to tree limbs. Everything was scattered.

The horse in falling had tumbled between the hunter and

the charging cubs. These few seconds' delay enabled the hunter to climb into a tree before the cubs could be upon him. As grizzly bears cannot climb he escaped. During the confusion the trapped cub had tugged violently at the trap chain, which was fastened to a small broken log, and dragged this log for some distance when it became caught. In the surges which followed the cub tore off his two trapped toes. As soon as he was freed all three cubs hurried off into the woods.

During two seasons of exploring the cubs had covered a mountainous country about forty miles long by thirty miles wide—about twelve hundred square miles. After they separated they may or may not have spent any time in this region. No matter how chummy and inseparable when tramping the woods together, after cubs separate they are not likely to meet again, or if they do meet as grown bears they are not likely to pay friendly attention to one another.

A grizzly, except a mother while with cubs, lives alone. Whether a cub simply wanders until he finds an unclaimed territory that he likes, or whether his mother sometimes selects his future home for him, is not known. But usually by the time a bear is three years old he has settled in some section. In this he lives alone, and in it, too, he dens up—hibernates—alone during the winter. Rarely does he leave his chosen locality, and then commonly for a short time only. A bear ever objects to another bear of the same species intruding on his claimed territory. So when a bear is away from home he is likely to keep on the move.

It is not known when or where these three loyal cub explorers finally parted. It may have been at the close of their second jolly summer when time to den up, or it may have been the spring following when they came forth from the den. After all their rambles, swims, feasts, and adventures together they separated. I wish I might have seen them at the time they parted for ever.

4.

Trailing without a Gun

I HAD GONE INTO WILD BASIN, hoping to see and to trail a grizzly. It was early November and the sun shone brightly on four inches of newly fallen snow; trailing conditions were excellent. If possible I wanted to get close to a bear and watch his ways for a day or two.

Just as I climbed above the last trees on the eastern slope of the Continental Divide, I saw a grizzly ambling along the other side of a narrow cañon, boldly outlined against the skyline. I was so near that with my field-glasses I recognized him as "Old Timberline," a bear with two right front toes missing. He was a silver-tip,—a nearly white old bear. For three days I followed Old Timberline through his home territory and camped on his trail at night. I had with me hatchet, kodak, field-glasses, and a package of food, but no gun.

The grizzly had disappeared by the time I crossed the cañon, but a clear line of tracks led westward. I followed them over the Divide and down into the woods on the other side. In a scattered tree-growth the tracks turned abruptly to the right, then led back eastward, close to the first line of tracks, as though Old Timberline had turned to meet any one who might be following him.

The most impressive thing I had early learned in trailing and studying the grizzly was that a wounded bear if trailed and harassed will sometimes conceal himself and lie in an ambush in wait for his pursuer. I never took a chance of walking into such danger. Whenever the trail passed a log, boulder, or bushes that might conceal a bear, I turned aside

Gem Lake

and scouted the ambush for a side view before advancing further.

Old Timberline's tracks showed that he had now and then risen on hind feet, listened, and turned to look back. He acted as though he knew I was following him, but this he had not yet discovered. All grizzlies are scouts of the first order; they are ever on guard. When at rest their senses do continuous sentinel duty, and when traveling they act exactly as though they believed some man was in pursuit.

Following along the trail and wondering what turn the grizzly would make next, I found where he had climbed upon a ledge in the edge of an opening, and had evidently stood for some seconds, looking and listening. From the ledge he had faced about and continued his course westward, heading for a spur on the summit of the Divide.

We were in what is now the southern end of the Rocky Mountain National Park. The big bear and myself were on one of the high sky-lines of the earth. We traversed a territory ten thousand to twelve thousand feet above sea-level, much of it above the limits of tree growth. There were long stretches of moorland, an occasional peak towering above us, and ridges long and short thrusting east and west, and cañons of varying width and depth were to be seen below us from the summit heights.

Crossing this spur of the Divide, the grizzly entered the woods. Here he spent so much time rolling logs about and tearing them open for grubs and ants that I nearly caught up with him. I watched him through the scattered trees from a rocky ledge until he moved on. This after a few minutes he did. As he came to an opening in the woods, I wondered whether he would go round it to the right or to the left. To my astonishment, without the least hesitation he sauntered across the opening, his head held low and swinging easily from side to side. But the instant he was screened by trees beyond, rising up, with fore paws resting against a tree, he peered cautiously out to see if he was being followed. When the next opening in the woods was reached, he went discreetly round it. You never know what a grizzly's next move will be nor how to anticipate his actions.

Old Timberline started down into a cañon as though to descend a gully diagonally to the bottom. I hastily made a short cut and was ready to take his picture when he should come out at the lower end. But he never came. After waiting some time, I back-tracked and found he had gone only a few hundred feet down the gully, then returned to the top of the canøn and followed along the rim for a mile. He had then descended directly to the bottom of the cañon and gone straight up to the top on the other side.

Autumn is the time when bears most search the heights for food. Old Timberline's trail headed again for the heights. When I next caught sight of him, he was digging above the tree-line, but as it was now nearly night, I went back a short distance into the woods and built a fire by the base of a cliff. Here all through the clear night I had a glorious view of the high peaks up among the cold stars.

Before daylight I left camp and climbed to the top of a treeless ridge, thinking that the bear might come along that

Trailing without a Gun

way. In the course of time he appeared, about a quarter of a mile east of me. After standing and looking about for a few minutes, he started along the ridge, evidently planning to recross the Continental Divide near where he had crossed the day before. As I could not get close to him from this point, I concluded to follow his trail of the preceding night and if possible find out what he had been doing.

A short distance below him I found his trail and backtracked to a place which showed that he had spent the night near the entrance of a recently dug den. I learned some weeks later that this den was where he hibernated that winter. A short distance farther on I came to where he had been digging when I saw him the evening before. Evidently he had been successful. A few drops of blood on the snow showed that he had captured some small animal, probably a cony. From this point I trailed Old Timberline forward and eastward, and near noon I caught a glimpse of him on the summit of the Divide.

While roaming above timber-line he did not take the precaution to travel with his face in the wind. He could see toward every point of the compass. He was ambling easily along, but I knew that his senses were wide awake—that his sentinel nose never slept and that his ears never ceased to hear. Climbing to the very summit of a snow-covered ridge, he lay down with his back to the wind. Evidently he depended upon the wind to carry the warning scent of any danger behind him, while he was on the lookout for anything in front of him. Nothing could approach nearer than half a mile without his knowing it. He looked this way and that. After only a short rest he arose and started on again.

I hope that some time I should be able to photograph Old Timberline at twenty-five or thirty feet. But at all times, too, I was more eager to watch him, to see what he was eating, where he went, and what he did. I was constantly trying to get as close as possible. Of course I had ever to keep in mind that he must not see, hear, nor scent me. I had to be particularly careful to prevent his scenting me. Often in hastening to reach a point of vantage I had to stop, note the topography, and change my direction, because a wind-current up an unsuspected cañon before me might carry news of my presence to the bear.

Near mountain-tops the wind is deflected this way and that by ridges and cañons. In a small area the prevailing west wind may be a north wind, and a short distance farther on it may blow from the southwest. Often, when the bear was somewhere in a cañon, I climbed entirely out of it, to avoid the likelihood of being scented, and scurried ahead on a plateau.

Usually I followed in the bear's trail, but sometimes I made short cuts. So long as Old Timberline remained on the moorland summit of this treeless ridge, I could not get close to him. But when he arose and started down the ridge, I hurried down the slope, hoping to get ahead and hide in a place of concealment near which he might pass. I kept out of sight in the woods and hastened forward for two miles, then climbed up and hid in a rock-slide on the rim of the ridge.

By and by I saw Old Timberline coming. When within five hundred feet of me he stopped and dug energetically. Buckets of earth flew behind, and occasionally a huge stone was torn out and hurled with one paw to the right or left. Once he stopped digging, rose on hind feet, and looked all around as though he felt that some one was slipping up on him. He dug for a few minutes longer and then again stood up and sniffed the air. Not satisfied, he walked quickly to a ledge from which he could see down the slope to the woods. Discovering nothing suspicious, he returned to his digging, stepping in his former footprints. He uncovered something in its nest, and through my glasses I saw him strike right and left and then rush out in pursuit of it. After nosing about in the hole where he had been digging, he started off again. He went directly to the ledge, walking in his former well-tracked trail, then descended the steep eastern slope of the Divide toward the woods. I hurried to the ledge from which he had surveyed the surroundings and watched him.

Arriving at a steep incline on the snowy slope, Old Timber-

Trailing without a Gun

line sat down on his haunches and coasted. A grizzy bear coasting on the Continental Divide! How merrily he went, leaning forward with his paws on his knees! At one place he plunged over a snowy ledge and dropped four or five feet. He threw up both fore paws with sheer joy. Soon he found himself exceeding the speed-limit. Looking back over one shoulder, and reaching out his paw behind him, he put on brakes; but as this did not check him sufficiently, he whirled about and slid flat on his stomach, digging in with both fingers and toes until he slowed down.

Then, sitting up on his haunches again, he set himself in motion by pushing along with rapid backward strokes of both fore paws. He coasted on toward the bottom. In going down a steep pitch of one hundred feet or more he either quite lost control of himself or let go from sheer enthusiasm. He rolled, tumbled, and slid recklessly along. Reaching the bottom, he rose on hind feet, looked about him for a few seconds, and then climbed halfway up the course for another coast. At the end of this merry sliding he landed on an open flat in the edge of the woods.

As it was nearly dark and I should not be able to see or follow the bear much longer, I concluded to roll a rock from the ledge down near him. Twice I had noticed that he had paid no attention to rocks that broke loose above and rolled near him. But he heard this rock start and rose up to look at it. It stopped a few yards from him. He sniffed the air with nose pointing toward it and then went up and smelled it. Rearing up instantly, he looked intently toward the mountain-top where I was hidden. After two or three seconds of thought he turned and ran. Evidently the stone had carried my scent to him. It was useless to follow him in the night.

The next morning I left camp and followed Old Timberline's trail through the woods. He had run for nearly ten miles almost straight south until coming to a small stream. Then for some distance he concealed, involved, and confused his trail with a cleverness that I have never seen equaled. Most animals realize that they leave a scent which enables other animals to follow them, but the grizzly is the only animal that I know who appears to be fully aware that he is leaving telltale tracks. He will make unthought-of turns and doublings to walk where his tracks will not show, and also tramples about to leave a confusion of tracks where they do show.

Arriving at the stream, the bear crossed on a fallen log and from the end of this leaped into a bushy growth beyond. I made a détour, thinking to find his tracks on the other side of the bushes, and I threw stones into the bushes, not caring to go into them. Both tracks and grizzly seemed to have vanished. I went down stream just outside the bushes bordering it, expecting every instant to find the grizzly's tracks, but not finding them. Then I returned to the log on which he had crossed the stream, and from which he had leaped into the bushes.

Examining the tracks carefully, I now discovered what I had before overlooked. After leaping into the bushes the bear had faced about and leaped back to the log, stepping carefully into his former tracks. From the log he had entered the water and waded up stream for a quarter of a mile. Of couse not a track showed. At a good place for concealing his trail he had leaped out of the water into a clump of willows on the north bank. From the willows he made another long leap into the snow and then started back northward, alongside his ten-mile trail and one hundred feet from it, as though intending to return to the place where I had rolled the stone down the slope near him.

I did not discover all this at once, however. In my search for his trail I went up stream on the north side and passed, without noticing, the crushed willows into which he had leaped. Crossing to where the bank was higher, I started back down stream on the other side, and in doing so chanced to look across and see the crushed clump of willows. But it took me hours to untangle this involved trail.

When I had followed the tracks northward for more than a mile, the trail vanished in a snowless place. Apparently the grizzly had planned in advance to use this bare place, because

Trailing without a Gun

the moves he made in it were those most likely to bewilder the pursuer. He did three things which are always more or less confusing and even bewildering to the pursuer, be he man or dog. He changed his direction, he left no tracks, and he crossed his former trail, thereby mixing the scents of the two. He confused the nose, left no record for the eye, and broke the general direction.

Unable to determine the course the bear had taken across this trackless place, I walked round it, keeping all the time in the snow. When more than halfway round I came upon his tracks leaving the bare place. Here he had changed his direction of travel abruptly from north to east, crossed his former trail, gone on a few yards farther, and then abruptly changed from east to north.

I hurried along his tracks. After a few miles I saw where perhaps the night before he had eaten part of the carcass of a bighorn. To judge from tooth marks, the sheep had been killed by wolves. The trail continued in general northward, parallel to the summit and a little below it. As I followed, the tracks approached timber-line, the trees being scattered and the country quite open.

Suddenly the trail broke off to the right for five or six hundred feet into the woods, as though Old Timberline had remembered an acquaintance whom he must see again. He had hustled along straight for a much-clawed Engelmann spruce, a tree with bear-claw and tooth marks of many dates, though none were recent. Old Timberline, apparently, had smelled the base of the tree and then risen up and sniffed the bark as high as his nose could reach. He had neither bitten nor clawed. Then he had gone to two near-by trees, each of which had had chunks bitten or torn out, and here smelled about.

Retracing his tracks to where the trail had turned off abruptly, the bear resumed his general direction northward. When he stopped on a ridge and began digging, I hurried across a narrow neck of woods and crept up as close as I dared. A wagon-load of dirt and stones had been piled up. While I watched the digging, a woodchuck rushed out, only to be overtaken and seized by the bear, who, having finished his meal, shuffled on out of sight.

I followed the trail through woods, groves, and openings. After an hour or more without seeing the grizzly, I climbed a cliff, hoping to get a glimpse of him on some ridge ahead. I could see his line of tracks crossing a low ridge beyond and felt that he might still be an hour or so in the lead. But, in descending from the cliff, I chanced to look back along my trail. Just at that moment the bear came out of the woods behind me. He was trailing me!

I do not know how he discovered that I was following him. He may have seen or scented me. Anyway, instead of coming directly back and thus exposing himself, he had very nearly carried out his well-planned surprise when I discovered him. I found out afterwards that he had left his trail far ahead, turning and walking back in his own footprints for a distance, and trampling this stretch a number of times, and that he had then leaped into scrubby timber and made off on the side where his tracks did not show in passing along the trampled trail. He had confused his trail where he started to circle back, so as not to be noticed, and slipped in around behind me.

But after discovering the grizzly on my trail I went slowly along as though I was unaware of his near presence, turning in screened places to look back. He followed within three hundred feet of me. When I stopped he stopped. He occasionally watched me from behind bushes, a tree, or a boulder. It gave me a strange feeling to have this big beast following and watching me so closely and cautiously. But I was not alarmed.

I concluded to turn tables on him. On crossing a ridge when I was out of sight, I turned to the right and ran for nearly a mile. Then, circling back into our old trail behind the bear, I traveled serenely along, imagining that he was far ahead. I was suddenly startled to see a movement of the grizzly's shadow from behind a boulder near the trail, only three hundred feet ahead. He was in ambush, waiting for me! At the place where I left the trail to circle behind him, he had stopped and evidently surmised my movements. Turning in his tracks, he had come a short distance back on the trail and lain down behind the boulder to wait for me.

I went on a few steps after discovering the grizzly, and he moved to keep out of sight. I edged toward a tall spruce, which I planned to climb if he charged, feeling safe in the knowledge that grizzlies cannot climb trees. Pausing by the spruce, I could see his silver-gray fur as he peered at me from behind the boulder, and as I moved farther away I heard him snapping his jaws and snarling as though in anger at being outwitted.

Just what he would have done had I walked into his ambush can only be guessed. Hunters trailing a wounded grizzly have been ambushed and killed. But this grizzly had not even been shot at nor harassed.

Generally, when a grizzly discovers that he is followed, or even if he only thinks himself followed, he at once hurries off to some other part of his territory, as this one did after I rolled the stone. But Old Timberline on finding himself followed slipped round to follow me. Often a grizzly, if he feels he is not yet seen,—that his move is unsuspected,—will slip round to follow those who are trailing him. But in no other case that I know of has a bear lingered after he realized that he was seen. After Old Timberline discovered that I had circled behind him, he knew that I knew where he was and what he was doing.

But instead of running away he came back along the trail to await my coming. What were his intentions? Did he intend to assault me, or was he overcome with curiosity because of my unusual actions and trying to discover what they were all about? I do not know. I concluded it best not to follow him farther, nor did I wish to travel that night with this crafty, soft-footed fellow in the woods. Going a short distance down among the trees, I built a rousing fire. Between it and a cliff I spent the night, satisfied that I had had adventure enough for one outing.

Trailing is adventurous. Many of the best lessons of woodcraft that I have learned, several of the greatest and most beneficial outings that I have had, were those during which I followed, sometimes day and night, that master of strategy, the grizzly bear. A few times in trailing the grizzly I have outwitted him, but more frequently he has outwitted me. Every grizzly has speed, skill, and endurance. He has mental capacity and often shows astounding plan, caution, courage, and audacity.

Trailing without a gun is red-blooded life, scouting of the most exacting and manly order. The trailer loses himself in his part in the primeval play of the wilderness. It is doubtful if any other experience is as educational as the trailing of the grizzly bear.

5.

The Story of a Thousand-Year Pine

THE PECULIAR CHARM and fascination that trees exert over many people I had always felt from childhood, but it was that great nature-lover, John Muir, who first showed me how and where to learn their language. Few trees, however, ever held for me such an attraction as did a gigantic and venerable yellow pine which I discovered one autumn day several years ago while exploring the southern Rockies. It grew within sight of the Cliff-Dwellers' Mesa Verde, which stands at the corner of four States, and as I came upon it one evening just as the sun was setting over that mysterious tableland, its character and heroic proportions made an impression upon me that I shall never forget, and which familiar acquaintance only served to deepen while it yet lived and before the axeman came. Many a time I returned to build my camp-fire by it and have a day or a night in its solitary and noble company. I learned afterwards that it had been given the name "Old Pine," and it certainly had an impressiveness quite compatible with the age and dignity which go with a thousand years of life.

When, one day, the sawmill-man at Mancos wrote, "Come, we are about to log your old pine," I started at once, regretting that a thing which seemed to me so human, as well as so noble, must be killed.

I went out with the axemen who were to cut the old pine down. A grand and impressive tree he was. Never have I seen

Veteran western yellow pine

so much individuality, so much character, in a tree. Although lightning had given him a bald crown, he was still a healthy giant, and was waving evergreen banners more than one hundred and fifteen feet above the earth. His massive trunk, eight feet in diameter on a level with my breast, was covered with a thick, rough, golden-brown bark which was broken into irregular plates. Several of his arms were bent and broken. Altogether, he presented a time-worn but heroic appearance.

The Story of a Thousand-Year Pine

It is almost a marvel that trees should live to become the oldest of living things. Fastened in one place, their struggle is incessant and severe. From the moment a baby tree is born—from the instant it casts its tiny shadow upon the ground—until death, it is in danger from insects and animals. It cannot move to avoid danger. It cannot run away to escape enemies. Fixed in one spot, almost helpless, it must endure flood and drought, fire and storm, insects and earthquakes, or die.

Trees, like people, struggle for existence, and an aged tree, like an aged person, has not only a striking appearance, but an interesting biography. I have read the autobiographies of many century-old trees, and have found their life-stories strange and impressive. The yearly growth, or annual ring of wood with which trees envelop themselves, is embossed with so many of their experiences that this annual ring of growth literally forms an autobiographic diary of the tree's life.

I wanted to read Old Pine's autobiography. A veteran pine that had stood on the southern Rockies and struggled and triumphed through the changing seasons of hundreds of years must contain a rare life-story. From his stand between the Mesa and the pine-plumed mountain, he had seen the panorama of the seasons and many a strange pageant; he had beheld what scenes of animal and human strife, what storms and convulsions of nature! Many a wondrous secret he had locked within his tree soul. Yet, although he had not recorded what he had *seen,* I knew that he had kept a fairly accurate diary of his own personal experience. This I knew the saw would reveal, and this I had determined to see.

Nature matures a million conifer seeds for each one she chooses for growth, so we can only speculate as to the selection of the seed from which sprung this storied pine. It may be that the cone in which it matured was crushed into the earth by the hoof of a passing deer. It may have been hidden by a jay; or, as is more likely, it may have grown from one of the uneaten cones which a Douglas squirrel had buried for winter food. Douglas squirrels are the principal nurserymen for all the Western pineries. Each autumn they harvest a heavy percentage of the cone crop and bury it for winter. The seeds in the uneaten cones germinate, and each year countless thousands of conifers grow from the seeds planted by these squirrels. It may be that the seed from which Old Pine burst had been planted by an ancient ancestor of the protesting Douglas who was in possession, or this seed may have been in a cone which simply bounded or blew into a hole, where the seed found sufficient mould and moisture to give it a start in life.

Two loggers swung their axes. At the first blow a Douglas squirrel came out of a hole at the base of a dead limb near the top of the tree and made an aggressive claim of ownership, setting up a vociferous protest against the cutting. As his voice was unheeded, he came scolding down the tree, jumped off one of the lower limbs, and took refuge in a young pine that stood near by. From time to time he came out on the top of the limb nearest to us, and, with a wry face, fierce whiskers, and violent gestures, directed a torrent of abuse at the axemen who were delivering death-blows to Old Pine.

The old pine's enormous weight caused him to fall heavily, and he came to earth with tremendous force and struck on an elbow of one of his stocky arms. The force of the fall not only broke the trunk in two, but badly shattered it. The damage to the log was so general that the sawmill-man said it would not pay to saw it into lumber and that it could rot on the spot.

I had come a long distance for the express purpose of deciphering Old Pine's diary as the scroll of his life should be laid open in the sawmill. The abandonment of the shattered form compelled the adoption of another way to getting at his story. Receiving permission to do as I pleased with his remains, I at once began to cut and split both the trunk and the limbs and to transcribe their strange records. Day after day I worked. I dug up the roots and thoroughly dissected them, and with the aid of a magnifier I studied the trunk, the roots, and the limbs.

I carefully examined the base of his stump, and in it I found 1047 rings of growth! He had lived through a thousand and

The Story of a Thousand-Year Pine

forty-seven memorable years. As he was cut down in 1903, his birth probably occurred in 856.

In looking over the rings of growth, I found that a few of them were much thicker than the others; and these thick rings, or coats of wood, tell of favorable seasons. There were also a few extremely thin rings of growth. In places two and even three of these were together. These were the result of unfavorable seasons,—of drought or cold. The rings of trees also show healed wounds, and tell of burns, bites, and bruises, of torn bark and broken arms. Old Pine not only received injuries in his early years, but from time to time throughout his life. The somewhat kinked condition of several of the rings of growth, beginning with the twentieth, shows that at the age of twenty he sustained an injury which resulted in a severe curvature of the spine, and that for some years he was somewhat stooped. I was unable to make out from his diary whether this injury was the result of a tree or some object falling upon him and pinning him down, or whether his back had been overweighted and bent by wet, clinging snow. As I could not find any scars or bruises, I think that snow must have been the cause of the injury. However, after a few years he straightened up with youthful vitality and seemed to outgrow and forget the experience.

A century of tranquil life followed, and during these years the rapid growth tells of good seasons as well as good soil. This rapid growth also shows that there could not have been any crowding neighbors to share the sun and the soil. The tree had grown evenly in all quarters, and the pith of the tree was in the centre. But had one tree grown close, on that quarter the old pine would have grown slower than the others and would have been thinner, and the pith would thus have been away from the tree's centre.

When the old pine was just completing his one hundred and thirty-fifth ring of growth, he met with an accident which I can account for only by assuming that a large tree that grew several yards away blew over, and in falling, stabbed him in the side with two dead limbs. His bark was broken and torn, but this healed in due time. Short sections of the dead limbs broke off, however, and were embedded in the old pine. Twelve years' growth covered them, and they remained hidden from view until my splitting revealed them. The other wounds started promptly to heal and, with one exception, did so.

A year or two later some ants and borers began excavating their deadly winding ways in the old pine. They probably started to work in one of the places injured by the falling tree. They must have had some advantage, or else something must have happened to the nuthatches and chickadees that year, for, despite the vigilance of these birds, both the borers and the ants succeeded in establishing colonies that threatened injury and possibly death.

Fortunately relief came. One day the chief surgeon of all the Southwestern pineries came along. This surgeon was the Texas woodpecker. He probably did not long explore the ridges and little furrows of the bark before he discovered the wound or heard these hidden insects working. After a brief examination, holding his ear to the bark for a moment to get the location of the tree's deadly foe beneath, he was ready to act. He made two successful operations. These not only required him to cut deeply into the old pine and take out the borers, but he may also have had to come back from time to time to dress the wounds by devouring the ant-colonies which may have persisted in taking possession of them. The wounds finally healed, and only the splitting of the affected parts revealed these records, all filled with pitch and preserved for nearly nine hundred years.

Following this, an even tenor marked his life for nearly three centuries. This quiet existence came to an end in the summer of 1301, when a stroke of lightning tore a limb out of his round top and badly shattered a shoulder. He had barely recovered from this injury when a violent wind tore off several of his arms. During the summer of 1348 he lost two of his largest arms. These were large and sound, and were more

The Story of a Thousand-Year Pine

than a foot in diameter at the points of breakage. As these were broken by a down-pressing weight or force, we may atttribute these breaks to accumulations of snow.

The oldest, largest portion of a tree is the short section immediately above the ground, and, as this lower section is the most exposed to accidents or to injuries from enemies, it generally bears evidence of having suffered the most. Within its scroll are usually found the most extensive and interesting autobiographical impressions.

It is doubtful if there is any portion of the earth upon which there are so many deadly struggles as upon the earth around the trunk of a tree. Upon this small arena there are battles fierce and wild; here nature is "red in tooth and claw." When a tree is small and tender, countless insects come to feed upon it. Birds come to it to devour these insects. Around the tree are daily almost merciless fights for existence. These death-struggles occur not only in the daytime, but in the night. Mice, rats, and rabbits destroy millions of young trees. These bold animals often flay baby trees in the daylight, and while at their deadly feast many a time have they been surprised by hawks, and then they are at a banquet where they themselves are eaten. The owl, the faithful nightwatchman of trees, often swoops down at night, and as a result some little tree is splashed with the blood of the very animal that came to feed upon it.

The lower section of Old Pine's trunk contained records which I found interesting. One of these in particular aroused my imagination. I was sawing off a section of this lower portion when the saw, with a buzz-z-z-z, suddenly jumped. The object struck was harder than the saw. I wondered what it could be, and, cutting the wood carefully away, laid bare a flint arrowhead. Close to this one I found another, and then with care I counted the rings of growth to find out the year that these had wounded Old Pine. The outer ring which these arrowheads had pierced was the six hundred and thirtieth, so that the year of this occurrence was 1486.

Had an Indian bent his bow and shot at a bear that had

stood at bay backed up against this tree? Or was there around this tree a battle among Indian tribes? Is it possible that at this place some Cliff-Dweller scouts encountered their advancing foe from the north and opened hostilities? It may be that around Old Pine was fought the battle that is said to have decided the fate of that mysterious race the Cliff-Dwellers. The imagination insists on speculating with these two arrowheads, though they form a fascinating clue that leads us to no definite conclusion. But the fact remains that Old Pine was wounded by two Indian arrowheads some time during his six hundred and thirtieth summer.

The year that Columbus discovered America, Old Pine was a handsome giant with a round head held more than one hundred feet above the earth. He was six hundred and thirty-six years old, and with the coming of the Spanish adventurers his lower trunk was given new events to record. The year 1540 was a particularly memorable one for him. This year brought the first horses and bearded men into the drama which was played around him. This year, for the first time, he felt the edge of steel and the tortures of fire. The old chronicles say that the Spanish explorers found the cliff-houses in the year 1540. I believe that during this year a Spanish exploring party may have camped beneath Old Pine and built a fire against his instep, and that some of the explorers hacked him with an axe. The old pine had distinct records of axe and fire markings during the year 1540. It was not common for the Indians of the West to burn or mutilate trees, and as it was common for the Spaniards to do so, and as these hackings in the tree seemed to have been made with some edged tool sharper than any possessed by the Indians, it at least seems probable that they were done by the Spaniards. At any rate, from the year 1540 until the day of his death, Old Pine carried these scars on his instep.

As the average yearly growth of the old pine was about the same as in trees similarly situated at the present time, I suppose that climatic conditions in his early days must have been similar to the climatic conditions of to-day. His records indi-

The Story of a Thousand-Year Pine

cate periods of even tenor of climate, a year of extremely poor conditions, occasionally a year crowned with a bountiful wood harvest. From 1540 to 1762 I found little of special interest. In 1762, however, the season was not regular. After the ring was well started, something, perhaps a cold wave, for a time checked its growth, and as a result the wood for that one year resembled two years' growth, but yet the difference between this double or false ring and a regular one was easily detected. Old Pine's "hard times" experience seems to have been during the years 1804 and 1805. I think it probable that these were years of drought. During 1804 the layer of wood was the thinnest in his life, and for 1805 the only wood I could find was a layer which only partly covered the trunk of the tree, and this was exceedingly thin.

From time to time in the old pine's record, I came across what seemed to be indications of an earthquake shock; but late in 1811 or early in 1812, I think there is no doubt that he experienced a violent shock, for he made extensive records of it. This earthquake occurred after the sap had ceased to flow in 1811, and before it began to flow in the spring of 1812. In places the wood was checked and shattered. At one point, some distance from the ground, there was a bad horizontal break. Two big roots were broken in two, and that quarter of the tree which faced the cliffs had suffered from a rock bombardment. I suppose the violence of the quake displaced many rocks, and some of these, as they came bounding down the mountain-side, collided with Old Pine. One, of about five pounds' weight, struck him so violently in the side that it remained embedded there. After some years the wound was healed over, but this fragment remained in the tree until I released it.

During 1859 some one made an axe-mark on the old pine that may have been intended for a trail-blaze, and during the same year another fire badly burned and scarred his ankle. I wonder if some prospectors came this way in 1859 and made camp by him.

Another record of man's visits to the tree was made in the

summer of 1881, when I think a hunting or outing party may have camped near here and amused themselves by shooting at a mark on Old Pine's ankle. Several modern rifle-bullets were found embedded in the wood around or just beneath a blaze which was made on the tree the same year in which the bullets had entered it. As both of these marks were made during the year 1881, it is at least possible that this year the old pine was used as the background for a target during a shooting contest.

While I was working over the old pine, a Douglas squirrel who lived near by used every day to stop in his busy harvesting of pine-cones to look on and scold me. As I watched him placing his cones in a hole in the ground under the pine-needles, I often wondered if one of his buried cones would remain there uneaten to germinate and expand ever green into the air, and become a noble giant to live as long and as useful a life as Old Pine. I found myself trying to picture the scenes in which this tree would stand when the birds came singing back from the Southland in the springtime of the year 3000.

After I had finished my work of splitting, studying, and deciphering the fragments of the old pine, I went to the sawmill and arranged for the men to come over that evening after I had departed and burn every piece and vestige of the venerable old tree. I told them I should be gone by dark. Then I went back and piled into a pyramid every fragment of root and trunk and broken branch. Seating myself upon this pyramid, I spent some time that afternoon gazing through the autumn sunglow at the hazy Mesa Verde, while my mind rebuilt and shifted the scenes of the long, long drama in which Old Pine had played his part, and of which he had given us but a few fragmentary records. I lingered there dreaming until twilight. I thought of the cycles during which he had stood patient in his appointed place, and my imagination busied itself with the countless experiences that had been recorded, and the scenes and pageants he had witnessed but of which he had made no record. I wondered if he had enjoyed the changing of seasons. I knew that he had often boomed or

The Story of a Thousand-Year Pine

hymned in the storm or in the breeze. Many a monumental robe of snow-flowers had he worn. More than a thousand times he had beheld the earth burst into bloom amid the happy songs of mating birds; hundreds of times in summer he had worn countless crystal rain-jewels in the sunlight of the breaking storm, while the brilliant rainbow came and vanished on the near-by mountain-side. Ten thousand times he had stood silent in the lonely light of the white and mystic moon.

Twilight was fading into darkness when I arose and started on a night-journey for the Mesa Verde, where I intended next morning to greet an old gnarled cedar which grew on its summit. When I arrived at the top of the Mesa, I looked back and saw a pyramid of golden flame standing out in the darkness.

6.

A Coyote Den by the River

LOOKING FROM MY SLEEPING BAG just at daylight, I saw a coyote on the other side of the river step from behind a clump of willows. He showed surprise at seeing me so close.

Arriving by starlight the night before, I had crawled into the sleeping bag without fire or noise. It is probable that this coyote had been off foraging at the time. On his return to the den neither sight nor scent had warned him of my presence.

But from his present actions he appeared to feel that he had been seen. This concerned him, because he was by the entrance to his well-concealed den, in which perhaps there were puppies.

He disappeared among the trees. A minute later he reappeared a short distance up the river and moved about, plainly trying to attract my attention. I watched him but did not let him know that I saw him. After making a number of moves calculated to catch my eye, he crossed to my side of the river and, pretending to be terribly crippled, started toward me. Only a minute before he had moved with light-footed agility. He was a good actor and pretended not to know that I was there.

But he was determined to make me notice him. He came within thirty feet but, still acting, looked away from me into the river. Evidently his keen nose must have told him that I had no gun. Coyotes are not mind readers, but they often

A Coyote Den by the River

show themselves to the hunter who is without a gun. He stopped and gave a yelp and howl.

Of course I had to look at him after that. Then he pretended to discover me. With show of alarm he made stumbling and vigorous efforts to escape.

He was badly crippled. His back and two legs were barely useful. I pursued him full speed. This was what he wished—to draw me away from the den—and I was eager to follow and see his tactics and learn how far he would lead me.

If there were puppies in the den, this would explain his boldly coming close to me and his clever manœuvres for leading me afar.

Crowding him closely, I caused him to plunge into the river. Desperately he struggled through the water and came out on the other side, acting the part of a wounded, exhausted animal. Had I not known his actual condition, and understood coyote cunning, I naturally should have concluded that he was badly hurt.

He allowed me almost to catch him. When I attempted to seize him he took to the water to save himself. He went crippling across the river on cobblestones. In climbing the steep bank he stood and breathed as if about to collapse, but this was just a ruse to allow me to catch up. As I scrambled up the bank he walked into the woods and entered a den. If he was a reasoning animal, as his actions seemed to show, he probably thought that he had lured me away from the den occupied by his mate and their puppies, and that I would linger by this other, unoccupied den, instead.

If a coyote family feel that their den is discovered they move. I hurried back to the den by the river and moved my sleeping bag. After making camp upstream I came back close to where I had slept and, concealed behind bushes, watched the entrance of the den.

It was well hidden in the bottom of a cañon at the foot of a cliff immediately behind a clump of willows. To reach it one had either to cross the river to climb down a precipitous cliff wall. The den was beneath the loose rocks that had fallen off the cliff, and the entrance was three feet or more above the level of the river.

Near noon the crippled coyote, completely recovered, came slipping back home. He deftly climbed down a steep place in the cliff that stood above the den. Every few steps he stopped, looked, and listened. His nose was ever open for man scent. But the air current was downstream and there was little likelihood of his scenting me.

He slipped out of sight behind the willows. Within a minute another coyote came out from the willows into full sight, hurried part way up the cliff, and stood to look around. A look through the glasses showed her to be the mother of young puppies. Her attitude betrayed suspicion—as if she realized that a man might be near. When she moved on out of sight I hurried over a detour downstream and then up the slope, trying to follow her.

But she had vanished, probably gone off for something to eat. Hoping to see her return, I strolled back and forth along her trail.

Two hours later she crossed an opening close to me, evidently with the intention of attracting my attention. She could readily have slipped by and on to the den without my seeing her. From an examination of her tracks, it appeared that she had scented me and had turned aside from her course to come in sight of me.

It was plain that she wanted to lead me away. As soon as I followed, she led up the slope—away from the den. Arriving on the edge of a thicket she smelled about this way and that with nose close to the earth, as if trailing something of importance. When I came close, she feigned surprise and darted into the thicket. I showed increased speed after her and off we hurried along a timbered slope. Finally she entered a den.

On the way back to my camp I kept well away from the den containing the puppies. Mr. Coyote who had played cripple was on scout duty. I travelled slowly and quietly and kept out of openings so that he would not discover me.

A Coyote Den by the River

Suddenly his nose caught a scent that told him that I was close. He had not heard me, and as I was behind a ridge covered with numbers of trees and rocks, he had not seen me. But a little movement of air and his nose received the information that I was to the west of him and less than one hundred feet away. Scent which all animals give off, its radiation and the news this tells to receiving noses, is the marvel of outdoor life.

He did not show himself but slipped along after me and tried to keep out of sight. Had I not been watching I should not have suspected his following. I walked on more rapidly and did nothing to indicate that I knew he was following me.

When I crossed to the other side of the stream he stopped where he could watch me. I sat down on my sleeping bag, screened by brush, where I could watch him. For minutes he stood still waiting for me to make a move. Then he changed his position but still kept guard. We were a quarter of a mile upstream from his den, and he evidently wanted to satisfy himself as to where I was camping. I started the campfire and went for water.

He saw me approach the stream, and eyed me as I stood and drank. All the time he stayed within ten feet, curiously alert. Near sundown I saw him move on. Evidently he was satisfied that he knew where I was to camp that night.

Coyotes are tireless and uncannily cunning for the care and the safety of their young, as well as for themselves. They are constantly on guard, and it appears that they are prepared with the next probable move, and the possible next two or three moves, to be made; and if danger arises they move in the right direction. Commonly a pair of coyotes have a number of dens. One of these is used regularly for a time, then a change is made to another.

The second afternoon I discovered another of these extra, camouflaged dens. A short distance up the slope from their used den I came unexpectedly upon one of the coyotes. He was surprised and ran off in a semicircle. I pursued for several minutes and he came back close to where I had discovered him, and entered a den the opening to which was not concealed.

In trying to keep him in sight I had climbed upon a rockpile just in time to see him enter this den. Then as I stood on these rocks, I chanced to see him slyly emerge from another exit, placed about twenty feet from the one through which he had gone in and concealed from it by a clump of trees.

He stood for a few seconds looking and listening, but without detecting me. Then with a long leap he slunk away to the top of the cliff, whence he descended to the den in use. By mere chance I had discovered this clever trick. Ordinarily, neither dog nor man would make the discovery of the real den after seeing the deceptive outlying one. A dog that had trailed a coyote to the entrance of this or a similar den would hardly understand the significance of the other, even though he discovered it.

I hoped that the pair were not alarmed and would not move their puppies. If they should move, it would probably deprive me of the opportunity of watching them further.

All the next morning I watched the den entrance with my glasses, keeping well away from the entrance itself, hoping they would feel that I did not suspect the place of their used den. I had discovered it by mere luck but had not gone close to it.

As neither coyote appeared during my watch of three hours I left the watching place for a time and went off exploring. Two miles upstream I came upon the track of Mr. Coyote on one side of a swamp. I walked around and explored the opposite edge. I found a den with his track in the entrance.

On the way back to camp I had a glimpse of a coyote watching me. Just a glimpse through the trees and it was gone. It had the appearance of being Mrs. Coyote. Evidently these coyotes were vigilant in their observation of me; perhaps partly through curiosity, but more through concern for their near-by puppies.

After a stop at my camp I went to the watching place by a triangular course. There were coyote tracks in the sand

A Coyote Den by the River

around where I had been hiding to watch. After a long wait Mrs. Coyote came down the cliff as quietly as a shadow. She entered the den and after the lapse of half an hour had not come out. The puppies were still there.

It proved unfortunate for the coyotes that they had not moved.

During the night a rain began falling. It seemed probable that I might have another day hunting coyotes with my eyes, for unless I had seriously alarmed them, with a rain falling they probably would not leave the old den that night.

It was raining steadily, and there was a splendid bombardment of thunder when I set off the following morning to watch the entrance to the den. After a few minutes in position I suddenly saw both coyotes standing in front of it. He was licking her shoulder. They appeared dry, and I do not know whether they had just come out or just arrived. Presently they entered the den.

As soon as they disappeared I went in search of a hiding-place near the top of the cliff above them. In crossing the stream, a short distance below, I noticed that the water was rising and was roily. Halfway up the cliff I came to a ledge from which I could look down on the entrance to the den, and stopped to watch from this place.

The rising stream soon began to roar. A heavy rain had fallen on the slopes tributary to an east fork and this water was now sweeping down. The river already was many times its normal volume. With increased roaring, a wide moving cataract of a flood from above came spreading among the trees. Leaves, trash, and a scattering of logs came down in the boiling torrent. A first rush of water filled the coyote den and second rush covered and remained above it.

The bedraggled old coyotes came out from their flooded home each with a puppy in his mouth. In a few seconds all the puppies had been carried out and placed near by upon a ledge a foot or two above the water level.

Six shivering puppies were curiously nosed about by the old coyotes. Each of the old ones took a puppy by the skin of the back of the neck and stepped into the stream, swimming for the opposite shore. The stream at this instant was about one hundred feet wide.

The current midstream was swift, and both coyotes were carried downstream at least one hundred feet. On reaching the bank they hurried upstream to a point opposite the den and dropped the puppies and at once reëntered the water, making toward the other puppies on the ledge. But the two puppies left behind stumbled about and mostly toward the water. Mother Coyote turned and swam back to them.

The father went on to rescue the others. Seizing one, he swam across, dropped it by the mother, and hurriedly reëntered the swift water. The fourth he brought across nicely. After picking it up he walked a short distance upstream before taking to the water. He used the same plan with the fifth one. He was tiring, however. The current, too, was stronger. But he landed the puppy and went upstream again before taking to the water.

With the advantage of the downstream current, he crossed without great effort. But he was a tired coyote. Why did not she take his place? Evidently she was needed to care for the little puppies. They perhaps were not more than a week old.

A log jam had formed in the stream among the boulders and trees a little below me. This dammed the stream, and although a volume poured over, there was a deepening and a backing up of water.

The sixth puppy, all alone, had become restless. Whether he fell off into the water or was swept off I know not. The old coyote dived two or three times and splashed about before he secured a hold on it.

Tired, he climbed out on a ledge to rest. He was breathing heavily. This time he started directly across instead of taking advantage of the current by going upstream as he had done with the two preceding trips across.

He had gone but a little way when the log jam below broke and a section of it went out. The pouring water greatly increased the current. The swimming coyote felt this. He was

A Coyote Den by the River

not going strong, and the trash and the powerful current worried him.

Mother Coyote, after moving the other coyotes back, came and stood at the edge of the stream to watch her mate. He was not making headway toward the shore and the current was carrying him rapidly downstream. Mother Coyote ceased looking over her shoulder at the puppies and kept her eyes upon him.

A mass of bushes and trash came rushing down and enveloped him. He lost his hold on the puppy. But again he seized it and swam desperately for the shore. He was weak and his efforts mostly wild. The current was carrying him toward the break in the log jam.

A rolling, rushing log pushed him aside but he caught this with his fore feet and after two attempts climbed upon it. This log might strike the jam or the bank and afford him a means of escape. But suddenly it rolled over.

Another section of the log jam broke out and the river-wide water rushed forward, rushing the log with it. The coyote came up, struggling, with the puppy still grasped by the skin of the neck.

In a few seconds he would either be swept through the wreck of the log jam or, possibly, would reach the bank. His fore feet caught a pole that was entangled. But the current was too strong. With his teeth he could have clung on and saved himself. But he held on to the puppy.

Just as I was roused and started to the rescue, Mother Coyote came full speed down the bank toward him. Before she could reach him his feet slipped off the pole. Still clinging to the puppy, he was swept through the broken jam and disappeared in the roaring rush of water.

As I climbed off the cliff I saw Mother Coyote collecting the five scattered puppies.

7.

Summer Travels of a Beaver

IN A BEAVER COLONY close to my cabin I found a small aspen stump freshly cut. The marks showed that the beaver that cut it had a broken front tooth. I watched for this beaver. A few days later I saw his track in the mud; part of the left front foot was missing—perhaps had been nipped off in a trap.

About the first of June each year the numerous beavers near my cabin left their houses and went off for the entire summer, I could not guess where. I had trailed a number, but usually after a few miles lost all trace.

Trailing a beaver is uncertain and usually impossible. He travels by water and may not for miles leave any sign of the bank. And then, the sign of one beaver—teeth marks on stumps and tracks in the mud—are much like those of any other.

But these two defects, a broken tooth and a toe or two missing, would be marks that would enable me to trail my beaver neighbour wherever he cut a tree or left a track.

He started off early June on his summer vacation, or, rather, on a long journey. He must have been gone a number of days before I missed him. I followed, hoping to trail him, go where he would.

At the first tributary stream I stopped to look for sign. There were tracks, a beaver had recently gone up. A short distance beyond I came to clean-cut footprints which showed that this beaver's feet were sound.

Summer Travels of a Beaver

So I returned to the main stream and followed it for four miles without seeing a sign of the broken-toothed beaver. Then the stream emptied into one much larger. Up this I went, examining the banks on both sides. There were several beaver colonies on the headwaters. A number of beavers had been up and down. There were two sets of tracks with toes missing, but these were not made by the beaver I was trailing.

After being closely shut up in a poorly ventilated house all winter beavers need days of air and sunshine. Summer is their vacation and travelling time. They scatter along streams and picnic with members of other colonies.

I found the tracks of a number of young beavers. Youngsters sometimes go away for the summer with their mothers, but they may go only a mile or two. And if there are many dangers the mother appears to stay close to their home.

I turned downstream and followed along the river bank, looking for tracks in the mud, and also examining each freshly cut stump. The broken-toothed beaver must have travelled rapidly. I had gone about five miles before I came upon the first sign of him. He had left footprints in the mud on the bank, and broken-tooth marks on an aspen stump.

A little below these signs the river united with the St. Vrain. The broken-toothed beaver had cut off an aspen at the entrance to the St. Vrain cañon. I was interested to know if he were going through the narrow, deep cañon, or upstream. After searching upstream for a mile without finding any sign, I concluded that he had gone downstream.

Miles of the cañon walls are several hundred feet apart with growths of trees and willows by the river; but several stretches are deep and narrow. In one of these steep, narrow sections, the closely crowding walls have just the rushing, swirling river between them. There was no way to get downstream without wading and swimming. I had not been through this part of the cañon, nor had I heard of any one who had. But down I started.

It was dark when I came out at its lower end. Then all my

matches were damp. After half an hour trying to dry them I gave up starting a fire. I pulled off my clothes and wrung a part of the water out of them. I went through a number of lively exercises that were warming. Finally I found a deep, dry bed of pine and spruce needles, and with wet clothes on, buried myself in them.

Two miles down from where I had entered the cañon I found the sign of the broken-toothed beaver on the north bank. He had stayed a day or two at this point, apparently. Two different aspens had been cut and the bark partly eaten. He had sunned himself for hours, as I judged from the marks where he had lain, moved, and lain down again.

From here on, about every mile, rarely was it two miles, he had stopped to cut an aspen for food and to sun himself. There short stretches between stops probably were the extent of twenty-four hours of travel.

This beaver had at least a week the start of me, but far down the river I caught up with him. Twice or more I passed him.

Now and then he turned and went upstream. Commonly it was for only a short distance, but once he travelled back three or four miles. I cannot guess why, unless he was playing with other beavers.

One evening I saw his sign a quarter of a mile downstream from my camp; that night he passed my camp and went upstream again and left his footprints on mine that had been made the afternoon before.

After fifteen miles from home I lost trace of him. Had a coyote or other beaver-eater captured him? I had last seen a stump cut by him up the river where a tributary entered. I went back up the river and up this tributary stream a short distance and once more found his chips.

I traced him up this side stream to a beaver colony whose inhabitants, like himself, probably were on an outing for the summer. After lingering for a time around this place he went on upstream, until he came to shallow water where he could no longer swim. Here he boldly left the water and started across a dry ridge to another stream. This was perilous.

A beaver is a swimming animal; in the water he goes easily and swiftly. But on land he goes slowly and with effort, and where there is hill climbing with logs and rocks to climb over, a cross-country trip is hard work. His speediest efforts down hill are slow, awkward going, compared with the agility and swiftness of his enemies.

The wild cat, the coyote, the lion, and the bear are fond of beaver flesh and for them to find a beaver away from a stream is like finding a fish out of water.

Leaving the stream the beaver crossed a sandy channel in which at night and early morning there was a thin trickle of water. But the beaver's tracks had been made here when the water was not running, so he must have started cross-country in daytime.

With man out of the scene it is safer for beaver to travel during the daytime. During the night bears, wolves, lions, and wild cats do most of their hunting. But coyotes often travel during daytime and cats sometimes do. In general, beaver never venture far from water. Only in emergencies will one do so.

The broken-toothed beaver climbed a long, steep slope just after leaving the stream. He left a muddy mark on a log that he climbed over and here and there a track in the soft, fine sand.

"Is this beaver travelling alone?" I had repeatedly asked myself, as I followed him down the river. Beaver traces were numerous where he had been, but at no time were there signs near his that showed anything peculiar.

At one place where a second aspen had been cut close to the other that carried his toothmarks both had been cut about the same time. Again, up the side stream I found two freshly cut trees. One stump carried the marks of a broken tooth, the other had been cut by a beaver with perfect teeth. It thus appeared certain that a pair of beavers were travelling together.

Tracks across the ridge showed this to be a fact. There were two sets of footprints and one line of these was made by a beaver having all his toes.

All the way across the ridge their tracks indicated that not a thing had troubled them except perhaps the dry heat, the lack of water to plunge in, and the steep climbing. But well down toward the other side of the ridge these beavers came upon the enemy.

They had passed near a cliff where there was a wild cat den. A cat was in. Whether he saw them or scented them cannot be guessed, but after them he went. He sneaked close at two places, hesitated, then crawled away, evidently to look for a better place of attack. Both were adult beaver, perhaps twice the weight of the cat.

Rarely does a beaver fight. His plan of life is to have an open line of retreat and escape into deep water. Once in deep water, probably no pursuer except an otter could cause him any trouble.

The cat had slipped ahead and squatted upon a stump by which the beavers would probably pass. There was a dim wild-life trail past this stump down to the brook. While the cat was flattened and waiting, a coyote appears to have come up from below. Possibly it scented the cat and had come near to have fun with her. His tracks and scratches all round the stump indicated that he had leaped at her several times. The cat at last sprang from the stump and started for its den full jump, with the coyote in pursuit.

Meantime, a stone's throw up the slope, the two beavers seem to have squatted against a log and waited. The line of the cat's retreat was near them. The coyote must have rushed the cat past them without suspecting their presence. But halfway to the den he stopped suddenly, wheeled, started this way then that, and finally rushed down the slope after the beavers.

They had probably hustled toward the brook as soon as the cat leaped off the stump. It matters not if the coyote heard their galloping or scented them. His far-apart tracks down the hill showed that he pursued them full speed.

They reached the shallow little brook in advance of their pursuer and were making haste downstream when he leaped for them. Again he leaped, but they dodged among the willows. Apparently they did not fight back.

They tumbled over a cascade in the stream that was only a few feet high. At its bottom were a deep pool, a log jam, and holes in the bank. Here they were able to get beyond the coyote. His muddy footprints stamped on the logs, his scratches on both banks, and his tracks under one bank showed that he had spent time and effort trying to reach them. There was one place just below the logs where he had lain down; the markings indicated that he had waited, possibly for hours.

Both beavers escaped. Nearly a mile below I found two freshly felled aspens, one of these the work of the broken-toothed beaver. This stream was a tributary of the one on the other side of the ridge. A number of beaver colonies were examined by the two travellers.

They went on down into the St. Vrain River two or three miles and turned up another small tributary. If anything of interest or adventure occurred while they explored its headwaters, I did not discover. They returned to the St. Vrain and went on downstream.

I had not yet seen these beavers. Their tree-cutting and an occasional track had enabled me to trail them. From the freshness of the sign I knew that I was close to them and might see them at any moment.

They were going leisurely, perhaps mostly at night. There were many indications of their having rolled about and lain in the sun for hours. From any of their loitering places they could have quickly dived beyond danger into deep water.

At the bottom of one steep bank that was six or seven feet above the river they had long sunned themselves in the sand. There was no chance for a coyote to slip up behind them. They had dug holes back into the bank where they could lie and be out of sight and had burrowed places in the dry sand that just fitted their bodies, and had lain and rolled about on the grass.

There were numerous other beavers loafing along the river. Every day I saw many, sometimes a dozen or more, frequently two and three at a time.

As far as I know I did not see the broken-toothed beaver but I may have seen him with other beavers a number of times without knowing him. In a few places I saw his tracks with those of the others. If ever I could have seen a lone beaver moving away from a freshly gnawed stump that was marked with his teeth, then I should have known that I had seen my beaver neighbour.

I came upon marked sand in one sunning place that showed that the travellers had had a narrow escape. A lion evidently had seen or scented them.

Along the opposite bank he had sneaked behind logs and rocks, without getting close enough to spring. Then he had looked down upon them from the opposite high bank. Perhaps if he had leaped, the overhang of the bank would have prevented his landing upon them.

A tree with long limbs had fallen across the river a little below where the beavers lay in the sun. On this he had crawled out and lain in wait probably a long time, possibly hours.

The beavers finally started down stream. The lion must have been lying on the log full length, otherwise they would have seen him. He either made an awkward leap, or did not notice the down-curving end of one of the long limbs of the fallen tree. His back struck the point of this limb; there were a few hairs still on it. He fell short and came down in the edge of the stream about three feet in front of the beavers. They dived from their tracks into deep water.

There were a number of small beaver houses and bank dens along this river. I examined the entrances of many, but in no case did I find the track of the broken-toothed beaver near them. Commonly, I think, beavers keep out of dens and houses in summer.

Sign showed that the two travellers had been joined by a third. A feeding place by which they had sunned themselves

Summer Travels of a Beaver

and eaten showed three felled trees instead of the usual two. At the next place downstream where they had stopped for food I found only two felled aspens, but the teeth marks showed that three different sets of teeth had eaten the bark.

It is possible that the three had been together for miles. But one thing is certain—only two had dared cross the dry ridge. If the third had been with them he must have dropped out and waited for the adventurers downstream.

On a small, tree-covered island in the river the three had had an adventure.

A fallen tree on the north bank made a bridge across the north channel. Near the lower end of the island I came to a half-cut aspen. The cutting was fresh, and it had been made by the broken-toothed beaver. Why had he not finished? I took a look around and found two other freshly half-cut aspens. All three of the beavers had been frightened from their cutting.

I looked for tracks. But not until I left the island and crossed on the fallen log to the north bank did I make a discovery. On the edge of a muddy place I found wild cat tracks. These led toward the island, then upon the fallen log bridge. But the tracks came to an end on the log with a blotch of thin, dry mud. This probably was where the beavers had taken fright and the cat had turned and jumped off the log.

My beaver neighbour was now more than thirty miles from his home. But he could have returned home in one hard night, or in two nights without hurrying. At this point the river left the mountains and started out across the Great Plains where with few trees along the shores the beaver would be more exposed to dangers, to traps and guns. Would they journey farther, I wondered, or start slowly homeward? It was still June, and they would have weeks for travel and exploration.

A trapper wrote me of finding the marks of the broken-toothed beaver on the Platte River, far out on the plains, mid-July. Evidently, this beaver from the swift, rocky streams of the mountains enjoyed the slow, sunny stream in the plains. No one knew his experiences and adventures.

Would this far-travelled beaver return to be my neighbour? Beavers that are away during the summer return usually by late August. But most beavers wander only a few miles from home while this explorer had gone sixty miles. Now and then a summer wanderer casts his or her lot with neighbour beavers and goes permanently to their colony. Often, also, two mate and start a new colony. And some, of course, lose their lives on their travels.

However, early in September I found fresh tooth and foot marks of the broken-toothed beaver in his old home by my cabin.

8.

The Ruined Colony

TWENTY-SIX YEARS AGO, while studying glaciation on the slope of Longs Peak, I came upon a cluster of eight beaver houses. These crude conical mud huts were in a forest pond far up on the mountainside. In this colony of our first engineers were so many things of interest that the fascinating study of the dead Ice King's ruins and records was indefinitely given up in order to observe Citizen Beaver's works and ways.

A pile of granite boulders on the edge of the pond stood several feet above the water-level, and from the top of these the entire colony and its operations could be seen. On these I spent days observing and enjoying the autumnal activities of Beaverdom.

It was the busiest time of the year for these industrious folk. General and extensive preparations were now being made for the long winter amid the mountain snows. A harvest of scores of trees was being gathered and work on a new house was in progress, while the old houses were receiving repairs. It was a serene autumn day when I came into the picturesque village of these primitive people. The aspens were golden, the willows rusty, the grass tanned, and the pines were purring in the easy air.

The colony-site was in a small basin amid morainal débris at an altitude of nine thousand feet above the sea-level. I at once christened it the Moraine Colony. The scene was utterly wild. Peaks of crags and snow rose steep and high above all; all around crowded a dense evergreen forest of pine and spruce. A few small swamps reposed in this forest, while here

From the Crags looking down on Lily Lake

and there in it bristled several gigantic windrows of boulders. A ragged belt of aspens surrounded the several ponds and separated the pines and spruces from the fringe of water-loving willows along the shores. There were three large ponds in succession and below these a number of smaller ones. The dams that formed the large ponds were willow-grown, earthy structures about four feet in height, and all sagged downstream. The houses were grouped in the middle pond, the largest one, the dam of which was more than three hundred feet long. Three of these lake dwellings stood near the upper

The Ruined Colony

margin, close to where the brook poured in. The other five were clustered by the outlet, just below which a small willow-grown, boulder-dotted island lay between the divided waters of the stream.

A number of beavers were busy gnawing down aspens, while others cut the felled ones into sections, pushed and rolled the sections into the water, and then floated them to the harvest piles, one of which was being made beside each house. Some were quietly at work spreading a coat of mud on the outside of each house. This would freeze and defy the tooth and claw of the hungriest or the strongest predaceous enemy. Four beavers were leisurely lengthening and repairing a dam. A few worked singly, but most of them were in groups. All worked quietly and with apparent deliberation, but all were in motion, so that it was a busy scene. "To work like a beaver!" What a stirring exhibition of beaver industry and forethought I viewed from my boulder-pile!

At times upward of forty of them were in sight. Though there was a general coöperation, yet each one appeared to do his part without orders or direction. Time and again a group of workers completed a task, and without pause silently moved off, and began another. Everything appeared to go on mechanically. It produced a strange feeling to see so many workers doing so many kinds of work effectively and automatically. Again and again I listened for the superintendent's voice; constantly I watched to see the overseer move among them; but I listened and watched in vain. Yet I feel that some of the patriarchal fellows must have carried a general plan of the work, and that during its progress orders and directions that I could not comprehend were given from time to time.

The work was at its height a little before midday. Nowadays it is rare for a beaver to work in daylight. Men and guns have prevented daylight workers from leaving descendants. These not only worked but played by day. One morning for more than an hour there was a general frolic, in which the entire population appeared to take part. They raced, dived, crowded in general mix-ups, whacked the water with their tails, wrestled, and dived again. There were two or three play-centres, but the play went on without intermission, and as their position constantly changed, the merrymakers splashed water all over the main pond before they calmed down and in silence returned to work. I gave most attention to the harvesters, who felled the aspens and moved them, bodily or in sections, by land and water to the harvest piles. One tree on the shore of the pond, which was felled into the water, was eight inches in diameter and fifteen feet high. Without having even a limb cut off, it was floated to the nearest harvest pile. Another, about the same size, which was procured some fifty feet from the water, was cut into four sections and its branches removed; then a single beaver would take a branch in his teeth, drag it to the water, and swim with it to a harvest pile. But four beavers united to transport the largest section to the water. They pushed with fore paws, with breasts, and with hips. Plainly it was too heavy for them. They paused. "Now they will go for help," I said to myself, "and I shall find out who the boss is." But to my astonishment one of them began to gnaw the piece in two, and two more began to clear a narrow way to the water, while the fourth set himself to cutting down another aspen. Good roads and open waterways are the rule, and perhaps the necessary rule, of beaver colonies.

I became deeply interested in this colony, which was situated within two miles of my cabin, and its nearness enabled me to be a frequent visitor and to follow closely its fortunes and misfortunes. About the hut-filled pond I lingered when it was covered with winter's white, when fringed with the gentian's blue, and while decked with the pond-lily's yellow glory.

Fire ruined it during an autumn of drouth. One morning, while watching from the boulder-pile, I noticed an occasional flake of ash dropping into the pond. Soon smoke scented the air, then came the awful and subdued roar of a forest fire. I fled, and from above the timber-line watched the stormcloud of black smoke sweep furiously forward, bursting and closing to the terrible leaps of red and tattered flames. Before noon several thousand acres of forest were dead, all leaves and twigs were in ashes, all tree-trunks blistered and blackened.

The Moraine Colony was closely embowered in a pitchy forest. For a time the houses in the water must have been wrapped in flames of smelter heat. Could these mud houses stand this? The beavers themselves I knew would escape by sinking under the water. Next morning I went through the hot, smoky area and found every house cracked and crumbling; not one was inhabitable. Most serious of all was the total loss of the uncut food-supply, when harvesting for winter had only begun.

Would these energetic people starve at home or would they try to find refuge in some other colony? Would they endeavor to find a grove that the fire had missed and there start anew? The intense heat had consumed almost every fibrous thing above the surface. The piles of garnered green aspen were charred to the waterline; all that remained of willow thickets and aspen groves were thousands of blackened pickets and points, acres of coarse charcoal stubble. It was a dreary, starving outlook for my furred friends.

I left the scene to explore the entire burned area. After wandering for hours amid ashes and charcoal, seeing here and there the seared carcass of a deer or some other wild animal, I came upon a beaver colony that had escaped the fire. It was in the midst of several acres of swampy ground that was covered with fire-resisting willows and aspens. The surrounding pine forest was not dense, and the heat it produced in burning did no damage to the scattered beaver houses.

From the top of a granite crag I surveyed the green scene of life and the surrounding sweep of desolation. Here and there a sodden log smouldered in the ashen distance and supported a tower of smoke in the still air. A few miles to the east, among the scattered trees of a rocky summit, the fire was burning itself out; to the west the sun was sinking behind crags and snow; near by, on a blackened limb, a south-bound robin chattered volubly but hopelessly.

While I was listening, thinking, and watching, a mountain lion appeared and leaped lightly upon a block of granite. He was on my right, about one hundred feet away and about an equal distance from the shore of the nearest pond. He was interested in the approach of something. With a nervous switching of his tail he peered eagerly forward over the crown of the ridge just before him, and then crouched tensely and expectantly upon his rock.

A pine tree that had escaped the fire screened the place toward which the lion looked and where something evidently was approaching. While I was trying to discover what it could be, a coyote trotted into view. Without catching sight of the near-by lion, he suddenly stopped and fixed his gaze upon the point that so interested the crouching beast. The mystery was solved when thirty or forty beavers came hurrying into view. They had come from the ruined Moraine Colony.

I thought to myself that the coyote, stuffed as he must be with the seared flesh of fire-roasted victims, would not attack them; but a lion wants a fresh kill for every meal, and so I watched the movements of the latter. He adjusted his feet a trifle and made ready to spring. The beavers were getting close; but just as I was about to shout to frighten him, the coyote leaped among them and began killing.

In the excitement of getting off the crag I narrowly escaped breaking my neck. Once on the ground, I ran for the coyote, shouting wildly to frighten him off; but he was so intent upon killing that a violent kick in the ribs first made him aware of my presence. In anger and excitement he leaped at me with ugly teeth as he fled. The lion had disappeared, and by this time the beavers in the front ranks were jumping into the pond, while the others were awkwardly speeding down the slope. The coyote had killed three. If beavers have a language, surely that night the refugees related to their hospitable neighbors some thrilling experiences.

The Ruined Colony

The next morning I returned to the Moraine Colony over the route followed by the refugees. Leaving their fire-ruined homes, they had followed the stream that issued from their ponds. In places the channel was so clogged with fire wreckage that they had followed alongside the water rather than in it, as is their wont. At one place they had hurriedly taken refuge in the stream. Coyote tracks in the scattered ashes explained this. But after going a short distance they had climbed from the water and again traveled the ashy earth.

Beavers commonly follow water routes, but in times of emergency or in moments of audacity they will journey overland. To have followed this stream down to its first tributary, then up this to where the colony in which they found refuge was situated, would have required four miles of travel. Overland it was less than a mile. After following the stream for some distance, at just the right place they turned off, left the stream, and dared the overland dangers. How did they know the situation of the colony in the willows, or that it had escaped fire, and how could they have known the shortest, best way to it?

The morning after the arrival of the refugees, work was begun on two new houses and a dam, which was about sixty feet in length and built across a grassy open. Green cuttings of willow, aspen, and alder were used in its construction. Not a single stone or handful of mud was used. When completed it appeared like a windrow of freshly raked shrubs. It was almost straight, but sagged a trifle downstream. Though the water filtered freely through, it flooded the flat above. As the two new houses could not shelter all the refugees, it is probable that some of them were sheltered in bank tunnels, while room for others may have been found in the old houses.

That winter the colony was raided by some trappers; more than one hundred pelts were secured, and the colony was left in ruins and almost depopulated.

The Moraine Colony site was deserted for a long time. Eight years after the fire I returned to examine it. The willow growth about the ruins was almost as thrifty as when the fire came. A growth of aspen taller than one's head clung to the old shore-lines, while a close seedling growth of lodge-pole pine throve in the ashes of the old forest. One low mound, merry with blooming columbine, was the only house ruin to be seen.

The ponds were empty and every dam was broken. The stream, in rushing unobstructed through the ruins, had eroded deeply. This erosion revealed the records of ages, and showed that the old main dam had been built on the top of an older dam and a sediment-filled pond. The second dam was on top of an older one still. In the sediment of the oldest—the bottom pond—I found a spearhead, two charred logs, and the skull of a buffalo. Colonies of beaver, as well as those of men, are often found upon sites that have a tragic history. Beavers, with Omar, might say,—

When you and I behind the veil are past,
Oh but the long long while the world shall last.

The next summer, 1893, the Moraine site was resettled. During the first season the colonists spent their time repairing dams and were content to live in holes. In autumn they gathered no harvest, and no trace of them could be found after the snow; so it is likely that they had returned to winter in the colony whence they had come. But early in the next spring there were reinforced numbers of them at work establishing a permanent settlement. Three dams were repaired, and in the autumn many of the golden leaves that fell found lodgment in the fresh plaster of two new houses.

In the new Moraine Colony one of the houses was torn to pieces by some animal, probably a bear. This was before Thanksgiving. About mid-winter a prospector left his tunnel a few miles away, came to the colony and dynamited a house, and "got seven of them." Next year two houses were built on the ruins of the two just fallen. That year's harvest-home was broken by deadly attacks of enemies. In gathering the harvest the beavers showed a preference for some aspens that were growing in a moist place about one hundred feet from the

The Ruined Colony

water. Whether it was the size of these or their peculiar flavor that determined their election in preference to nearer ones, I could not determine. One day, while several beavers were cutting here, they were surprised by a mountain lion which leaped upon and killed one of the harvesters. The next day the lion surprised and killed another. Two or three days later a coyote killed one on the same blood-stained spot, and then overtook and killed two others as they fled for the water. I could not see these deadly attacks from the boulder-pile, but in each case the sight of flying beavers sent me rushing upon the scene, where I beheld the cause of their desperate retreat. But despite dangers they persisted until the last of these aspens was harvested. During the winter the bark was eaten from these, and the next season their clean wood was used in the walls of a new house.

One autumn I had the pleasure of seeing some immigrants pass me *en route* for a new home in the Moraine Colony. Of course they may have been only visitors, or have come temporarily to assist in the harvesting; but I like to think of them as immigrants, and a number of things testified that immigrants they were. One evening I had been lying on a boulder by the stream below the colony, waiting for a gift from the gods. It came. Out of the water within ten feet of me scrambled the most patriarchal, as well as the largest, beaver that I have ever seen. I wanted to take off my hat to him, I wanted to ask him to tell me the story of his life, but from long habit I simply lay still and watched and thought in silence. He was making a portage round a cascade. As he scrambled up over the rocks, I noticed that he had but two fingers on his right hand. He was followed, in single file, by four others; one of these was minus a finger on the left hand. The next morning I read that five immigrants had arrived in the Moraine Colony. They had registered their footprints in the muddy margin of the lower pond. Had an agent been sent to invite these colonists, or had they come out of their own adventurous spirit? The day following their arrival I trailed them backward in the hope of learning whence they came and

Snow-covered beaver lodge

why they had moved. They had traveled in the water most of the time; but in places they had come out on the bank to go round a waterfall or to avoid an obstruction. Here and there I saw their tracks in the mud and traced them to a beaver settlement in which the houses and dams had been recently

The Ruined Colony

wrecked. A near-by rancher told me that he had been "making it hot" for all beavers in his meadow. During the next two years I occasionally saw this patriarchal beaver or his tracks thereabout.

It is the custom among old male beavers to idle away two or three months of each summer in exploring the neighboring brooks and streams, but they never fail to return in time for autumn activities. It thus becomes plain how, when an old colony needs to move, some one in it knows where to go and the route to follow.

The Moraine colonists gathered an unusually large harvest during the autumn of 1909. Seven hundred and thirty-two sapling aspens and several hundred willows were massed in the main pond by the largest house. This pile, which was mostly below the water-line, was three feet deep and one hundred and twenty-four feet in circumference. Would a new house be built this fall? This unusually large harvest plainly told that either children or immigrants had increased the population of the colony. Of course, a hard winter may also have been expected.

No; they were not to build a new house, but the old house by the harvest pile was to be enlarged. One day, just as the evening shadow of Longs Peak had covered the pond, I peeped over a log on top of the dam to watch the work. The house was only forty feet distant. Not a ripple stirred among the inverted peaks and pines in the clear, shadow-enameled pond. A lone beaver rose quietly in the scene from the water near the house. Swimming noiselessly, he made a circuit of the pond. Then for a time, and without any apparent purpose, he swam back and forth over a short, straight course; he moved leisurely, and occasionally made a shallow, quiet dive. He did not appear to be watching anything in particular or to have anything special on his mind. Yet his eyes may have been scouting for enemies and his mind may have been full of house plans. Finally he dived deeply, and the next I saw of him he was climbing up the side of the house addition with a pawful of mud.

By this time a number of beavers were swimming in the pond after the manner of the first one. Presently all began to work. The addition already stood more than two feet above the waterline. The top of this was crescent-shaped and was about seven feet long and half as wide. It was made mostly of mud, which was plentifully reinforced with willow cuttings and aspen sticks. For a time all the workers busied themselves in carrying mud and roots from the bottom of the pond and placing these on the slowly rising addition. Eleven were working at one time. By and by three swam ashore, each in a different direction and each a few seconds apart. After a minute or two they returned from the shore, each carrying or trailing a long willow. These were dragged to the top of the addition, laid down, and trampled in the mud. Meantime the mud-carriers kept steadily at their work; again willows were brought, but this time four beavers went, and, as before, each was independent of the others. I did not see how this work could go on without some one bossing the thing, but I failed to detect any beaver acting as overseer. While there was general coöperation, each acted independently most of the time and sometimes was apparently oblivious of the others. These beavers simply worked, slowly, silently, and steadily; and they were still working away methodically and with dignified deliberation when darkness hid them.

9.

The Forest Fire

FOREST FIRES LED ME to abandon the most nearly ideal journey through the wilds I had ever embarked upon, but the conflagrations that took me aside filled a series of my days and nights with wild, fiery exhibitions and stirring experiences. It was early September and I had started southward along the crest of the continental divide of the Rocky Mountains in northern Colorado. All autumn was to be mine and upon this alpine skyline I was to saunter southward, possibly to the land of cactus and mirage. Not being commanded by either the calendar or the compass, no day was to be marred by hurrying. I was just to linger and read all the nature stories in the heights that I could comprehend or enjoy. From my starting-place, twelve thousand feet above the tides, miles of continental slopes could be seen that sent their streams east and west to the two far-off seas. With many a loitering advance, with many a glad going back, intense days were lived. After two great weeks I climbed off the treeless heights and went down into the woods to watch and learn the deadly and dramatic ways of forest fires.

This revolution in plans was brought about by the view from amid the broken granite on the summit of Longs Peak. Far below and far away the magnificent mountain distances reposed in the autumn sunshine. The dark crags, snowy summits, light-tipped peaks, bright lakes, purple forests traced with silver streams and groves of aspen,—all fused and faded away in the golden haze. But these splendid scenes were being

Forest cañon with Longs Peak in the distance

blurred and blotted out by the smoke of a dozen or more forest fires.

Little realizing that for six weeks I was to hesitate on fire-threatened heights and hurry through smoke-filled forests, I took a good look at the destruction from afar and then hastened toward the nearest fire-front. This was a smoke-clouded blaze on the Rabbit-Ear Range that was storming its way eastward. In a few hours it would travel to the Grand River, which flowed southward through a straight, mountain-walled valley that was about half a mile wide. Along the river, occupying about half the width of the valley, was a picturesque grassy avenue that stretched for miles between ragged forest-edges.

There was but little wind and, hoping to see the big game that the flames might drive into the open, I innocently took my stand in the centre of the grassy stretch directly before the fire. This great smoky fire-billow, as I viewed it from the heights while I was descending, was advancing with a formidable crooked front about three miles across. The left wing was more than a mile in advance of the active though lagging

The Forest Fire

right one. As I afterward learned, the difference in speed of the two wings was caused chiefly by topography; the forest conditions were similar, but the left wing had for some time been burning up a slope while the right had traveled down one. Fire burns swiftly up a slope, but slowly down it. Set fire simultaneously to the top and the bottom of a forest on a steep slope and the blaze at the bottom will overrun at least nine-tenths of the area. Flame and the drafts that it creates sweep upward.

Upon a huge lava boulder in the grassy stretch I commanded a view of more than a mile of the forest-edge and was close to where a game trail came into it out of the fiery woods. On this burning forest-border a picturesque, unplanned wild-animal parade passed before me.

Scattered flakes of ashes were falling when a herd of elk led the exodus of wild folk from the fire-doomed forest. They came stringing out of the woods into the open, with both old and young going forward without confusion and as though headed for a definite place or pasture. They splashed through a beaver pond without stopping and continued their way up the river. There was no show of fear, no suggestion of retreat. They never looked back. Deer straggled out singly and in groups. It was plain that all were fleeing from danger, all were excitedly trying to get out of the way of something; and they did not appear to know where they were going. Apparently they gave more troubled attention to the roaring, the breath, and the movements of that fiery, mysterious monster than to the seeking of a place of permanent safety. In the grassy open, into which the smoke was beginning to drift and hang, the deer scattered and lingered. At each roar of the fire they turned hither and thither excitedly to look and listen. A flock of mountain sheep, in a long, narrow, closely pressed rank and led by an alert, aggressive bighorn, presented a fine appearance as it raced into the open. The admirable directness of these wild animals put them out of the category occupied by tame, "silly sheep." Without slackening pace they swept across the grassy valley in a straight line and vanished in the wooded slope beyond. Now and then a coyote appeared from somewhere and stopped for a time in the open among the deer; all these wise little wolves were a trifle nervous, but each had himself well in hand. Glimpses were had of two stealthy mountain lions, now leaping, now creeping, now swiftly fleeing. Bears were the most matter-of-fact fellows in the exodus. Each loitered in the grass and occasionally looked toward the oncoming danger. Their actions showed curiosity and anger, but not alarm. Each duly took notice of the surrounding animals, and one old grizzly even struck viciously at a snarling coyote. Two black bear cubs, true to their nature, had a merry romp. Even these serious conditions could not make them solemn. Each tried to prevent the other from climbing a tree that stood alone in the open; around this tree they clinched, cuffed, and rolled about so merrily that the frightened wild folks were attracted and momentarily forgot their fears. The only birds seen were some grouse that whirred and sailed by on swift, definite wings; they were going somewhere.

With subdued and ever-varying roar the fire steadily advanced. It constantly threw off an upcurling, unbroken cloud of heavy smoke that hid the flames from view. Now and then a whirl of wind brought a shower of sparks together with bits of burning bark out over the open valley.

Just as the flames were reaching the margin of the forest a great bank of black smoke curled forward and then appeared to fall into the grassy open. I had just a glimpse of a few fleeing animals, then all became hot, fiery, and dark. Red flames darted through swirling black smoke. It was stifling. Leaping into a beaver pond, I lowered my own sizzling temperature and that of my smoking clothes. The air was too hot and black for breathing; so I fled, floundering through the water, down Grand River.

A quarter of a mile took me beyond danger-line and gave me fresh air. Here the smoke ceased to settle to the earth, but extended in a light upcurling stratum a few yards above it. Through this smoke the sunlight came so changed that every-

The Forest Fire

thing around was magically covered with a canvas of sepia or rich golden brown. I touched the burned spots on hands and face with real, though raw, balsam and then plunged into the burned-over district to explore the extensive ruins of the fire. A prairie fire commonly consumes everything to the earth-line and leaves behind it only a black field. Rarely does a forest fire make so clean a sweep; generally it burns away the smaller limbs and the foliage, leaving the tree standing all blackened and bristling. This fire, like thousands of others, consumed the litter carpet on the forest floor and the mossy covering of the rocks; it ate the underbrush, devoured the foliage, charred and burned the limbs, and blackened the trunks. Behind was a dead forest in a desolate field, a territory with millions of bristling, mutilated trees, a forest ruin impressively picturesque and pathetic. From a commanding ridge I surveyed this ashen desert and its multitude of upright figures all blurred and lifeless; these stood everywhere,—in the gulches, on the slopes, on the ridges against the sky,—and they bristled in every vanishing distance. Over the entire area only a few trees escaped with their lives; these were isolated in soggy glacier meadows or among rock fields and probably were defended by friendly air-currents when the fiery billow rolled over them.

When I entered the burn that afternoon the fallen trees that the fire had found were in ashes, the trees just killed were smoking, while the standing dead trees were just beginning to burn freely. That night these scattered beacons strangely burned among the multitudinous dead. Close to my camp all through that night several of these fire columns showered sparks like a fountain, glowed and occasionally lighted up the scene with flaming torches. Weird and strange in the night were the groups of silhouetted figures in a shadow-dance between me and the flickering, heroic torches.

The greater part of the area burned over consisted of mountain-slopes and ridges that lay between the altitudes of nine thousand and eleven thousand feet. The forest was made up almost entirely of Engelmann and Douglas spruces, alpine fir, and flexilis pine. A majority of these trees were from fifteen to twenty-four inches in diameter, and those examined were two hundred and fourteen years of age. Over the greater extent of the burn the trees were tall and crowded, about two thousand to the acre. As the fire swept over about eighteen thousand acres, the number of trees that perished must have approximated thirty-six million.

Fires make the Rocky Mountains still more rocky. This bald fact stuck out all through this burn and in dozens of others afterward visited. Most Rocky Mountain fires not only skin off the humus but so cut up the fleshy soil and so completely destroy the fibrous bindings that the elements quickly drag much of it from the bones and fling it down into the stream-channels. Down many summit slopes in these mountains, where the fires went to bed-rock, the snows and waters still scoot and scour. The fire damage to some of these steep slopes cannot be repaired for generations and even centuries. Meantime these disfigured places will support only a scattered growth of trees and sustain only a sparse population of animals.

In wandering about I found that the average thickness of humus—decayed vegetable matter—consumed by this fire was about five inches. The removal of even these few inches of covering had in many places exposed boulders and bedrock. On many shallow-covered steeps the soil-anchoring roots were consumed and the productive heritage of ages was left to be the early victim of eager running water and insatiable gravity.

Probably the part of this burn that was most completely devastated was a tract of four or five hundred acres in a zone a little below timberline. Here stood a heavy forest on solid rock in thirty-two inches of humus. The tree-roots burned with the humus, and down crashed the trees into the flames. The work of a thousand years was undone in a day!

The loss of animal life in this fire probably was not heavy; in five or six days of exploring I came upon fewer than three dozen fire victims of all kinds. Almong the dead were ground-

The Forest Fire

hogs, bobcats, snowshoe rabbits, and a few grouse. Flying about the waste were crested jays, gray jays ("camp birds,") and magpies. Coyotes came early to search for the feast prepared by the fire.

During the second day's exploration on the burn, a grizzly bear and I came upon two roasted deer in the end of a gulch. I was first to arrive, so Mr. Grizzly remained at what may have been a respectful distance, restlessly watching me. With his nearness and impolite stare I found it very embarrassing to eat alone. However, two days of fasting had prepared me for this primitive feast; and, knowing that bears were better than their reputation, I kept him waiting until I was served. On arising to go, I said, "Come, you may have the remainder; there is plenty of it."

The fire was followed by clear weather, and for days the light ash lay deep and undisturbed over the burn. One morning conditions changed and after a few preliminary whirlwinds a gusty gale set in. In a few minutes I felt and appeared as though just from an ash-barrel. The ashen dust-storm was blinding and choking, and I fled for the unburned heights. So blinding was the flying ash that I was unable to see; and, to make matters worse, the trees with fire-weakened foundations and limbs almost severed by flames commenced falling. The limbs were flung about in a perfectly reckless manner, while the falling trees took a fiendish delight in crashing down alongside me at the very moment that the storm was most blinding. Being without nerves and incidentally almost choked, I ignored the falling bodies and kept going.

Several times I rushed blindly against limb-points and was rudely thrust aside; and finally I came near walking off into space from the edge of a crag. After this I sought temporary refuge to the leeward of a boulder, with the hope that the weakened trees would speedily fall and end the danger from that source. The ash flew thicker than ever did gale-blown desert dust; it was impossible to see and so nearly impossible to breathe that I was quickly driven forth. I have been in many dangers, but this is the only instance in which I was ever irritated by Nature's blind forces. At last I made my escape from them.

From clear though wind-swept heights I long watched the burned area surrender its slowly accumulated, rich store of plant food to the insatiable and all-sweeping wind. By morning, when the wind abated, the garnered fertility and phosphates of generations were gone, and the sun cast the shadows of millions of leafless trees upon rock bones and barren earth. And the waters were still to take their toll.

Of course Nature would at once commence to repair and would again upbuild upon the foundations left by the fire; such, however, were the climatic and geological conditions that improving changes would come but slowly. In a century only a good beginning could be made. For years the greater portion of the burn would be uninhabitable by bird or beast; those driven forth by this fire would seek home and food in the neighboring territory, where this influx of population would compel interesting readjustments and create bitter strife between the old wild-folk population and the new.

This fire originated from a camp-fire which a hunting-party had left burning; it lived three weeks and extended eastward from the starting-place. Among most of its course it burned to the timber-line on the left, while rocky ridges, glacier meadows, and rock fields stopped its extension and determined the side line on the right; it ran out of the forest and stopped in the grassy Grand River Valley. Across its course were a number of rocky ridges and grassy gorges where the fire could have been easily stopped by removing the scattered trees,—by burning the frail bridges that enabled the fire to travel from one dense forest to abundant fuel beyond. In a city it is common to smother a fire with water or acid, but with a forest fire usually it is best to break its inflammable line of communication by removing from before it a width of fibrous material. The axe, rake, hoe, and shovel are the usual fire-fighting tools.

A few yards away from the spot where the fire started I found, freshly cut in the bark of an aspen, the inscription:

The Forest Fire

JSM
Yale 18

A bullet had obliterated the two right-hand figures.

For days I wandered over the mountains, going from fire to smoke and studying burns new and old. One comparatively level tract had been fireswept in 1791. On this the soil was good. Lodge-pole pine had promptly restocked the burn, but these trees were now being smothered out by a promising growth of Engelmann spruce.

Fifty-seven years before my visit a fire had burned over about four thousand acres and was brought to a stand by a lake, a rocky ridge, and a wide fire-line that a snowslide had cleared through the woods. The surface of the burn was coarse, disintegrated granite and sloped toward the west, where it was exposed to prevailing high westerly winds. A few kinnikinnick rugs apparently were the only green things upon the surface, and only a close examination revealed a few stunted trees starting. It was almost barren. Erosion was still active; there were no roots to bind the finer particles together or to anchor them in place. One of the most striking features of the entire burn was that the trees killed by the fire fifty-seven years ago were standing where they died. They had excellent root-anchorage in the shattered surface, and many of them probably would remain erect for years. The fire that killed them had been a hot one, and it had burned away most of the limbs, and had so thoroughly boiled the pitch through the exterior of the trunk that the wood was in an excellent state of preservation.

Another old burn visited was a small one in an Engelmann spruce forest on a moderate northern slope. It had been stopped while burning in very inflammable timber. It is probable that on this occasion either a rain or snow had saved the surrounding forest. The regrowth had slowly extended from the margin of the forest to the centre of the burn until it was restocked.

One morning I noticed two small fires a few miles down

the mountain and went to examine them. Both were two days old, and both had started from unextinguished camp-fires. One had burned over about an acre and the other about four times that area. If the smaller had not been built against an old snag it probably would have gone out within a few hours after the congressman who built it moved camp. It was wind-sheltered and the blaze had traveled slowly in all directions and burned a ragged circle that was about sixty feet across.

The outline of the other blaze was that of a flattened ellipse, like the orbit of many a wandering comet in the sky. This had gone before the wind, and the windward end of its orbit closely encircled the place of origin. The camp-fire nucleus of this blaze had also been built in the wrong place,—against a fallen log which lay in a deep bed of decaying needles.

Of course each departing camper should put out his camp-fire. However, a camp-fire built on a humus-covered forest floor, or by a log, or against a dead tree, is one that is very difficult to extinguish. With the best of intentions one may deluge such a fire with water without destroying its potency. A fire thus secreted appears, like a lie, to have a spark of immortality in it.

A fire should not be built in contact with substances that will burn, for such fuel will prolong the fire's life and may lead it far into the forest. There is but little danger to the forest from a fire that is built upon rock, earth, sand, or gravel. A fire so built is isolated and it usually dies an early natural death. Such a fire—one built in a safe and sane place—is easily extinguished.

The larger of these two incipient fires was burning quietly, and that night I camped within its orbit. Toward morning the wind began to blow, this slow-burning surface fire began to leap, and before long it was a crown fire, traveling rapidly among the tree-tops. It swiftly expanded into an enormous delta of flame. At noon I looked back and down upon it from a mountain-top, and it had advanced about three miles into a primeval forest sea, giving off more smoke than a volcano.

I went a day's journey and met a big fire that was coming

The Forest Fire

aggressively forward against the wind. It was burning a crowded, stunted growth of forest that stood in a deep litter carpet. The smoke, which flowed freely from it, was distinctly ashen green; this expanded and maintained in the sky a smoky sheet that was several miles in length.

Before the fire lay a square mile or so of old burn which was covered with a crowded growth of lodge-pole pine that stood in a deep, criss-crossed entanglement of fallen fire-killed timber. A thousand or more of these long, broken dead trees covered each acre with wreckage, and in this stood upward of five thousand live young ones. This would make an intensely hot and flame-writhing fire. It appears that a veteran spruce forest had occupied this burn prior to the fire. The fire had occurred fifty-seven years before. Trees old and young testified to the date. In the margin of the living forest on the edge of the burn were numerous trees that were fire-scarred fifty-seven years before; the regrowth on the burn was an even-aged fifty-six-year growth.

That night, as the fire neared the young tree growth, I scaled a rock ledge to watch it. Before me, and between the fire and the rocks, stood several veteran lodge-pole pines in a mass of dead-and-down timber. Each of these trees had an outline like that of a plump Lombardy popular. They perished in the most spectacular manner. Blazing, wind-blown bark set fire to the fallen timber around their feet; this fire, together with the close, oncoming fire-front, so heated the needles on the lodge-poles that they gave off a smoky gas; this was issuing from every top when a rippling rill of purplish flame ran up one of the trunks. Instantly there was a flash and white flames flared upward more than one hundred feet, stood gushing for a few seconds, and then went out completely. The other trees in close succession followed and flashed up like giant geysers discharging flame. This discharge was brief, but it was followed by every needle on the trees glowing and changing to white incandescence, then vanishing. In a minute these leafless lodge-poles were black and dead.

The fire-front struck and crossed the lodge-pole thicket in a flash; each tree flared up like a fountain of gas and in a moment a deep, ragged-edged lake of flame heaved high into the dark, indifferent night. A general fire of the dead-and-down timber followed, and the smelter heat of this cut the green trees down, the flames widely, splendidly illuminating the surrounding mountains and changing a cloud-filled sky to convulsed, burning lava.

Not a tree was left standing, and every log went to ashes. The burn was as completely cleared as a fireswept prairie; in places there were holes in the earth where tree-roots had burned out. This burn was an ideal place for another lodge-pole growth, and three years later these pines were growing thereon as thick as wheat in a field. In a boggy area within the burn an acre or two of aspen sprang up; this area, however, was much smaller than the one that the fire removed from the bog. Aspens commonly hold territory and extend their holdings by sprouting from roots; but over the greater portion of the bog the fire had either baked or burned the roots, and this small aspen area marked the wetter part of the bog, that in which the roots had survived.

After destroying the lodge-pole growth the fire passed on, and the following day it burned away as a quiet surface fire through a forest of scattered trees. It crept slowly forward, with a yellow blaze only a few inches high. Here and there this reddened over a pile of cone-scales that had been left by a squirrel, or blazed up in a pile of broken limbs or a fallen tree-top; it consumed the litter mulch and fertility of the forest floor, but seriously burned only a few trees.

Advancing along the blaze, I came upon a veteran yellow pine that had received a large pot-hole burn in its instep. As the Western yellow pine is the best fire-fighter in the conifer family, it was puzzling to account for this deep burn. On the Rocky Mountains are to be found many picturesque yellow pines that have a dozen times triumphed over the greatest enemy of the forest. Once past youth, these trees possess a thick, corky, asbestos-like bark that defies the average fire.

The Forest Fire

Close to this injured old fellow was a rock ledge that formed an influential part of its environment; its sloping surface shed water and fertility upon its feet; cones, twigs, and trash had also slid down this and formed an inflammable pile which, in burning, had bored into its ankle. An examination of its annual rings in the burned hole revealed the fact that it too had been slightly burned fifty-seven years before. How long would it be until it was again injured by fire or until some one again read its records?

Until recently a forest fire continued until stopped by rain or snow, or until it came to the edge of the forest. I have notes on a forest fire that lived a fluctuating life of four months. Once a fire invades an old forest, it is impossible speedily to get rid of it. "It never goes out," declared an old trapper. The fire will crawl into a slow-burning log, burrow down into a root, or eat its way beneath a bed of needles, and give off no sign of its presence. In places such as these it will hibernate for weeks, despite rain or snow, and finally some day come forth as ferocious as ever.

About twenty-four hours after the lodge-pole blaze a snow-storm came to extinguish the surface fire. Two feet of snow—more than three inches of water—fell. During the storm I was comfortable beneath a shelving rock, with a fire in front; here I had a meal of wild raspberries and pine-nuts and reflected concerning the uses of forests, and wished that every one might better understand and feel the injustice and the enormous loss caused by forest fires.

During the last fifty years the majority of the Western forest fires have been set by unextinguished camp-fires, while the majority of the others were the result of some human carelessness. The number of preventable forest fires is but little less than the total number. True, lightning does occasionally set a forest on fire; I have personal knowledge of a number of such fires, but I have never known lightning to set fire to a green tree. Remove the tall dead trees from forests, and the lightning will lose the greater part of its kindling.

In forest production, the rivers, ridge-tops, rocky gulches, rock-fields, lake-shores, meadows, and other natural fire-resisting boundary lines between forests are beginning to be used and can be more fully utilized for fire-lines, fire-fighting, and fire-defying places. These natural fire-barriers may be connected by barren cleared lanes through the forest, so that a fire-break will isolate or run entirely around any natural division of forest. With such a barrier a fire could be kept within a given section or shut out of it.

In order to fight fire in a forest it must be made accessible by means of roads and trails; these should run on or alongside the fire-barrier so as to facilitate the movements of fire patrols or fire-fighters. There should be with every forest an organized force of men who are eternally vigilant to prevent or to fight forest fires. Fires should be fought while young and small, before they are beyond control.

There should be crows'-nests on commanding crags and in each of these should be a lookout to watch constantly for fires or suspicious smoke in the surrounding sea of forest. The lookout should have telephonic connection with rangers down the slopes. In our national forests incidents like the following are beginning to occur: Upon a summit is stationed a ranger who has two hundred thousand acres of forest to patrol with his eyes. One morning a smudgy spot appears upon the purple forest sea about fifteen miles to the northwest. The lookout gazes for a moment through his glass and, although not certain as to what it is, decides to get the distance with the range-finder. At that instant, however, the wind acts upon the smudge and shows that a fire exists and reveals its position. A ranger, through a telephone at the forks of the trail below, hears from the heights, "Small fire one mile south of Mirror Lake, between Spruce Fork and Bear Pass Trail, close to O'Brien's Spring." In less than an hour a ranger leaps from his panting pony and with shovel and axe hastily digs a narrow trench through the vegetable mould in a circle around the fire. Then a few shovelfuls of sand go upon the liveliest blaze and the fire is under control. As soon as there lives a good, sympathetic public sentiment concerning the forest, it will be comparatively easy to prevent most forest fires from starting and to extinguish those that do start.

With the snow over, I started for the scene of the first fire, and on the way noticed how much more rapidly the snow melted in the open than in a forest. The autumn sun was warm, and at the end of the first day most of the snow in open or fireswept places was gone, though on the forest floor the slushy, compacted snow still retained the greater portion of its original moisture. On the flame-cleared slopes there was heavy erosion; the fire had destroyed the root-anchorage of the surface and consumed the trash that would ordinarily have absorbed and delayed the water running off; but this, unchecked, had carried off with it tons of earthy material. One slope on the first burn suffered heavily; a part of this day's "wash" was deposited in a beaver pond, of half an acre, which was filled to the depth of three feet. The beavers, finding their subterranean exits filled with wash, had escaped by tearing a hole in the top of their house.

Leaving this place, I walked across the range to look at a fire that was burning beyond the bounds of the snowfall. It was in a heavily forested cove and was rapidly undoing the constructive work of centuries. This cove was a horseshoe-shaped one and apparently would hold the fire within its rocky ridges. While following alone one of these ridges, I came to a narrow, tree-dotted pass, the only break in the confining rocky barrier. As I looked at the fire down in the cove, it was plain that with a high wind the fire would storm this pass and break into a heavily forested alpine realm beyond. In one day two men with axes could have made this pass impregnable to the assaults of any fire, no matter how swift the wind ally; but men were not then defending our forests and an ill wind was blowing.

Many factors help to determine the speed of these fires, and a number of observations showed that under average conditions a fire burned down a slope at about one mile an hour; on the level it traveled from two to eight miles an hour, while up a slope it made from eight to twelve. For short distances fires occasionally roared along at a speed of fifty or sixty miles an hour and made a terrible gale of flames. I hurried up into the alpine realm and after half an hour scaled a promontory and looked back to the pass. A great cloud of smoke was streaming up just beyond and after a minute tattered sheets of flame were shooting high above it. Presently a tornado of smoke and flame surged into the pass and for some seconds nothing could be seen. As this cleared, a succession of tongues and sheets of flame tried to reach over into the forest on the other side of the pass, but finally gave it up. Just as I was beginning to feel that the forest around me was safe, a smoke-column arose among the trees by the pass. Probably during the first assault of the flames a fiery dart had been hurled across the pass.

Up the shallow forested valley below me came the flames, an inverted Niagara of red and yellow, with flying spray of black. It sent forward a succession of short-lived whirlwinds that went to pieces explosively, hurling sparks and blazing bark far and high. During one of its wilder displays the fire rolled forward, an enormous horizontal whirl of flame, and then, with thunder and roar, the molten flames swept upward into a wall of fire; this tore to pieces, collapsed, and fell forward in fiery disappearing clouds. With amazing quickness the splendid hanging garden on the terraced heights was crushed and blackened. By my promontory went this magnificent zigzag surging front of flame, blowing the heavens full of sparks and smoke and flinging enormous fiery rockets. Swift and slow, loud and low, swelling and vanishing, it sang its eloquent death song.

A heavy stratum of tarlike smoke formed above the fire as it toned down. Presently this black stratum was uplifted near the centre and then pierced with a stupendous geyser of yellow flame, which reddened as it fused and tore through the tarry smoke and then gushed astonishingly high above.

A year or two prior to the fire a snow slide from the heights had smashed down into the forest. More than ten thousand trees were mowed, raked, and piled in one mountainous mass

The Forest Fire

of wreckage upon some crags and in a narrow-throated gulch between them. This wood-pile made the geyser flames and a bonfire to startle even the giants. While I was trying to account for this extraordinary display, there came a series of explosions in rapid succession, ending in a violent crashing one. An ominous, elemental silence followed. All alone I had enjoyed the surprises, the threatening uncertainties, and the dangerous experiences that swiftly came with the fire-line battles of this long, smoky war; but when those awful explosions came I for a time wished that some one were with me. Had there been, I should have turned and asked, while getting a better grip on my nerves, "What on earth is that?" While the startled mountain-walls were still shuddering with the shock, an enormous agitated column of steam shot several hundred feet upward where the fiery geyser had flamed. Unable to account for these strange demonstrations, I early made my way through heat and smoke to the big bonfire. In the bottom of the gulch, beneath the bonfire, flowed a small stream; just above the bonfire this stream had been temporarily dammed by fire wreckage. On being released, the accumulated waters thus gathered had rushed down upon the red-hot rocks and cliffs and produced these explosions.

In the morning light this hanging terraced garden of yesterday's forest glory was a stupendous charcoal drawing of desolation.

10.

The Love Song of Little Blue

A MOUNTAIN BLUEBIRD and his mate arrived at my home one March day, alighting on the pole fence by my uncompleted log-cabin, as though surprised to see me. Perhaps they had been reared in the region, while I was a newcomer. After a moment's pause, Mr. Bluebird flew away to examine a hollow limb in a near-by pine. He looked in and went in, flew back to his mate and then to the tree again, and finally returned and persuaded her to come and examine this possible nesting-site. She went reluctantly, and after a look or two evidently condemned the location. Both resumed this position on the fence, content to rest after their long journey from the Southland.

The bluebird is the confidential messenger of the life-moving season of the year, his cheerful presence assuring us that summer will arrive tomorrow for a long and glorious stay. This was good news to me, a boy of sixteen, anxious to complete my cabin, which I had started the summer before to build by myself.

This pair of bluebirds lingered near day after day. They had leisure and enjoyed it lovingly. They were in no hurry to start nest-building. They were weeks ahead of the birds that migrated farther northward, several thousand miles, to secure the same climatic and food conditions which my birds found here in the mountains. Being day travelers, combining food-hunting with travel, they had covered only a short distance

The Love Song of Little Blue

Aspen grove and stream

each day on their migratory flight from the South. It is probable that they had had opportunity to do their mating on the way; or they may have nested in these scenes before, possibly even in the near-by pine.

My cabin stood in a grove of pine and aspen on a steep mountain-side, sloping south and west. It was nine thousand feet above sea-level. I had few neighbors, and so was eager to make friends with the wild birds and animals that lived near me. Often, as I stood in the doorway, looking across at Longs Peak, which towered more than five thousand feet above me, the rabbits, squirrels, and chipmunks hopped by unafraid. I moved about quietly, never harmed them, and they soon came to know that they were in a safety zone around my home.

The two bluebirds evidently liked the surroundings and often appeared to be watching the slow building of my cabin. At last, one morning before the front of the house was finished, they took possession. I lived in my cabin that summer without completing it, unwilling to disturb the bluebirds and the building of their nest above the ridge-pole. From this nest scores of little girls and boys in blue have looked out upon the world.

I had much opportunity to enjoy bluebird ways and companionship. It was not long before they were accustomed to my watching them, and in a month we were friendly. By September they would come into my cabin, and frequently they lunched with me on my writing-table or one on each shoulder as I stood outdoors near the cabin.

The bluebirds were affectionate and devoted. He was a handsome fellow, cheerful, fearless, and calm through all emergencies. Faithfully he performed his daily duties, and ever was free from curiosity or contempt, appearing to have complete indifference for the rest of the world. His favorite seat was the top pole of the fence, about fifteen feet distant from the nest. Here he sat very erect and motionless, like a philosopher. He was interested in no one's affairs but his own.

His trim, modestly attired little mate did most of the work, assumed all the responsibility, and was just a trifle nervous. Occasionally, indifferent to my nearness, these two sat on the pole fence lovingly, close together—he perfectly perpendicular, though in repose, she restless, facing first one side of the fence, then the other. Once in a while she would pull herself up for a moment of deliberation, or to speak low, loving

The Love Song of Little Blue

words to her blue prince. To these terms of endearment the prince listened with greatest interest, though he sat motionless and held himself up like an Indian.

The mountain bluebird is the bluest of the blue. No bird that I know carries a color that more completely matches the turquoise or cerulean blue of mountain skies.

The male is bright blue above and pale blue beneath, while she has an ashen-colored coat, thinly, unevenly washed with blue. The youngsters wear ashen brown; around the throat this is dark, and beneath a pale wash over white. This famous color-bearer displays the blue of the sky throughout the middle mountain zone of all western North America, from central Alaska to central Mexico.

One day, as the pair sat side by side on the fence, a robin alighted on a post only a few yards away, apparently without seeing them. Certainly the robin did not know that he was intruding, and he manifested not the slightest evil intentions. Instantly, however, Mother Bluebird hurled herself at the intruder as though to annihilate him, though she was provokingly small for such a task. The robin, apparently chagrined, and certainly surprised and frightened, made haste to escape. Mrs. Bluebird returned to the pole and edged up close to her mate. While they exchanged conversational twitters, he looked at her tenderly and then made haste to bring her a worm. It was offered with much gallant show and accepted demurely.

Another day, after they had had a few loving moments on the fence, he suddenly unbent and faced her with fluttering wings and worshipful attention. I do not know what had been said, but she becomingly received these attentions with quiet dignity. After another moment of admiration he flew to the nest hurriedly, then back again; went to it a second time, looked in, lingered a moment, and then returned to his mate. After a little more gallantry on his part, they flew away to lunch together.

There were five light-blue eggs laid, and thirteen days later both father and mother worked overtime supplying the crying needs of these helpless mites. I was completely ignored in the busy life of these devoted parents. I found that this was true throughout the bird world. During feeding-time, mid-June and later, I made the acquaintance of other bird families nesting in hollow trees, in brushes and branches, and on the ground around my cabin.

While Mrs. Bluebird was brooding the second nestful of eggs, her blue prince took the first brood in hand; patiently he fed and trained them after the ways considered good by bluebirds. These youngsters saw but little of their mother for three weeks after they left the nest, but almost constantly followed their busy father about.

When the second brood hatched, these children were early on hand to see the babies, and, as soon as allowed, they carried them food. Three of the grown-up children worked faithfully in food-hunting and in feeding the nestful of babies, and apparently they did their task well, for Mother Bluebird stayed close by, supervising or serenely looking on. One of the sisters often lingered by the nest after bringing food, watching them with lively curiosity and almost maternal interest.

The two broods of children and their parents lingered around my cabin till late summer, instead of flying farther up the mountain-side, as did so many families, to feed and frolic around timber-line. But autumn appeared to make them uneasy. They knew they must start for the southland before the coming of the cold days.

One glorious September day they joined a flock of bluebirds passing through. Here and there some golden leaves still shone on the aspens; occasionally there was a whisper from the air and the pines. I had marked the old birds, and as they flew away with their two broods of children, I called out: "Come back early next spring. I'll be looking for you. And be sure to bring those copper threads I have placed around your ankles."

Many birds mate for life and return to the same locality year after year. Food scarcity, increased dangers, or better opportunities may cause them sometimes, like people, to go to a better, new home.

These bluebirds returned the next spring, and the two following. They lived around my cabin for four successive summers. They had found it a good place in which to bring up their children.

The first bluebirds to arrive near my cabin reported about the first week of March. But these bluebirds were bound farther north. My birds rarely arrived earlier than the 25th of March. This was a month in advance of nesting—a month for relaxation and picnicking. Commonly after arrival they remained in the region, though they sometimes disappeared for two or three days. A late spring snow always sent them out of the storm zone where food could still be obtained on the wing.

I was glad to have my bluebirds over the ridge log again. These cheerful, loving mates had two broods each summer and raised thirty-three children in three years. After all the care that these children had required, they began housekeeping the fourth season as eagerly and as lovingly as though it was the first time.

The nest used three previous summers was renovated and partly rebuilt according to the latest models. From this summer residence and nursery little girls and little boys in blue again looked out with wondering interest upon the strange, big world while their wings were growing.

I had little opportunity during the fourth summer of our friendship to watch over Mr. and Mrs. Bluebird. But it was a joy to see them each day, and to know that they were safe. They had chosen one of the best of places for their family, and I could not imagine anything bringing them harm.

Early one June morning I left my cabin for a day by the timber-line. The bluebirds sat on the fence by the gate. I bade them good-bye and touched them with my hand. We were old friends. They seemed to watch me as I went on up the mountain.

During my absence a boy from a tourist camp near by visited my cabin. He was enthusiastic over barbaric sport, to which he had been reared. Having heard nothing of wild-life conservation, and having nothing else to do, he amused himself by shooting at the bluebirds. They, together with other birds, squirrels, chipmunks, and rabbits around my cabin had learned to trust man. The fearless mother and father bluebirds allowed him to come close. Regardless of the fact that they were tame, he shot one, then the other, and carried the mangled birds to camp to recount his feat to proud parents.

Even with isolation and watchfulness, the fatal day had come to this little bluebird home beneath the end of my cabin ridge log. Returning home after dark that night, I realized that the bluebirds had been betrayed. In vain five speckled-bibbed babies opened wide their mouths for food; in vain these hungry, forlorn bird children cried and called for their parents.

I carried the nest into my cabin. Here was I, a bachelor, with a family to bring up! Fate had given me five hungry, poorly dressed orphans, and I was to be both mother and father to them.

One little fellow died the first day. A week later, while they were huddled on the floor together, a merry chipmunk tipped a book off the shelf, crushing another. The remaining three came to depend upon me for everything. I tried to understand the youngsters and to care for them according to their needs.

After the first week I put the babies to bed in an old hat on the bookshelf. A handkerchief was spread over them, and three or four towels piled on top to keep them from climbing or tumbling out of bed. Later they had the freedom of the cabin floor during the daytime and were allowed to spend their nights where they pleased. Generally they went to sleep cuddled together in the corner.

I can never know how much or how deeply this tragedy influenced and colored my life. I had planned simply to enjoy seeing the parents feed and train these children for their brief and busy existence. Then came the sad event that changed the

The Love Song of Little Blue

even tenor of passing days and asked me to be far more than I had ever been and different than I had ever dreamed of being.

It was fortunate for me, and also for these little orphans, that I had watched their mother and father feed, train, and raise a number of bluebird families. The old birds were my first wild-life acquaintance, and I had entered into their daily manners and customs.

I already knew that young birds, like young boys, were always hungry. But, although I worked constantly, apparently there was no filling them up. For a time each of these birds must daily have eaten its weight in combinations of worms, crumbs, grubs, flies, and grasshoppers. They compelled me to work for them, rain or shine. But they developed on the diet supplied, and slowly their speckled bibs and baby clothes were replaced by those for which the bluebird is known.

My bluebirds learned to walk long before they learned to fly. At first they toddled along with most amusing and tumbly short steps. They did much more walking perhaps in this one summer than the average bluebird does in a lifetime. But rarely did they venture far without me, although during the daytime the door was usually open.

Occasionally they came out to me as I sat on the doorstep, and lolled about on the grass and gravel in the sunshine. One sometimes lay down with both legs and wings outstretched. Or one would slowly spread first one wing, then the other; then daintily in turn stretch its legs. For minutes while arranging feathers and enjoying stretching exercises they were unmindful of all else.

Sometimes in the midst of their exercises a chipmunk came along. They would pause a few seconds to look at him, whether from fear or curiosity I could not tell, then continue what they were doing, even though he lingered near. Their parents had not tolerated the chipmunks until their second season was well advanced. If the old birds met a chipmunk in the cabin, or one came close to the door, they promptly assailed the striped visitor, battering him with bill and wings, and sent him scampering. If thoughtlessly a chipmunk climbed up the front of the cabin toward the sacred nest, he was routed. But the young birds finally learned that at least these chipmunks were harmless. They would sometimes sit quietly in one hand while the chipmunks ate from the other. The day I took the little bluebirds out for their first long walk they were excited, puzzled, and happy. They kept together, close at my heels. Apparently they looked neither to the right nor to the left except when I stopped. We went below to the brook, about one hundred feet down the trail. The movement and the splash of the water aroused curious looks. Then they scattered. But when I called, saying, "Let's go back," they hastened to start and made every effort to keep up with me.

There were times when I had to shut the children in the cabin and go away for the day. They understood the early morning preparations which preceded a day's absence. I left a little food and plenty of water, but this long shut-in period without any one to play with them they plainly did not like. During these preparations they walked soberly about and did but little else than watch me until I left. How merrily they greeted me on my return, forgetting even hunger for a time in their gladness!

One day, when I was away, a friend of mine called at the cabin. The lonesome little birds were apparently glad to have a caller. But they did not offer to play with him. They received him politely, but without demonstration.

It was different the day a loud-voiced man came into the cabin. Before he had finished the first sentence the birds scampered away and hid behind the wood-box. In fact it was several minutes after he had gone and the room had become quiet again, before they would come out. Then they came ever so cautiously, looking and listening for the first sign of danger.

One day a mother wren who had a nest in a near-by hollow tree, chanced to light in front of the door. Seeing the little bluebirds inside, she ventured in, too. I was seated on the floor, and the bluebirds were scampering around me. Wrens are trustful little birds, but rarely are they curious. But her curiosity was deeply aroused; she was interested almost to excitement, as she stood watching the bluebirds and myself. When one of them alighted on my head, she leaned back on her upturned tail with every attitude and expression of amazement.

Sometimes a young bluebird insists on coming off the nest before the mother is ready, but more often the mother has to encourage and persuade the youngsters to try their wings in flight the first time.

My little bluebirds did not learn to fly in the regular way, nor at the regular time. One day I had placed them on the pole fence, when I happened to notice a gentian, and stooped to look at it, then at another and another near by. I do not know whether I forgot them too long, or if they became curious. Their wings were well grown, but with the exception of stretching exercises, had not been used. They evidently felt this was the opportunity to try them.

As I looked up, one little bird pitched forward and aimed straight for my head with a rapid beating of wings. He went over me and tumbled with an awkward roll on the grass. The other two followed close upon the first, one going some yards beyond him and the other falling short. After this flying experiment they flew about when there was need of it, and sometimes when there was not.

These youngsters, like all children, being intensely interested in food, were generally clamorous if the demand was not promptly supplied. Hunger was so insistent with them that they never forgot it nor allowed me to forget it long at a time. They quickly learned that when I went outdoors with the shovel a supply of grubs would naturally be forthcoming. Then they began following me whenever I picked up the shovel.

One day, shovel in hand, I went up the mountain-side to uproot and transplant an attractive cluster of kinnikinnick. The little birds were not in mind, in fact they were almost independent of me now. But while digging I chanced to look back and discovered that they were coming after me with all their might.

They stood three abreast waiting for something to appear as I dug into the earth by a log. When I turned up a grub or worm, all three seized it at once. But after a tug or two, and without any squabbling, two let go and the other took the prize. I never saw these children disagree; their manners were always perfect. With other birds, too, they acted quietly and with thoughtful consideration, and among themselves there was no trouble. I never saw a quarrel in the family.

A pair of Rocky Mountain gray jays, "campbirds," called on me one day. Of all birds they are the most easily tamed, seeming to enjoy the companionship of man. One lighted on my head and the other on my shoulder as I stood in front of the cabin. The little bluebirds were just walking out of the door. They showed no alarm at the arrival of these big birds, but were greatly interested in seeing them eat from my hand. One of the gray jays occasionally flew to the fence, then back to my head or shoulder. The bluebirds stood still, moving only their heads to follow these flights with their eyes. When the camp-birds finally flew off, the little bluebirds came out and went about their affairs as usual. If they had any feeling of jealousy or antipathy toward these callers, they did not show it.

On another occasion we had a most interesting visit from a bluebird, one who probably was a relative. All four of us were sitting on the fence, when this stranger alighted on the top pole just beyond the farthest bird. After a few seconds he fluttered up to where the nest had been, under the edge of the ridge log, and then back to the fence again. Soon followed a purr-like chatter between the stranger and these three little birds. I felt certain he must be an older brother, born under the end of the ridge log a year or two before. Just before he left I noticed six young bluebirds shyly peeping at us from a near-by tree. They were the same age as my birds. Our visitor flew to them, and from their actions I judged he was their father. From what I saw afterwards he was caring for the first

The Love Song of Little Blue 115

brood of the season while his mate hatched the second nestful of eggs. Their home was in an old woodpecker hole in a pine a short distance from the cabin.

Though the three little bluebirds and I became intimately acquainted, only one was named. He was the smallest, the brightest-colored, and always the most alert of the three. I called him "Little Blue." He came to me most frequently, and I unconsciously gave him more attention than the other two.

Kittens and puppies, I knew, played and played. When I realized that baby bluebirds, too, would play intently through all their young days, I tried to make Nature's great way as pleasant and as beneficial as possible by providing playthings.

An envelope was hung by a string from the ridge log so that it just cleared the floor, and this was daily enjoyed. Occasionally all tugged at it at once from different directions; sometimes all stood by to watch it dance, swing, and whirl after one had jostled or pulled or struck it.

A hollow, bright-striped rubber ball gave them hours of eager activity. They rolled it about, racing after it and following it all over the floor. When I dropped it, they stood still, watching it curiously as it bounced up and down. When I rolled it against the wall and it came back to them, they dodged and scampered about, pretending to be frightened. A box of shavings afforded them many a mysterious delight. When all played together in it, trampling and plowing through the shavings, they showed as much excited earnestness as children do when playing bear.

Most youngsters like to make a noise, and I found that even gentle, quiet young bluebirds are no exception. One day when in a hurry I placed a tin pan containing a handful of dry beans on the floor. In a moment three children were in the pan stamping about, having a rattling good time. Many a time afterwards when too busy to play with them I took down the tin basin and its ration of dry beans.

They always enjoyed sitting on the pole fence, but expected me to be near them. I was talking to them one day as they sat there, when two little girls and their mother called. It was probably the closest that the children had ever come to bird-life, and it certainly was the first meeting of these bird children with human children. For some seconds the birds looked down, gladly but somewhat bashfully; the little girls looking up with quiet eagerness, hoping to be allowed to touch them. When the little birds were cuddled and talked to in turn, they received it as a matter of course, but appeared happier to be back on the pole fence again.

All three of these blue children were at different times greatly interested in different things, but to the very end of the summer my writing-table never ceased to fascinate Little Blue. It was for him a real fairy place, and he insisted on playing there much of the time.

Generally he entertained himself quietly, but occasionally he indulged in vigorous pranks. Seizing the end of a pencil or penholder in his bill, he backed off to the edge of the table and dropped or pushed it overboard. Then he peered after it, listening with tilted head for it to strike the floor. Each time the rattle made him leap for joy or look up at me with an expression of happy satisfaction. Then he made haste to find something else to throw overboard.

While Little Blue was one day busy on the table, the other two birds were outdoors. The door presently blew shut. Bye and bye Little Blue flew to the floor. Not seeing the other birds, he gave a puzzled chirp and began exploring every corner of the room. Greatly mystified, he stood in the center of the floor for several seconds, listening and apparently thinking. Then slowly, seriously, he began looking for them again. His attitude was one of responsibility. He appeared worried about them rather than lonesome. I opened the door, and out he rushed. Curiously and with grave concern he looked them over, then quickly dismissed his fears when he discovered that they were all right.

Sometimes, while I was writing, Little Blue made it too lively for me. Partly to divert him, I began keeping a covered tin box of crumbs on the table. Often, when he wanted something to eat, he hovered with beating wings just above the

The Love Song of Little Blue

box until I opened it. On one occasion he found the box uncovered. Alighting on its edge, he bent forward and peered in, and then looked up at me. The box was empty. He wiped his bill on the edge a time or two and looked at me again. I pretended not to have noticed either him or the empty box. He then clutched the edge of the box in his claws and hammered the table vigorously with it.

One morning, while making merry on the table, he overturned a quart bottle of ink. It fell smash on the floor, and after it tumbled the tin crumb-box. Little Blue, in happiest mood, looked down from the edge of the table, while I gathered up the pieces of the broken bottle. I saved a little of the ink, a scarce article in my part of the world, pouring this into the empty tin box until I could find something better. This gave Little Blue an idea!

Usually each morning the little birds had the opportunity for a bath. Watching the splashy enthusiasm of robins in the brook had suggested to me that the bluebirds might like to try it. They did. But on this particular morning they had not yet been given the opportunity, and Little Blue evidently thought it was time. Just as I returned with an empty bottle he squatted in the tin box and began splashing ink with his wings. I almost drowned him in the water bucket before putting him out in the sun to dry.

Little Blue so greatly confused things in his intense enjoyment of the table that I sometimes covered it when I left the cabin. If I put on my hat, took up the water-bucket, or made other unmistakable preparations to go out, he instantly watched to see whether or not the table would be covered. If not, and I was slow to go after making preparations, he became excited. It was so much in his mind that the instant I was outdoors he pounced upon the table and at once made all haste to clear it off completely.

One day the table was uncovered and he playing with the other birds in the shavings on the floor, when I rose and put on my hat. He at once ceased playing and flew to the back of the chair by the table. I started for the door, with him watching my every move. But on reaching the door I stopped, picked up a pamphlet, and with my back toward him pretended to read. I was watching him closely in the looking-glass. He was all eagerness and excitement at my delay. He stood watching me for a moment, and then the situation appeared to dawn on him—that I could not see him. Anyway, he stretched his neck, looked the table over, and then took a glance at me. Then he hopped over upon the table. I made no move, and after turning for another look at me, he proceeded to enjoy himself.

Toward the close of summer I kept the table covered when not in use. For this purpose I used a burlap cloth that was barely large enough. Little Blue found a way to uncover it. He one day alighted on a corner of the table and looked at me; then, reaching over and catching the edge of the cover in his bill, he lifted it, tilted his head, and tried to peep under it. Then he let it drop and again looked up at me. As with many a mother, the child triumphed.

Dry climate one day gave him a surprise. He alighted on my shoulder and then hopped upon my head. The weather was extra dry and my crowded, curly hair electrical. Apparently the soles of his feet were strangely tickled. He tried standing on one foot like a stork. Then he tried the other foot. He changed places and feet repeatedly, and finally squatted down in my hair.

I was writing, and on reaching the end of a line I asked, "Little Blue, can you read that?" Leaning forward and downward, he stared closely at the writing as though trying to understand it.

I frequently talked to the birds in a natural, conversational way, apparently to their great enjoyment. I always talked about something definite, told stories or endeavored to speak sympathetically as though talking to a child. I avoided detached words and meaningless chatter. Often I have won the attention and sometimes the affection of an animal or bird simply by talking calmly, kindly to it.

Little Blue was simply charmed when I did this, especially

The Love Song of Little Blue

when I addressed myself to him alone. He sometimes lighted on my table, I think, for the purpose of having me talk to him. I spoke slowly, gently, and cheerfully. After the first few words he looked up into my face and stopped all activities, listening to the end with perfect attention. I sometimes explained to him the ways of other birds, spoke of birds he would meet in the South during the winter. Often I talked to him about his parents, and the ways of bluebirds I had known. Many times he listened with the greatest interest for minutes. But his was almost a silent attention. The bluebird as a species has few chirps, peeps, or calls; it is mostly silent.

One morning I paused in my writing to talk to Little Blue. Pen in hand stood by the last word written. After listening with his usual eagerness, he hopped upon my hand and looked up wonderingly into my face. I continued talking quietly and earnestly. Suddenly, with half-opened and fluttering wings, he began a low, sweet, whispered warble—the love song of the bluebird—all the while looking intensely at me with almost passionate interest. It continued for a little less than a half minute.

This was a dear experience to have with a dumb friend, and it was deep enough for tears.

The day before the birds were called South, I had been talking to Little Blue on the table, when he again sang the whispered warble—I suppose the love song of his heart for his mate.

During early autumn the little bluebirds were uneasy and restless. Evidently they were ready to be off for the southland and to take the great migration journey.

The call came to them when all four of us were sitting close together on the top pole of the fence one still, sunny, thoughtful September morning. I was wondering what the winter had in store for them, for I felt that their migratory instinct would be irresistible. I said: "Some day you will start on a long and wonderful journey which will carry you over rivers, hills, and fields into the warm southland. Your bluebird companions will travel slowly, in flocks, picnicking on the way. You will have new things to eat in every country where you stop. Before Thanksgiving you should be in central Mexico, or, if you do not go to Mexico you will be in Texas. Wherever you are, you will find thousands of bluebirds, perhaps millions of robins, and hundreds of other species of birds. But bluebirds make short stays in the southland, and long before our winter is over, you will be starting slowly northward. Bluebirds often pass here by the first of March and sometimes rest for a day or two before going on farther. I hope I shall see you next spring; perhaps some of you will stay and nest with me again."

Suddenly, the plaintive, stirring call of a bluebird was heard. Then several bluebirds alighted on a pole in the next panel of the fence. Leaving my birds interested in the visiting travelers, I backed away to watch them from my cabin. Here and there golden leaves shone on the aspen, and occasionally the serene air of autumn whispered in the pines.

I stood in the doorway watching, and wondering if these three little birds whom I had raised would fly away and leave me. For a time there was an exchange of conversational twitterings and warblings. Then, the far, far-away, mysterious and irresistible migration instinct called, I suppose. True to this, all presently took wing and started south.

But Little Blue circled from the flock and came back to me as I stood in the cabin door. On beating wings he paused in the air just before me, looked at me intently a few seconds, then flew away over the pine grove toward the south after the flock. I felt certain that next spring he would return with a mate to nest beneath my cabin ridge log.

Early in the autumn many local bluebirds ascend the mountains to about twelve thousand feet and sometimes spend two or three weeks along the timber-line. Here they feed on insects and late berries. This autumn in the heights I saw a number of small bluebird flocks of from eight to fifteen, perhaps they were families. I looked and called repeatedly for Little Blue, but there was no response. One day, however, I

The Love Song of Little Blue

felt certain that I saw his older brother, the bird who had called upon us, but whose six bashful children remained in the near-by pine.

A few days after the little bluebirds flew away I left my cabin for a winter in Montana and the Northwest, and I did not return until early the following July. On arrival I paused just long enough to see that there was a nest of baby bluebirds in the old place, then hurried in to examine some papers. Leaving the cabin door open, I took a seat at the table. Suddenly there was a flutter of wings, and a bird alighted on my shoulder, then on the table. He was looking up into my face with worshipful satisfaction.

"Are you Little Blue?" I asked. "Are those your babies in the nest?"

The answer was the low, sweet, whispered warble—the bluebird's song of love and memory.

11.

A Mountain Pony

OUR STAGE IN THE San Juan Mountains had just gained the top of the grade when an alert, riderless pony trotted into view on a near-by ridge. Saddled and bridled, she was returning home down a zigzag trail after carrying a rider to a mine up the mountain-side. One look at this trim, spirited "return horse" from across a narrow gorge, and she disappeared behind a cliff.

A moment later she rounded a point of rocks and came down into the road on a gallop. The stage met her in a narrow place. Indifferent to the wild gorge below, she paused unflinchingly on the rim as the brushing stage dashed by. She was a beautiful bay pony.

"That is Cricket, the wisest return horse in these hills," declared the stage-driver, who proceeded to tell of her triumphant adventures as he drove on into Silverton. When I went to hire Cricket, her owner said that I might use her as long as I desired, and proudly declared that if she was turned loose anywhere within thirty miles she would probably come home or die. A trip into the mountains beyond Telluride was my plan.

A "return horse" is one that will go home at once when set free by the rider, even though the way be through miles of trailless mountains. He is a natural result of the topography of the San Juan Mountains and the geographic conditions therein. Many of the mines in this region are situated a thousand feet or so up the precipitous slopes above the valleys. The railroads, the towns, society, are down in the cañons,

A Mountain Pony

—so near and yet so far,—and the only outlet to the big world is through the cañon. Miners are willing to walk down from the boarding-house at the mine; but not many will make the vigorous effort, nor give the three to four hours required, to climb back up the mountain. Perhaps some one wants to go to a camp on the opposite side of the mountain. As there is no tunnel through, he rides a return horse to the summit, turns the horse loose, then walks down the opposite side. The return horse, by coming back undirected, meets a peculiar transportation condition in a satisfactory manner.

The liverymen of Silverton, Ouray, and Telluride keep the San Juan section supplied with these trained ponies. With kind treatment and experience the horses learn to meet emergencies without hesitation. Storm, fallen trees, a landslide, or drifted snow may block the way—they will find a new one and come home.

The local unwritten law is that these horses are let out at the owner's risk. If killed or stolen, as sometimes happens, the owner is the loser. However, there is another unwritten law which places the catching or riding of these horses in the category of horse-stealing,—a serious matter in the West.

I rode Cricket from Silverton to Ouray, and on the way we became intimately acquainted. I talked to her, asked questions, scratched the back of her head, examined her feet, and occasionally found something for her to eat. I walked up the steeper stretches, and before evening she followed me like a dog, even when I traveled out of the trail.

For the night she was placed in a livery-barn in Ouray. Before going to bed I went out and patted and talked to her for several minutes. She turned to watch me go, and gave a pleasant little whinny as the barn-door closed.

Telluride and Ouray are separated by a mountain that rises four thousand feet above their altitude. By trail they are twelve miles apart; by railroad, forty miles. Many people go by trail from one to the other, usually riding to the summit, one half the distance, where the horse is set free, and walking the rest of the way.

Cricket at the summit

When Cricket and I set out from Ouray, we followed the road to the Camp Bird Mine. We met horses returning with empty saddles, each having that morning carried a rider from Ouray to the mine. Three of these horses were abreast, trotting merrily, sociably along, now and then giving a pleasant nip at one another.

We stopped at the Camp Bird Mine, and while in the office I overheard a telephone inquiry concerning a return horse, Hesperus, who had been sent with a rider to the summit and was more than an hour overdue. Half a mile above the mine we met Hesperus coming deliberately down. He was not loafing, but was hampered by a loose shoe. When he reached the Camp Bird barn he stopped, evidently to have the shoe removed. As soon as this was done, he set off on a swinging trot down the trail.

As Cricket and I went forward, I occasionally gave her attention, such as taking off her saddle and rubbing her back. These attentions she enjoyed. I walked up the steep places, an act that was plainly to her satisfaction. Sometimes I talked to

A Mountain Pony

her as if she were a child, always speaking in a quiet, conversational manner, and in a merry make-believe way, pretending that she understood me. And doubtless she did, for tone is a universal language.

At the summit Cricket met some old friends. One pony had been ridden by a careless man who had neglected to fasten the bridle-reins around the saddle-horn,—as every rider is expected to do when he starts the pony homeward. This failure resulted in the pony's entangling a foot in the bridle-rein. When I tried to relieve him there was some lively dodging before he would stand still enough for me to right matters. Another pony was eating grass by walking in the bottom of a narrow gully and feeding off the banks. Commonly these horses are back on time. If they fail to return, or are late, there is usually a good reason for it.

The trail crossed the pass at an altitude of thirteen thousand feet. From this point magnificent scenes spread away on every hand. Here we lingered to enjoy the view and to watch the antics of the return ponies. Two of them, just released, were rolling vigorously, despite their saddles. This rolling enabled me to understand the importance of every liveryman's caution to strangers, "Be sure to tighten the saddle-cinches before you let the pony go." A loose cinch has more than once caught the shoe of a rolling horse and resulted in the death of the animal. A number of riderless ponies who were returning to Telluride accompanied Cricket and me down the winding, scene-commanding road into this picturesque mining town.

I spent a few days about Telluride riding Cricket up to a number of mines, taking photographs on the way. Whenever we arrived at an exceptionally steep pitch, either in ascending or in descending, Cricket invited me to get off and walk. Unbidden she would stop. After standing for a few seconds, if I made no move to get off, she turned for a look at me; then if I failed to understand, she laid back her ears and pretended to bite at my feet.

One day we paused on a point to look down at a steep

trail far below. A man was climbing up. A riderless pony was trotting down. Just as they met, the man made a dash to catch the pony. It swerved and struck with both fore feet. He dodged and made another bold, swift grab for the bridle-rein, but narrowly missed. He staggered, and, before he could recover, the pony wheeled and kicked him headlong. Without looking back, the pony trotted on down the trail as though nothing had happened. For a moment the man lay stunned, then, slowly rising, he went limping up the slope.

A well-meaning tenderfoot, that afternoon in Telluride, saw a riderless pony and concluded that he had broken loose. After lively work he cornered the pony in an alley and caught it. The owner appeared just as the stranger was tying the pony to a hitching-post. A crowd gathered as the owner, laughing heartily, dragged the stranger into a saloon. I leaped off Cricket and went into the saloon after them. To the astonishment of every one Cricket also walked in.

We left Telluride one sunny October morning with a sleeping-bag and a few supplies. I had made plans to have a few days for the study of forest conditions around Lizard Head and Mt. Wilson. In the neighborhood of Ophir Loop, the first night out, the moonlight on the mountains was so enchanting that I rode on until nearly morning.

Cricket and I were chummy. The following afternoon, while waiting for sunset over Trout Lake, I lay down for a sleep on the grass in a sun-filled opening surrounded by clumps of tall spruces. Trusting Cricket to stay near, I threw her bridle-rein over her head to the ground and thus set her free. In the sunny, dry air I quickly fell asleep. An hour later, a snorting explosion on the top of my head awakened me. Though I was somewhat startled, the situation was anything but alarming. Cricket was lying beside me. Apparently, while dozing, she had dropped her head against mine, and had snorted while her nostrils were against my ear.

We wandered far from the trail, and, after a few perfect days in the mountain heights, big clouds came in and snow fell thickly all night long. By morning it was nearly two feet

A Mountain Pony

deep, and before noon several snow-slides were heard. Being a good rustler, Cricket had all the morning been pawing into the snow, where she obtained a few mouthfuls of snowy grass. But she must be taken where she could get enough to eat.

After thirty-six hours of storm we started down a cañon out of the snowy wilderness under a blue sky. No air stirred. The bright sun cast purple shadows of the pines and spruces upon the clean white snow. After a few hours we came to a blockade. The cañon was filled with an enormous mass of snow. A snow-slide had run in from a side gulch. We managed to get into the upper edge of this snow, where it was thin and not compressed.

Cricket fought her way through in the most matter-of-fact manner, notwithstanding her head and neck were all that showed above the snow. As these return horses are often caught out in deep drifts, it is important that they be good "snow horses." She slowly forced her way forward, sometimes pawing to make an opening and again rearing and striking forward with both fore feet. From time to time she paused to breathe, occasionally eating a mouthful of snow while she rested. All the time I talked encouragingly to her, saying, "Of course you can make it!" "Once more!"

When more than halfway through the snowslide mass, one of the saddle-cinches caught on the snag of a fallen log and held her fast. Her violent efforts were in vain. Wallowing my way along the rocks several yards above, I descended to her side, cut both saddle-cinches, threw the saddle and the sleeping-bag off her back, and removed the bridle. Cricket was thus left a naked horse in the snow.

When after two hours she had made her way out, I went for the saddle and sleeping-bag. As it was impossible to carry them, I attached the bridle to them and wallowed my way forward, dragging them after me. Meantime Cricket was impatiently waiting for me and occasionally gave an encouraging hurry-up neigh.

When I had almost reached her, a mass of snow, a tiny slide

from a shelving rock, plunged down, sweeping the saddle and the bag down into the cañon and nearly smothering me. As it was almost night, I made no attempt to recover them. Without saddle or bridle, I mounted Cricket and went on until dark. We spent the night at the foot of an overhanging cliff, where we were safe from slides. Here we managed to keep warm by a camp-fire. Cricket browsed aspen twigs for supper. I had nothing. A number of slides were heard during the night, but none were near us.

At daylight we again pushed forward. The snow became thinner as we advanced. Near Ophir Loop, we passed over the pathway of a slide where the ground had been swept bare. Having long been vigilant with eyes and ears for slides, while on this slide-swept stretch, I ceased to be alert. Fortunately Cricket's vigilance did not cease. Suddenly she wheeled, and, with a quickness that almost took her from beneath me, she made a frantic retreat, as a slide with thunderous roar shot down into the cañon. So narrowly did it miss us that we were heavily splashed with snow-fragments and almost smothered by the thick, prolonged whirl of snow-dust. Cricket's vigilance had saved my life.

The masses of snow, stones, and broken timber brought down by this slide blockaded the cañon from wall to wall. These walls were too steep to be climbed, and, after trying until dark to make a way through the wreckage, we had to give it up.

We spent a cold night alongside a cliff. Cricket and I each ate a few willow twigs. The night was of refined clearness, and from time to time I moved away from the pungent camp fire smoke to look at the myriads of stars that pierced with icy points the purple sky.

The clear morning brought no solution of my problem of getting Cricket through. I could not abandon her. While she was trying to find something to eat, I made my way up a side gulch, endeavoring to find a way for her to the summit. From the top we could get down beyond the slide blockade. After a time a way was found that was impossible for her at only one

A Mountain Pony

point. This point was a narrow gulch in the summit. I climbed along a narrow ledge, swept bare by the slide, then turned into a rocky gulch which came in from the side. I was within fifteen feet of success. But this was the width of a rocky gulch. Beyond this it would be comparatively easy to descend on the other side of the slide wreckage and land in the road to Telluride.

But how was Cricket to get to the other side of this gorge? Along the right I made my way through great piles of fallen fire-killed timber. In places this wreckage lay several logs deep. I thought to find a way through the four or five hundred feet of timber-wreckage. Careful examination showed that with much lifting and numerous detours there was a way through this except at four places, at which the logs that blocked the way were so heavy that they could not be moved. Without tools the only way to attack this confusion of log-masses was with fire. In a short time the first of these piles was ablaze. As I stepped back to rub my smoke-filled eyes, a neigh came echoing to me from the side cañon below.

Cricket had become lonesome and was trying to follow me. Reared in the mountains, she was accustomed to making her way through extremely rugged places, over rocks and fallen trees. Going to the rim of the cañon, I looked down upon her. There she stood on a smoothly glaciated point, a splendid statue of alertness. When I called to her she responded with a whinny and at once started to climb up toward me. Coaching her up the steep places and along narrow ledges, I got her at last to the burning log obstruction. Here several minutes of wrestling with burning log-ends opened a way for her.

The two or three other masses were more formidable than the first one. The logs were so large that a day or more of burning and heavy lifting would be required to break through them. More than two days and nights of hard work had been passed without food, and I must hold out until a way could be fought through these other heavy timber-heaps. Cricket, apparently not caring to be left behind again, came close to me and eagerly watched my every move. To hasten the fire, armfuls of small limbs were gathered for it. As limbs were plentiful on the other side of the gorge, I went across on a large fallen log for a supply, shuffling the snow off with my feet as I crossed. To my astonishment Cricket came trotting across the slippery log after me! She had been raised with fallen timber and had walked logs before. As she cleared the edge, I threw my arms around her neck and leaped upon her back. Without saddle, bridle, or guiding, she took me merrily down the mountain-side into the wagon-road beyond the snow-slide blockade. At midnight we were in Telluride.

12.

Trailing Utah's Shore Lines

I ASSUMED THAT EVERYONE in Utah knew the wonderful story of old Lake Bonneville. But the hotel clerk to whom I mentioned the historical ancestor of Great Salt Lake looked up from the morning paper with a fossil stare—nothing more. A First Settlers Club referred me to the State Historical Society. But this organization, dealing in recent human affairs, was not even interested in prehistorical geology. And the secretary of a Chamber of Commerce suggested, kindly but firmly, if I had in mind the publication of a story concerning a wholly imaginary lake, that I locate it in some other region, as they did not care for that kind of advertising.

I had failed to impress any one with my enthusiasm for trailing ancient shore lines when I at last encountered an old prospector outside the city limits.

"Yes," he said reflectively, "old Bonneville was a thousand feet deep and covered half of Utah. Its waves wore an enduring shore line upon the slopes of the Oquirrh Range; and, in fact, all the Great Basin shows evidence of the old lake level, high and dry on the mountain-sides. Lake Bonneville was fresh water. Its sediments and its abandoned shores are strewn with fresh-water fossils. This immense, dried-out lake basin, in which half a million people now have their homes, schools, farms, mines, and factories, is the largest fossil known."

After a few more illuminating remarks concerning this dead lake and the records which it had left in shore lines, sediments, and evidences of long submergence, the prospector turned away and I started off for the Oquirrh Range.

As I skirted Great Salt Lake, which occupies a small area of the old lake bottom, the shore seemed strangely like that of the sea. Gulls were flying over and waves were forming and thundering along the beach. Deltas had formed where streams poured in, and on beaches and headlands winds, like happy children, were building and shifting their piles of sand. The breezes had a goodly tang of salt, as though sea rivers were flowing into the lake; but none flowed out; its waters left only in clouds.

The old shore lines showed boldly in the distance, like highways along the mountain walls and around mountain peaks that had stood as islands in the ancient inland sea. In places, a dozen shore lines, one above the other, formed gigantic terraces. Each marked the level at which the slow-changing surface of the lake remained sufficiently long to wear an enduring record. The many shore lines tell of a fluctuating existence, of ups and downs, while old Bonneville had a place in the sun.

I climbed up for a closer view and, near sundown, paused in a gulch on an old shore line wide enough for a four-track Lincoln Highway. Here was the high-water mark of Lake Bonneville, one thousand feet above the surface of Great Salt Lake. At its height, Lake Bonneville comprised about nineteen thousand square miles—the area of Lake Michigan—and covered more than half of Utah and a small area in Nevada and Idaho. It was about three hundred and fifty miles long and one hundred and forty-five wide, with a three-thousand-mile shore line stretching across desert plains and mountains and extending far back into mountain cañons for slender bays. Mountain-tops large and small were its rocky islands.

As darkness came on, I made camp on this ancient beach line, alone and happy—my camp fire and I, beneath desert stars, by a fossil lake on which the waves had not rolled for at least twenty thousand years, possibly not for twice as long. For years I had been hoping to explore this long-deserted

Trailing Utah's Shore Lines

ruin. As I thought of trailing the old beach line, my imagination was stirred. When the waves of this vast lake were washing and wearing its boundary, there were elephants, camels, horses, and other mammals feeding along its beaches or trampling the headlands above its shores. Possibly, primitive man was also in the scene. In the sediments of near-by fossil Lake Lahontan a primitive spear head has been found beneath twenty feet of sediment. For thousands of years, the old shore line has endured wind, frost, and rain; running water and landslides have also done their work. Today, modern man fills and stirs the scene of this geological story. Miles of radiating railroads with their bands of steel are firmly bedded in the bottom of this deserted and deserty lake bed.

The next morning the shore-line highway brought me out on a long, outthrusting ridge that had been a peninsula in the old lake. As the shore line folded around it, I looked down on the shallow shore of Great Salt Lake miles away and a thousand feet below.

Immediately below the Bonneville shore line, on which I stood, the mountain-side was terraced with five shore lines in close succession. These, so the wave sediment showed, were made by five pauses of the rising surface of the lake. When high water reached the Bonneville shore line, the lake found an outlet north at Red Rock Pass, Idaho. Through this outlet, the waters eagerly rushed, rapidly deepening the outlet. In a short time, it was cut three hundred and seventy-five feet down to the Provo shore line—the boldest of them all. At the Provo level, the lake surface appears to have lingered many thousand years. Finally, it sank below the outlet, lingered, made other shore lines, and became salty.

I climbed down to reach the Provo shore line and followed it around the mountain all day long. Long segments of it were missing; these had been washed off by running water or had slipped away with landslides. Stretches were covered with landslide débris or sediment that had washed and rolled from above. Wind erosion and windblown sand in places had cut it to pieces or had buried it. But, though broken, miles of it were so well preserved it seemed almost incredible that the waves had not splashed it for ages.

Back in a cañon I found the remnants of a delta. Here a small stream flowing into the lake had dropped its burden of sediment—an enormous dump. After the lake lowered, the stream had washed a part of the delta away. These deltas, with upper surface roughly level with the old lake level, had filled in and built outward at the stream's mouth just as deltas are formed to-day.

As I walked along, noticing gulleys, eroded deltas, and débris piles left by streams and landslides, I became conscious that the shore line was tilted, and that the water had run over it in the same direction in which I was travelling.

But the arrangement of accumulated sediment on the surface of the shore line showed that at a low point streams from opposite directions—from the east and the west—had met, then overflowed in this break.

This warping puzzled me and I accounted for it with local landslip and local cave-in. Made by the horizontal surface of a lake, these old shore lines were originally dead level. The Wasatch Mountains are still rising. Many faultings and warpings of the crust of recent date are seen. A water-pipe main was recently broken near where the pipe crossed a fault in the underlying crust.

One night, I camped in a sheltering niche of the Provo shore line. The lurid and many-coloured clouds over the desert horizon made sunset worth crossing the continent to see, but gorgeous horizons are common in the Salt Lake Desert.

Great Salt Lake now is about six hundred and twenty-five feet below the Provo shore line. It has an average depth of thirteen feet. Bonneville was a thousand feet deeper. Salt Lake, like Bonneville, has made many shore lines and the records of its rise and fall have been kept since 1850. Twice—in 1903 and 1905—its surface dropped a few feet below the shore line of 1850; twice—in 1858 and 1877—it rose ten feet above this level. Its surface now is several feet above the level of 1850.

Trailing Utah's Shore Lines

The next day, I left the Provo and went out into the desert plain. Here the mirage put on an exhibition of old shore lines for my especial benefit. Evidently segments of real shore lines had been reflected and projected. Lines from the Promontory Mountains, the Oquirrh Range and Fremont Island were shown, mingled, magnified, and wrecked with greatly exaggerated tilts and depressions.

Unexpectedly, while crossing the old lake bed, I came upon lava that had poured red hot into the lake. Volcanic action has now and then been recorded in the Basin since its creation. Volcanic ash shows in many layers of the lake's sediments. The spectacular part that had been played by these old craters was as exciting as any of the lake's records. One of the most telling volcanic exhibitions was near Deseret, Utah. One mound-like crater stood out in the desert plain belted with two shore lines. Lava was buried beneath the oldest Bonneville sediments; an old shore line, evidently made by the first Bonneville existence, had been partly covered by lava of later date. Then, too, lava had flowed out into the water during the second stage of the lake and on the dry desert floor.

When miles out in the desert plain, I turned for another look at this fossilized volcano. Boiling over the top was a black, convulsed, and fire-tinged mass like a rolling flood of lava; while, still staring, a heavy cloud like smoke and ashes settled before me. Was I seeing the beginning of another volcanic outburst? I was ready to believe it when the scene shifted and I added another specialty to the master producer of movies — the Mirage.

A year later, there was another mirage demonstration. This was by the Promontory Mountains to the north of Great Salt Lake. I had climbed one of the many mountains which had once stood a rocky island in the ancient lake. Its base was deeply buried beneath sediments. Across the far-reaching sea of sand rose many island-like, barren mountains in the barren Basin.

The entire scene before me suddenly became a mirage. With a rush, the old lake was restored. Most of Utah vanished beneath clear water. The surface of this mirage lake appeared to be a few hundred feet beneath me. I moved to another point and had a glimpse down into camp and of a young geology student who had been with me for a few days. He had been examining a delta near camp for gold, and now loafed about as though waiting for a train.

I called to him to look at the mirage. He looked, but plainly saw nothing unusual from where he stood. He started up, and when about one hundred feet below me called: "Did you see the reflection?"

But when I looked again, the mirage lake was still perfect. Not a wave moved along the rocky shores of the peaks that pierced it.

However, not seeing any reflection, I hurried down to him and there reflected was the Wasatch mountain range and the white clouds in the sky. Often I had seen a mirage simulate lake or a section of the sea. Here was double deception, perfectly reflecting mountain and horizon, the clouds and the sky.

Lake Bonneville may be said to have been twice upon the earth. During the Ice Age, the flood of water which followed the melting brought Bonneville into existence for its first stage. It appears to have had a place in the sun for several thousand years and then to have dried up altogether. After a long period with the basin dry, it was again filled during the melting of the ice which followed the last glacial advance.

Though there were many down-reaching, out-reaching glaciers, at one place only do these giant ice tongues appear to have reached the shore of the lake. This is in Little Cottonwood Cañon. Here the shore-line deposits and moraines mingle; from the steep, sloping Wasatch, the Ice King probably launched many an iceberg on this inland Bonneville sea.

Bonneville's first existence appears to have been long. The water rose slowly, with many fluctuations, to the depth of more than nine hundred feet. Though within ninety feet of a possible outlet, it slowly shrank and dried out altogether without sending its waters to the sea.

The sediments deposited during the first existence of the lake were deeply eroded by running water, and in places quantities of débris were washed and blown upon them, before the sediments of the second existence were deposited.

Its second existence, shorter than the first, was more of the nature of flooding. Its waters rose speedily to the depth of several hundred feet, paused briefly, rose higher, paused again, and finally rose to the depth of more than a thousand feet. This was the Bonneville level and this allowed the waters to flow north out through Red Rock Pass.

Eagerly the long-imprisoned waters made their escape through this high mountain pass, thence through the Snake and Columbia rivers into the sea. This is the first time that water had flowed out of the Great Basin, perhaps after the existence of a million years.

That Bonneville was a fresh-water lake is shown by the presence of several species of freshwater fossils found at varying depths in the sediments of the lake bottom. During the existence of Bonneville, Lake Lahontan was in existence in Nevada. This Nevada lake had long existence and no outlet, but during its long, deep stage it too was a fresh-water lake.

The Wasatch Mountains were composed of sedimentary rocks—rocks formed in the salt waters of the sea and which carried a percentage of salt. The erosion and weathering of the mountains gave a percentage of salt in solution to the streams that flowed from them into the basin. This salt must have accumulated as the repeated lakes dried out in the basin before the coming of Bonneville. With the basin lined with salt deposits it would appear that Bonneville should have been intensely salty from the beginning. But before Bonneville came, the salt that lay deep in its basin had been buried beyond the reach of its water.

During explorations, I came upon a number of small salt or soda deposits in the beds of extinct lakes. A few of these deposits were deeply though not completely buried. One deposit of salt was more than one half covered beneath a twenty-one-foot layer of drifted sand; another deposit was nine tenths covered beneath a twelve-foot layer which was forming from the sediments abundantly washed in during floods from cloudbursts. The natural cements in this sediment would in time form over the salt a rock strata that no surface water could penetrate.

Deeply buried in sediments are the bases of many mountains which pierce the surface of the old basin. With buttresses, lowlands, and approaches buried, they stand like mountain-top islands in the sea, and in Great Salt Lake.

A few years ago, the Southern Pacific Railroad drilled many deep wells seeking water in the desert Bonneville basin miles to the west of Salt Lake. The drilling penetrated lake sediments for from several hundred to a thousand feet. It would take a long epoch for a thousand feet of lake sediment to accumulate. These sediments must have been accumulating untold ages before the coming of Bonneville. Their varying character suggests the deposits of alternating periods of moisture and drought. Evidently several fossil lakes, one above the other, were buried beneath these layers of salty sediments. Eight ruined, buried Troys are beneath the existing city of Troy. Evidently, many fossil lake beds, including Bonneville the first, are buried with their salt, soda, and borax deposits beneath Salt Lake. But these vast salty deposits of ages—of many fossil lakes—are overlaid with cemented, watertight sediments of rock and shale.

The Great Basin was neither round nor smooth bottomed. Its rim was broken and its bottom roughened with mountain peaks and cañons.

The lowlands of the Basin are from 4,000 to 5,000 feet above sea level, and the mountains rise 3,000 to 7,000 feet higher. The mountain summits have more precipitation than the lowlands, perhaps more than three times, and snow, during the winter, lies sometimes deeply.

A mountain revolution which began, perhaps, three million years ago made vast changes in the surfaces of the West. The Sierras were uplifted, numerous large areas sank, and the Wasatch Mountains were upraised. This revolution produced

Trailing Utah's Shore Lines

the Great Basin, an area between the Wasatch and the Sierra about the size of France. Rivers poured into this basin, but for ages it did not send a single drop of water to the sea. Embraced within the Great Basin are parts of Utah, Nevada, California, Wyoming, Idaho, and Oregon. It is the result of a mountain revolution which extended over a long age of time during which blocks of the basin were uplifted and adjacent ones subsided. The Sierras and the Wasatch were the great boundary uplifts. This shut the drainage off from the sea and nearly cut off incoming moisture-laden clouds.

After two explorations of the region, I went away planning to return and follow the Provo shore line from Ogden to the old outlet of the lake. This would take me through a long-settled and populated section of the old Basin.

Meantime, I wrote for information concerning it. A governor took pains to explain to me that Bonneville could not have emptied into Snake River, as this would require it to run uphill. "I financed an irrigation ditch," he wrote, "which the engineer built for the water to run up grade, and it would not work." A few days later, he wired me, "Bonneville did it once and has been a dead one ever since."

At last I went to investigate for myself. Before leaving Ogden, I spent a day on Observation Peak, a few miles to the southwest. I could see into three or four states, and what was better, into most of the old lake's basin.

I could outline the shore lines and the islands of present Salt Lake and trace hundreds of miles of the fossil shore lines of Lake Bonneville. The Provo shore line showed distinctly on Antelope Island, and it also came out on the Promontory Mountains to the northwest. Below and just before me were two vast deltas against the bold Provo shore line at Ogden. In places, these enormous overlapping deltas, roughly level on top, outreached six to eight miles into the old lake. One section, deeply channeled by a river since the lowering of Bonneville below Provo level, was occupied by a railroad. A part of Ogden sat serene on one shore-line terrace and acres of cherry orchards were rooted in the rich delta sediments. Many miles of stretches of these old shore lines now are automobile roads.

The entire ninety-mile walk along the Provo shore line between Ogden and the old outlet in Idaho was over the old lake bed and in places four hundred feet below the Bonneville level. The Oregon Short Line is in this lake bottom. Several times I wished there had been children with me to enjoy the romance of it, for none of the older people along the way caught the story.

I passed a plant that was making brick out of clay from the old lake bed; saw hundreds of cattle grazing the grass-grown sediments and hundreds of acres of peach trees upon old deltas. Thousands of Utah's farms are in the old lake bed. In places I saw three distinct shore lines on the mountains above us, and in Boxelder Cañon the lines were on both sides of the cañon. At several places, the shore lines folded back into a cañon, and across on the mountain wall of a narrow valley I saw the Provo, which I was following, the Bonneville nearly four hundred feet above me, and four or five less obvious lines between.

The region had been long populated and prosperous. Local people were ever pleasant, and a miner reminded me that a number of rich Utah mines were below the level of the old lake.

Everywhere, during these lake explorations, I had interesting glimpses into human nature—and our school system.

Near the Idaho line, I came to a country school that stood in an extensive plain, evidently the level sediments of the old lake bed. It was noon, and the teacher, a college man of forty years, and the collected pupils revealed no interest in my fossil geology, and when I pointed out before them a butte, broadly, boldly belted with an old shore line, that had been an island in Lake Bonneville, I found that their interest, like in many sections of the Provo line, was absent.

Around Red Rock Pass, by the old outlet of Bonneville, I found the people most responsive, but completely oblivious

Trailing Utah's Shore Lines 141

of the stirring geological scenes that have been shown in their mountain valley.

Across the Pass, a railroad runs for a few miles through the old outlet channel of the Bonneville River. Immediately on arriving in the Pass, I climbed from the Provo up to the Bonneville at the summit where the water had first flowed over. From this place and level, the outrushing Bonneville River had speedily eroded down to solid limestone 375 feet below. After tracing the Bonneville line to its farthest point, I descended to the Provo and asked questions of the railroad agent. He had been stationed there a number of years and had not heard of it, and felt that if there ever had been such an outlet that it must have been elsewhere. Other local people along the miles of outlet visited had not heard of it, and only one had heard of Lake Bonneville. A few even remarked that there might recently have been an outlet of the state asylum. Still, this lack of interest in local geography is common, as I found when looking over the glaciology of the Park section of Manhattan Island and asking local people concerning the morainal story of Long Island.

The Red Rock Pass region is rich in geological stories. Through this pass, perhaps for a few thousand years, poured the only running water that has come from the Great Basin, and this basin may have been in existence more than a million years.

This pass, when the eager waters of Bonneville hurried to escape across it, was deeply covered with loose, gravelly sediment washed down from the heights. This loose material was quickly washed away, and the outgoing Bonneville River speedily cut down three hundred and seventy-five feet. Then, dense, durable limestone was struck. This held, and at this level the lake cut the deep, broad, and well-marked Provo shore line, inside and against which incoming streams accumulated deltas.

The lowering of this pass removed its steep approaches and changed it into a mountain valley. The down-cutting of the river shifted the summit of the pass to Swan Lake, seven miles to the south of Red Rock. The broad, deep channel or valley worn by Bonneville River now seems like an abandoned channel, so small is the stream—Marsh Creek—which uses it. In places it is dammed, or nearly so, and for miles along its moderate slope there are ponds and marshes. This stream, on reaching the nearly level grade through the pass, drops much of the carried sediment. In time, a delta-like dam is formed. This temporarily blocks the flow. As a result, at times Marsh Creek flows down into Bear Creek, and into old Bonneville basin; at other times, down its regular channel to the north to Snake River.

The wide old channel of the Bonneville River is one hundred feet below the level of a lava plateau. Perhaps twenty miles below the summit, the Portneuf River breaks into this countersunk valley and flows down this east side of it. In the west side of the valley is Marsh Creek. This is separated from Portneuf by a narrow tongue of lava. After several miles of paralleling, these streams unite and empty, where Bonneville briefly poured, into the Snake River near Pocatello, Idaho.

13.

Ups and Downs of the Grand Cañon

THE OVERTURNING OF MY BOAT in the upper end of the Grand Cañon caused me to rise from the waters heavily laden. In less than a minute, my clothes picked up fifteen to twenty pounds of sand, fine rock flour, mica, marble, and iron, and suddenly developed a strange stiffening overload of armour that impeded every move.

There are two pounds of sediment in each gallon of water of the Colorado River. Multiply this overload of sediment a few million times for each gallon of water that has flowed through the river bed down through the ages, and one has a small conception of the vast quantities of material that have been eroded off the 15,000 square miles of the Colorado plateau and washed away by the caving in of the walls.

The Colorado River has made a distinct showing on the globe. It flows through a series of twenty vast cañons that have a total length of about one thousand miles. Rising on the western slope of the Rocky Mountains, snow-born streams bring to it contributions from high peaks and mountain valleys, and the eroded material from several states. Added to this is wind-blown dust and sand from desert plateaus. Continual carving and caving of the walls compel the river to spend most of its time and energy in breaking up this débris and carrying it forward to the sea—building up the delta of the Colorado. There are long stretches of quiet water through gentle valleys and low hills, and numerous turbulent currents between steep rocky walls where wild, foaming rapids spend their energy against the river bed. Through its thousand miles of cañons it has a fall of more than four thousand feet, unevenly divided.

Erosion is the artistic agency which causes old landscapes to melt away and new ones to advance upon the scene. This planet is old, and all the material in it, all that is now on the surface and much that is miles beneath the surface, has been through countless changes. Starting as a lifeless mass of solid rock, without a particle of soil, the earth has been given its present surface by time and the elements; erosion and decay have been lowering and levelling the heights, cutting valleys and cañon walls, washing the loosened material upon the lowlands, and building up new shore lines in ten thousand deltas out into the sea. What is deposited to-day will be eroded to-morrow. In how many times and places has each particle been deposited, vulcanized, stratified, cut to pieces, and broken up, then transported by wind, water, and ice to form new landscapes in the sun? Through erosion's agent—running water—the earth flows from one form into another.

The triumph of geology is in demonstrating that the forces which we see in operation to-day are sufficient—given time enough—to explain the sculpturing of the earth's surface.

The Colorado River has been working overtime for untold ages in producing that masterpiece of erosion, the Grand Cañon, which might well be called the greatest wonder in the world. Its immensity alone would be sufficient to attract the attention of the world. But combine with its vastness the marvellous and intricate sculpturing of its walls, the display of all of nature's colours in orderly array, and the appealing geological story revealed in the rocks of sea-born origin, and you cannot find its equal or any to compare with it the world over.

The Grand Cañon is the eighteenth of the series of cañons of the Colorado, counting downstream. This stupendous cañon, one mile deep and twelve miles wide, has been cut by the scratching of the sand and gravel dragged along by the river during an inconceivable period of time. Written in the

Ups and Downs of the Grand Cañon

two hundred miles of its exposed rock strata is a wonderful story of the past. The world-making processes are graphically exhibited in a stupendous panorama of prehistoric horizons. In no other place in the world are all the geological ages displayed in such a magnificent and complete array.

The Grand Cañon is a monument to Nature—to her achievements in uplift and subsidence, rock-making and breaking, sedimentation and erosion. Here are the original Archean rocks—granite and gneiss; sedimentary rocks as formed and as changed through heat, pressure, and other metamorphosing forces; lava new and old, by itself and forced between strata of other rocks; displays of uplift and subsidence; faults, displacement, crystallization, and colour; rocks folded, crumpled, deformed, and tilted; a thousand illustrations of sedimentation and the ever-changing story of erosion.

The Grand Cañon plateau has had seven separate lives or existences; three times it has been sea bottom and the ocean covered the region it now occupies; during its three separate submergences, not less than 30,000 feet of rock layers were deposited upon it, 26,000 of which were eroded away. Two of these ancient deposits were completely eroded off, and at present there are 4,000 feet of sedimentary deposits remaining upon it, through which the Colorado River has cut its river bed, and it has cut still another 1,000 feet into the original granite of the earth.

A tourist to-day picks up sea shells on the rim of the cañon, now 6,000 feet above sea level. This plateau surface of the cañon was formed beneath the sea. In its ups and downs, the Grand Cañon country has been 15,000 feet or more above sea level; as sea bottom, it has been 15,000 feet or more below the waves. Each time it was beneath the sea, numerous strata were deposited upon it. Each time it has been land, the surface has been levelled off and worn down by wind and water.

The outer surface of the earth was never long, if ever, in repose. Parts of the first land areas sank beneath the level of the sea, while other sea-covered areas, commonly those close to the original land, were uplifted into the sunlight. The surfaces raised and lowered have been both the original granite and surfaces of sandstone, limestone, and other rock layers formed upon the original granite.

The Grand Cañon plateau shows a mile of sedimentary rock, layer upon layer, in the original order in which the deposits were laid down. These sedimentary rocks, as well as their embedded fossils, tell definite information. A microscopic examination reveals whether they were deposited in fresh or in salt water; whether the sediments were brought by wind or by water. Cross-bedded sandstone often is of wind-blown desert sand. Sediments deposited in arid regions commonly form red rocks—the red beds of geology. Most limestone is formed of the minute remains of marine animals. Rock salt and gypsum commonly are the dried-up remains of lakes or sea arms and are the result of evaporation exceeding rainfall. From a thousand ages of the past, the plants and animals of ages indefinitely removed are brought to light in rocks formed of sands, muds, and limes laid down as sediments. Uplifts have raised many of these deposits, and erosion has uncovered and exposed the fossil records made long ago.

Near the El Tovar Hotel, the Colorado River flows in a narrow river bed 5,000 feet below the rim of an age-old cañon. Between the rim and the river are 4,000 feet of sedimentary rock layers, limestone, sandstone, and shale, and a thousand feet of the ancient Archean rock—the original granite and gneiss of the earth's surface. The history of the cutting of the Grand Cañon covers an inconceivable period and takes us back to the earliest history of time. But from the enduring records told in rocks, we can rebuild the past.

This Continent, if mapped a few million years ago, would have been very different in its land and water areas. The Gulf of California reached far up into the north, extending into Nevada and covering the areas now occupied by the Mohave and the Colorado deserts. The Gulf of Mexico was vastly larger, extending up into the Mississippi Valley toward the

Ups and Downs of the Grand Cañon

Great Lakes, and completely covering Florida. Slight uplifts along an inland sea brought new lands into existence. And every bit of land above the waves was material to be battled with by wind and water, frost and ice, and all the elements helping to wear it away.

If we can imagine the Grand Cañon country when it arose from the primeval sea, we can see its surface being slowly changed in form and appearance, until the original granite was worn down to a level plain and the eroded material was reposing in the shallow waters of the inland sea.

The Archean rocks slowly subsided. During the ages that the inland sea regained possession, erosion was going on upon all the surrounding land areas, and 12,000 feet of sediments were laid down under water. These deposits formed layer upon layer of limestone, sandstone, and shale. At this time, so fossils found in the remnants of the Algonkian strata show, the earliest forms of life were developing. During this epoch, which lasted an interminable time, the region was the scene of volcanic disturbances, as evidence in dykes and chimneys of lava shows. These disturbances shattered, cracked, and seamed the strata.

Then came a mountain-making movement which uplifted these 12,000 feet of rock layers into the sky. It was accompanied by faulting and tilting. While the uplift was occurring, erosion was working away at the tilted material, and eventually about 11,500 feet of the 12,000 feet that had been deposited were worn away. During the long period of erosion, a mountain range was reduced to a rolling plain again, and only small remnants of this brilliant red tilted and faulted Algonkian strata remain as insets in the base level surface of the old original granite and gneiss foundation of the earth. There were probably rivers then, as now, but the Colorado River had not yet taken its place on the plateau.

Another long period of submergence and sinking of the plain followed, allowing the incoming of the Tonto Sea, which worked upon the surface, still further wearing it away. From near-by peaks erosion carried off material to be deposited upon the submerged plain. The sea was salt and shallow and it is very likely that the submergence of the old Archean granite and Algonkian plain was going on simultaneously with the depositing of mud and sand of the Cambrian epoch. Then a rest, and these deposits were cemented into sandstone and shale—the strata now seen resting on the remnants of the Algonkian strata and in places upon the original granite. Two hundred feet of deep buff and greenish-gray strata of the Cambrian epoch show strikingly in the lower walls of the cañon, beneath the Tonto platform. They are much duller in colour than either the brilliant crimson of the Algonkian below or the red of the Carboniferous strata above. The Tonto platform forms a distinct, wide terrace, owing to the capping of these more resisting materials.

The records of the Ordovician, Silurian, and Devonian epochs are almost a blank, and it is probable either that the sea retreated for a time and no deposits were laid down, or that there was a slight uplift and sediments laid down were exposed to erosion. Only slight evidence of Devonian deposits has been found in the region.

During the Carboniferous epoch two thousand to three thousand feet of deposits were laid down. These formed the red-wall limestone, cross-bedded sandstone, and cherty limestone now exposed by the cutting of the Colorado River. The strata of red-wall limestone are the most striking in the cañon, forming the greater height of the present wall. There was no coal formed in this region during the Carboniferous epoch, the arid conditions of the climate and the lack of vegetation determining the materials laid down in the water. The purity of the limestone is evidence of the clearness of the waters in which the deposits were laid down and the presence of large cup corals shows that the sea was warm. The sea was probably shallow for a time, as alternating deposits of sand and mud were laid down, forming the shales and sandstone. On top of the Carboniferous, continuous deposits were probably forming during the Permian, Triassic, Jurassic, and Cretaceous epochs, until two miles of rocks accumulated.

Ups and Downs of the Grand Cañon

A great mountain movement occurred in early Eocene times, accompanied by violent disturbances of the earth's crust and many changes in the plateau country. The Cretaceous rocks and underlying strata were uplifted and subjected to the fierce attack of erosion. The records are not complete, but it is assume that a great warping occurred; some of the plateau sank and other portions arose, forming an inland sea. Vast deposits occurred again, their weight sinking the plateau deeper and deeper. Alternating uplifts and subsidences without record were at working during a great extent of time.

During the continued slow process of uplift, the Eocene lake was drained and 15,000 feet of deposit that had accumulated since Carboniferous times rose above the sea. During eons of erosion, this 15,000 feet of rock strata was entirely washed away. Only slight traces of the Permian, Triassic, Jurassic, and Cretaceous epochs are found in detached underlying strata of the Grand Cañon. And the subsequent deposits of Tertiary times were entirely removed upon the Grand Cañon rim. Peripherally some distance back, north and south from the rim, the eroded and broken strata of rock layers subsequent to the Carboniferous epoch are well defined.

The Colorado River was probably the outlet of the freshwater Eocene lake that disappeared during uplift. During this time, the river flowed in an easy-going shallow channel, in a comparatively level plateau. As continued uplift gave it impetus it cut its channel deeper, and as erosion was hastened, the débris-laden water sawed ever deeper as it slid over the surface of its inclined plateau. There were pauses in the uplift and a slowing down in erosion, but with each new steepening of the grade, the opportunities for erosion were increased. The climate was probably one of increased precipitation, and erosion of the entire plateau was undoubtedly going on at a rapid pace.

Enormous periods of time are represented in the fact that all the later geological epochs are missing along the rim of the Grand Cañon. The epochs had their existence, as rocks deposited elsewhere show, but in this region these thick layers, slowly deposited, were again slowly eroded. Sections of the adjacent plateaus show more recent periods of geology, and from the remnants of these strata, geologists restore the formations which once rested upon the Grand Cañon rim. Not all the strata are complete in one place, but where in horizontal position, or preserved by the cappings of volcanic material, they have endured through periods of subsidence, uplift, and erosion. The remnants give the most complete and logical abstract of all the geologic epochs anywhere to be found.

It may have been fifty million years since the original granite of the Grand Cañon region first rose above the surface of the sea. And it may have been twice as long. Slowness is the keynote to the marvellous story of geology. Slow upheaval and slow settling; slow erosion and slow forming of rock layers. One hundred years or more for each foot of uplift might be called average; an entire century for a few inches of subsidence would be normal.

A few small land areas are being thickened by additions of sediment or dust, volcanic ash or lava, but most of the surface of the earth is being lowered by erosion, which goes steadily on, much less than an inch a century. Sea bottom over most of its area is being built up by hundreds of millions of tons of rock sediment annually poured in by rivers and the dusts contributed by winds and volcanoes. Sedimentary rocks are deposited inch by inch, in some cases less than a foot a century; in other cases or places, the rate of deposit might be trebled. This material is combined into many kinds of rocks. A little more of this mineral or that chemical, a trifle more or less heat or pressure, and the rock produced is distinctive. Limestone intensely heated becomes marble.

Layers having a thickness of approximately 15,000 feet have been washed off the present surface of the plateau. And this surface still is being lowered by erosion, and possibly, too, it is also being uplifted by upheaval. But if conditions were to go on very much as now for, say, one million years, in this time the walls of the cañon would widen and flatten

Ups and Downs of the Grand Cañon

out into moderate slopes. The removal of 4,000 feet more of sedimentary rocks would uncover the original granite. Sometime this 4,000 feet may be completely removed; sometime this old granite may again slowly sink, give the plateau region over to the sea, while, for the fourth time, as sea bottom, it receives another covering of sedimentary rocks.

Of all the works of nature of which we have record, the Grand Cañon has been the slowest and the most eloquent. Three times submerged beneath the sea, four times uplifted into the sky. What time and transformation are represented in the strata laid down by the slow processes of the elements! then slowly, tediously uplifted into a mountainous plateau, to be slowly planed down again by running water, ceaseless winds, rains, frost, and extremes of temperature; more accumulations of sediments through thousands of years, and another prolonged battle with the elements. Two complete deposits entirely worn away, washed out of the landscape, and 4,000 feet now in process of being removed to other scenes.

Four prominent factors have been favourable to the production of this architectural wonder: the elevation of the plateau, the horizontal stratification, the varying degrees of softness and firmness of the rock layers, and the aridity of the climate.

A narrow ditch will widen by the gradual caving in of its walls. But the sharpness of these cañon walls is due to the peculiar climatic conditions, the short rainy seasons and long periods of drought. The lack of vegetation is everywhere evident, giving erosion little resistance and displaying to the best advantage the relief work of rock sculpturing. Spasmodic rainfall and cloudbursts, followed by long dry seasons, turn dry rivers into torrents, with an eroding and carving power of magnitude. And during dry periods, the ever-busy wind takes up the work. It is likely that, through the ages, winds have ever been a factor in erosion, in shaping the topography of the earth. Much of the cross-bedded sandstone which abounds in the walls of the Grand Cañon had its dry day with sifting, shifting winds; in dunes and drifts, it marched and dashed beneath cloudy screens of dust and the sweeping roar of storm.

In the desert of the Grand Cañon plateau, one may see the ancient cross-bedded sandstone now on the surface being eroded away by the wind. The closest call I ever had of becoming a desert fossil was on the Painted Desert, not many miles from the Grand Cañon. After thirty-six choking, thirsty hours in a sleeping bag, I crawled out and found myself almost sealed in one end of a new-formed sand dune that was more than two hundred feet long, forty feet wide, and three to eight feet deep. All in one storm it formed, by a rocky outcrop, and much of it must have been swept more than a mile. The air was so full of rock powder during the storm that for hours I was threatened with strangulation. Horses, men, and wild animals occasionally are buried alive in the dust drifts of these desert storms. In this storm, as far as the eye could reach, the low-lying desert topography in every direction changed.

Geological records show that the desert has ever had large land holdings—about one fifth of the solid surface of the earth. Many millions of years ago, this same sand now being broken from the surface sandstone was being blown and drifted about on the prehistoric desert of the Grand Cañon region. Erosion, rebuilding, submergence, stratification, uplift, and slow erosion again in which the wind has had its part is the story of the sculpturing of the Grand Cañon walls.

But the making of the Grand Cañon has not ceased. Running water, the smooth-edged winds, and the silent frost—the age-old tools of the elements—never wear out. They work with every varying device known to nature, changing with the material which they meet. Even the gentle raindrop grapples eagerly with mountains of solid rock, the softer materials receiving the deeper impression, the harder strata resisting longer.

When one beholds this marvellous sculptured cañon for the first time, other scenes and places are forgotten—there is

Ups and Downs of the Grand Cañon

no comparison, for there is no object in nature on the same scale of grandeur. And with a longer acquaintance comes a desire for a thousandfold capacity of greater feeling and comprehension.

I have boated in many of the cañons of the Colorado and have camped and tramped along their rims. I have looked down into broken depths when they were filled with mists; when coloured clouds hung over them, at sunrise and sunset, I have watched the mysterious changing lights transform the age-old strata with the intenseness of rainbow hues.

While the extent of the river through the Grand Cañon plateau is 217 miles, this does not suggest the ins and outs of the cañon walls around out-jutting peninsula-like promontories and into deep recesses, all carrying their orderly banding of red, brown, gray, buff, and crimson. It is like looking down upon an inverted, hollow mountain range, with ridges, spurs, plateaus, cliffs, shattered pinnacles, broad platforms, detached peaks and buttes. Stratified colour in a magnificent assortment; walls of brown and red, deep layers of gray, yellow, grayish brown, and green—all combine to produce a landscape in form and colour unrivalled, and so harmoniously balanced as to height and breadth as to suggest perfect architectural achievement.

Lying in the still, clear air of the western desert it seems finished, complete and unchanging. But even in a torrential rain, the serrated cliffs and pinnacles and sloping taluses stand unmoved. Rocks may roll and cliffs may fall while streams wash on, but standing out in the heart of the cañon, four thousand to seven thousand feet above the river bed, the massive buttes and terraces are all one sees. The scale is too immense to distinguish detail. It is the whole that makes it all, like the thousand whitecaps on the lapping waves that break and mingle to form again; the myriad leaves of a forest that lift and stir the sun and air. And then the alchemy of colour that binds it all in one, that underlies the mystery and the magic of the sculpturing, bursting from the hidden recesses of the deepest strata, edging the serrated cliffs, and outlining the buttes and mesas abutting the wider sections of the cañon. Even the air is filled with mystical lights of blue, violet, and lavender, or gold and yellow, according to the time of day, as though caught up in light rays streaming through the cañon walls.

Colour is the impressive characteristic of the Grand Cañon. Desert chemistry develops colours of the most brilliant dye. But the absence of vegetation allows the fire-toned and time-coloured rocks to be seen in all their brilliant richness.

This arid land makes the most lavish and artistic displays of deep rich colours. Many a sunset I have seen in which the broken horizon clouds were of melting opals or melting gold. Dawn often came up, not like thunder, but lurid, as though below the horizon were only volcanic flame and smoke. Under the slanting evening light the heights, spacings and outlines of the mountain walls show with bold distinctness and their colours with all their freshness. The cañons fill with solid purple while the white upshooting last rays give the upstanding peaks their blackest silhouettes and sharpest outlines.

Geology is intensely filled with information appealing to the imagination and, as well, vital to our welfare: the story of coal, the romance of soil, the history of minerals, the combining and recombining of materials of this old earth. But for its cycles of change through unknown periods of time, its stories revealed in rocks, fossils, and erosion, its existence through uplifts and subsidence, the greatest production in nature yet revealed is the Grand Cañon of the Colorado.

14.

Trees at Timberline

ALL DAY I FOLLOWED the dwarfed, battered, uppermost edge of the forest through the heights of the Rockies. My barometer steadily said that we were two miles higher than the sea. From a stand of dead timber I cut eleven small trees and carried them in one load to my camp-fire. They were so gnarled and ancient-looking that they aroused my curiosity, and with a magnifier I counted the annual rings in each. The youngest was 146 years of age, and the oldest 258! The total age of these eleven trees was 2,191 years! These and other trees had blazed in my fire and fallen to ashes long before I fell to sleep beneath the low and crowded stars.

With rare exceptions the trees at timberline are undersized and of imperfect form. A forest only eight feet high is not uncommon. One winter a tough staff that I used was almost an entire tree which had been nearly 400 years in growing. A tree that I carried home in my pocket the microscope showed to be more than three score and ten years old! Annual rings in many of these timberline trees are scarcely 1-100 of an inch in diameter, while a fate-favoured cottonwood or eucalyptus may in one season envelop itself with a ring that is more than an inch in diameter.

The age of a timberline tree cannot be approximated by its size or appearance or by the size or the age of its neighbours. It may have lived twice as long, and it may have endured more hardships than its near-by fellows of similar size and appearance.

Environment has shaped many timberline trees into huge

Sand-blasted limber pine

and crooked vines. Still others are picturesque, bell-shaped individuals formed by the deeply drifting snows pressing the limbs downward and against the trunk. During the summer months the limbs partly regain their natural position, and the result is a slender bell shape in tall trees and a heavy bell outline in stocky ones. Instead of symmetrical limb development many trees are one-sided. Imagine a tree with storm-threshed limbs all flung out on one side of the trunk, like a tattered, wind-blown banner! Then imagine thousands of

Trees at Timberline

bannered trees scattered and grouped, in a mountainside forest front!

The climatic conditions at the forest frontier are trying, but timberline trees are hardy and probably have as long or even longer lives than the majority of their more fortunately placed relatives. The oldest timberline settler that I ever studied had been permanently located at an altitude of 11,437 feet for 1,182 years when finally killed by fire. Much-branched and stocky, its height was twelve feet, and its diameter a foot above the earth was four feet six inches. What these timberline trees lack in symmetry and heroic size they make up in hardiness and aggressiveness.

Timberland in the far northland marks the latitudinal limits, while the mountain timberline shows the altitudinal limits of the forest-life zone. The forest farthest north ends in a ragged, battered edge against the Arctic prairies. The polar storms that sweep across broken icefields and barren lands meet with first resistance in the advanced low-crouching timberline of sturdy spruces.

Timberline far up the sides of high mountains is as strange and as abrupt a boundary as the crooked and irregular shoreline of the sea. This mountainside timberline is the forest's uppermost edge. Above are the treeless distances and barren heights of the Arctic-alpine zone. Below and away from the ragged edge drapes and rolls the dark and broken robe of forest. Like old ocean's shifting and disputed boundary line, timberline is a place where contending forces ever surge and roar.

Nowhere does this forest frontier—the ever-contending line of battle between woods and weather—appear more stormy or striking than in the high mountains of the West. For miles this timberline extends away in a front of dwarfed and distorted trees—millions of them—ever fiercely fighting a relentless enemy. The veterans show the intense severity of the struggle as they stand resolutely in their inhospitable heights.

Timberline trees are among the distinct attractions of our national parks. Timberline is probably the most telling in the

Rocky Mountain National Park, but in the Yosemite, Mount Rainier, and Glacier National Parks it has striking phases. It is an illustrated and graphic story—one of the most powerful in the book of Nature.

In Colorado this mountainside tree line is two vertical miles above the shore line of the sea. Like the ocean's edge, timberline has miles that are straight and level as a die; but in places it sweeps outward around a peninsula and follows the crooked line of an invading cañon. There are forested bays, beautiful coves, and wooded islands. Stretches of forest climb high ridges, and invading outposts make a successful stand in favourable spots among the snowfields far above the main forest front.

Violent, dry winds that blow ever from the same quarter are a powerful, relentless foe of many a forest frontier. They either point all limbs toward the leeward or prevent all limbs except leeward ones from growing. Trees are pushed out of plumb and entire forests are pushed partly over. Then overweighted with snow, they are forced down to earth and flattened out. The wind and snow never allow them to rise again, and they become in effect huge vines or low, long-bodied, prehistoric animals headed to the leeward. They refuse to die, and may live on for centuries.

Snow, cold, and dryness are the chief factors which determine where the forest may or shall not grow. In some localities the snow line is the barrier that forms the timberline. Dryness of locality combined with dry winds resists forestation. But the sand blasts of dry, windy localities play havoc by beating and flaying the trees. This sand beats off the bark on the trees' stormward quarter, exposing their very bones. Often it eats its way into the already half-flayed trunks. The stormward half of many trees is dead and lifeless, a sand-graven totem pole, while the living half holds long, tattered limbs streaming leeward.

This gale-blown sand frequently prevents trees from growing higher than the shelter behind which they stand. In places so-called trees may be seen with trunks one to three feet in

Trees at Timberline

diameter and only one or two feet high, cut off by the sand fire of the high winds. Numerous long limbs reach out from the trunk in all directions. The shoots which these limbs send up are clipped off by the wind-shot sand. In time this tree-top is a table or brush of bristles twenty feet across, and trimmed off as level as a lawn. Hundreds of these trees are often crowded together until the identity of each is lost, forming acres of clipped, low tree lawn. The wide-spreading mass is too low to crawl under and not quite strong enough to allow one to walk on the surface. It is a good mattress to sleep on; often I have rolled out of one of these tree-top beds without discovering the tumble till morning!

Snowslides, landslides, and other factors often pile up embankments of débris, and these form large windbreaks whose shelter allows trees to grow in places formerly windswept and inhospitable. Trees at timberline are eternally vigilant and promptly seize every new opportunity or opening. One spring a landslide on the slope of Mt. Clarence King piled a shipload of stones on a windswept, treeless flat. A few years later several dozen spruce were growing up in the leeward of this chance-made shelter.

But slides or other forces occasionally remove shelters behind which a forest front was formed. Or they place an obstruction which changes the course of the prevailing winds. Snowslides occasionally cut an avenue down into a forest, which exposes the trees on the edges of the new avenue. Or an old stretch of forest front is sheared off by a slide. With the hardened front ranks removed, the less hardy trees thus exposed are slashed and shot to pieces by the cutting edges of the prevailing gales.

One day I came out upon a long, hedge-like growth of trees extending down the slope. Here the high, sand-flinging winds blew from west to east. A lone boulder about six feet in diameter at the west end of the hedge had sheltered the first tree that had grown up to the leeward of it. Then another tree had risen in the shelter of this one, and still others in order and in line eastward, until the long hedge was grown. The straight line of the hedge from west to east showed that the high winds were always from the same quarter, and the topography of the place had compelled them to rush along the straight line which they had followed. The front of this hedge was the diameter of the boulder, and the farther end, about two hundred feet away, was about a foot higher. Each summer thousands of shoots and twigs grew out on the top and sides, but each succeeding winter the winds trimmed them off. Long afterward, in pursuit of a woodchuck one day, a grizzly dug out a few tons of earth and stones by the side of this boulder. Frost and water undermined, until gravity caused the boulder to roll over. The hedgerow was quickly sandblasted to pieces, and in a few years all that remained was a number of stubby trunks, half round, with the flattened, stormward side fantastically ground and engraved by the wind and sand.

I have followed the timberline for hundreds of miles, in the Sierras, the Cascades, and the Rocky Mountains. One evening I camped on the rim of Wild Basin in what is now the Rocky Mountain National Park. Out of the opposite side of the Basin, Longs Peak swept ruggedly far up into the sky. I was on the eastern slope of the Continental Divide. Great light bars, miles in length, and long shadow pennants of peaks lay across the basin. As the sun descended, these lengthened and pushed down the descending slopes. Finally they reached out upon the Great Plains nearly a hundred miles distant. Near by a solitaire sang with inspiring and unrivalled eloquence. He sang from a crag and from a tree-top, and then with intense ecstasy, while darting and dropping, wheeling and gliding, he gladdened the air above his nesting mate. Once he rose high above the shadows and for a moment poured forth his song in the bright sunlight above.

As he ceased, the beavers began making merry in a pond just below. I watched them and the purple ripples they made. Presently the ripples faded from sight, but in the darkness the easy movements and dividing wavelets of the swimmers were revealed by the rocking of the reflected stars.

In the night a white-crowned sparrow repeatedly sang

Trees at Timberline

briefly. A camp-bird quietly waited for my awakening. Later a tiny chipmunk bashfully called. An astonished squirrel first stared in silence, then with jerky note scolded and bluffed from a safety-first distance, but at last gave way to curiosity and came closer.

Big game is common along the boundary of woodland and grassland. Deer and elk frequent timberline during the summer, and mountain sheep may be seen at any time. In the autumn it is frequented by bears. The mountain lion, coyote, and fox come to this edge of the woods to watch and wait, and here concealed gaze out upon the upland open.

Beautiful lakes, gouged by glaciers out of solid rock, are scattered along the farthest edge of the forest. They are one of the distinctive charms of these Arctic gardens. With a border of wild cliff, a waterfall, a fringe of brilliant flowers, grassy spaces, picturesque trees in clusters and singly, these lakes are wildly, poetically lovely.

On the whole, the heights are becoming dryer. Many summits are no longer tolerant to the trees. Parts of the Rocky Mountains are in the arid belt, and their winters are often extremely dry. Dry, high winds frequently sweep their summits, sucking moisture from all vegetation. The unprotected trees in the forest front of dry ridges suffer greatly, thousands perishing during a single dry winter.

I walked for hours along a dry summit slope strewn with the bleaching bones of millions of veteran pines and spruces. Here over a long front the battle had gone against the forest. The nearest frontier was half a mile down the slope.

Timberline is not fixed. In places it is creeping forward and upward; in other reaches it is being driven back. Still other boundary lines, like those of nations, are stationary for years, then suddenly these are obliterated and redrawn, as territory is lost or won.

Only a few of the earth's numerous tree people dwell at timberline. Those most commonly found both at timberline in the heights and the low levels of the north are pine, spruce, fir, aspen, birch, and willow. On the eastern slope of Longs

Peak timberline is approximately two miles above sea-level. Here, in a moist place by a tiny tributary of the Mississippi, grow Engelmann spruce, Alpine fir, black birch, aspen, and Arctic willow. On a near-by dry slope all the trees are limber pines.

On Mount Orizaba, close to the equator, timberline is maintained above the altitude of 13,000 feet. In the Rockies of Colorado and in the Sierras it is at approximately 11,500 feet. The highest timberline of normal trees in the United States that I have found is on a gulch of the San Juan Mountains at an altitude of 12,300 feet. Here are upright trees more than a foot in diameter and 60 feet high. Timberline in Switzerland is about 6,500 feet; on Mount Washington about 5,000; on Mount Rainier about 7,000. In most localities it is higher on the southerly mountain slopes than on the northerly. In the far north the altitudinal and latitudinal timberlines converge and form the defensive outpost of the forest on the edge of the polar world.

Broken wild-flower gardens crowd and colour every ragged opening among the picturesque tree groups on the forest frontier. Many of these flowers are dwarfed and tiny but in moist places they grow thickly and tall. Among the last trees I have seen wild sheep wading shoulder deep through wide meadows of coloured bloom.

A typical timberline garden is a ragged-edged acre fenced off and sheltered by a weird, low wall of trees. Here and there a blooming open way connects it with an adjoining garden. A young tree clump and a boulder pile add artistic touches; here and there appear low-growing, many-tinted phlox; tall, stately columbines with silver and blue ribbons at the top; blue mertensia, taller still; paint brushes touched with a variety of shades; anemones; gentians; white monkshood; and, bending upon its stem, a ray-faced, golden-brown gaillardia.

One winter the snow drifted deeply over a stretch of forest as large as a huge circus tent. The following summer it partly melted. The next winter new snow was added, and the following spring the drift was larger than before. It did not melt

Trees at Timberline

away until the third summer. In the meantime, the several hundred spruce trees were kept asleep in a natural cold storage and had failed to grow. This is why their annual rings were two less in number than those of the neighbouring trees of the same age.

Trees have tongues. They record in their annual rings the larger experiences of the years, the triumphs of friendly seasons, and the batterings and the burns that fall to the lot of those in the front ranks of high mountain forests. A timberline veteran might tell of the wealth of moonlight on a winter night, with forest outposts half buried in the white snow; of crowded stars in the field of space; of terrific winds and irresistible avalanches of vast snow piles.

With flying snow, in perfect autumn days and during mist-filled nights, I have slept and communed with my camp-fire at timberline. Timberline gives one the feeling of being on the edge of things. Envelop it in unevenly moving mist and everything seems a mystery. The strangely shaped trees and the weird forms of tree clumps half revealed are a part of the indefinite, the uncomprehended. Add to this vague realm the magic of a camp-fire, and one loses the experience of ages and again is a primitive, crouching fire worshipper in a new and unexplored world. A camp-fire ever recalls the ages long past, and paints primeval scenes. Through all the centuries the camp-fire has been a place of safety and comfort, of hope and cheer.

Though they stand in one place all their years, trees have adventurous lives from their seedling days to battered old age, and stored in their unrolled and untranslated annual rings are their records and perhaps glimpses of the everchanging scenes in which they grew. Sometimes while watching my changing camp-fire blaze I have half believed that the blazing tree was picturing with fire the story of its life—the larger experiences of the years; the triumphs of the good seasons and the failures of the bad; the battles with wind and frost, with fire and insect foes. Surely no picture ever painted is more suggestive than the camp-fire. With it the imagination brings the dead past back to life, and its people in fitting scenes act again the parts they once played.

The Big Trees of California are the greatest living wonders of the world. In the serene Sierras they have achieved the dignity befitting the largest and the oldest living things upon this earth. Compared with these Big Trees the timberline trees of the Rockies are pygmies and infants. Yet who shall say that the life story of the timberline tree is the less inspiring. To stand beneath the Big Trees is to feel the silent eloquence of the "noblest of a noble race." To stand above the dwarfed and battered front ranks of the intrepid timberline forests, where the Storm King reigns and the eagle soars, is to live with fired imagination through all the long years of battle, and to feel the triumphs of the unconquerable. Timberline touches the heart with a sense of universal kinship.

15.

Wild Mountain Sheep

ONE DAY IN GLACIER GORGE, Colorado, I was astonished to see a number of sheep start to descend the precipitous eastern face of Thatch-Top Mountain. This glaciated wall, only a few degrees off the perpendicular, rises comparatively smooth for several hundred feet. Down they came, slowly, with absolute composure, over places I dared not even try to descend. The nearness of the sheep and the use of field-glasses gave me excellent views of the many ways in which they actually seemed to court danger.

It is intensely thrilling to watch a leaping exhibition of one of these heavy, agile, alert, and athletic animals. Down precipitous places he plunges head foremost, turning and checking himself as he descends by striking his feet against walls and projections—perhaps a dozen times—before alighting on a ledge for a full stop. From this he walks overboard and repeats the wild performance!

Wild mountain sheep are perhaps the most accomplished and dare-devil acrobats in the animal world. They are indifferent to the depths beneath as they go merrily along cañon-walls. The chamois and the wild mountain goat may equal them in climbing among the crags and peaks, but in descending dizzy precipices and sheer walls the bighorn sheep are unrivaled. When sheep hurriedly descend a precipice, the laws of falling bodies are given a most spectacular display, and the possibilities of friction and adhesion are tested to the utmost.

A heavily horned ram led the way down Thatch-Top. He was followed by two young rams and a number of ewes, with two small lambs in the rear. They were in single file, each well separated from the others. Down this frightful wall the lambs appeared to be going to certain death. At times they all followed the contour round small spurs or in niches. In places, from my point of view they appeared to be flattened against the wall and descending head foremost.

There was one long pitch that offered nothing on which to stand and no place on which to stop. Down this the old ram plunged with a series of bouncing drops and jumps,—falling under control, with his fall broken, checked, and directed, without stopping, by striking with the feet as frequently as was necessary. First came three or four straightforward bouncing dives, followed by a number of swift zigzag jumps, striking alternately right and left, then three or four darts to the right before again flying off to the left. At last he struck on a wide ledge, where he pulled up and stopped with masterly resistance and stiff-legged jumps! Mind controlled matter! This specialty of the sheep requires keen eyesight, instant decision, excellent judgment, a marvelous nicety in measuring distances, and a complete forgetfulness of peril. Each ewe in turn gave a similar and equally striking exhibition; while the lambs, instead of breaking their necks in the play of drop and bounce, did not appear to be even cautious. They showed off by dropping farther and going faster than the old ones! This was sheer frolic for these children of the crags.

Down a vertical gulley—a giant chimney with one side out—they went hippety-hop from side to side, and at the bottom, without a stop, dropped fifteen feet to a wide bench below. The ram simply dived off, with front feet thrust forward and with hind feet drawn up and forward, and apparently struck with all four feet at once. A number of others followed in such rapid succession that they appeared to be falling out of the air. Each, however, made it a point to land to the right or the left of the one it was following. Two ewes turned broadside to the wall as they went over and dropped vertically,—stiff-legged, back horizontal, and with head held well up. The lambs leaped overboard simultaneously only a

Wild Mountain Sheep

second behind the rear ewe, each lamb coming to a stop with the elastic bounce of youth.

Beneath this bench where all had paused, the wall was perilously steep for perhaps one hundred feet. A moment after the lambs landed, the ram followed the bench round the wall for several yards, then began to descend the steep wall by tacking back and forth on broken and extremely narrow ledges, with many footholds barely two inches wide. He was well down, when he missed his footing and fell. He tumbled outward, turned completely over, and, after a fall of about twenty feet, struck the wall glancingly, at the same time thrusting his feet against it as though trying to right himself. A patch of hair—and perhaps skin—was left clinging to the wall. A few yards below this, while falling almost head first, he struck a slope with all four feet and bounded wildly outward, but with checked speed. He dropped on a ledge, where with the utmost effort he regained control of himself and stopped, with three or four stiff plunges and a slide. From there he trotted over easy ways and moderate slopes to the bottom, where he stood a while trembling, then lay down.

One by one his flock came down in good order. The leaps of flying squirrels and the clever gymnastic pranks of monkeys are tame shows compared with the wild feats of these masters of the crags.

The flock, after playing and feeding about for an hour or more, started to return. The injured leader lay quietly on the grass, but with head held bravely erect. The two lambs raced ahead and started to climb the precipice over the route they had come down. One ewe went to the bottom of the wall, then turned to look at the big-horned leader who lay still upon the grass. She waited. The lambs, plainly eager to go on up, also waited. Presently the ram rose with an effort and limped heavily away. There was blood on his side. He turned aside from the precipice and led the way back toward the top by long easy slopes. The flock slowly followed. The lambs looked at each other and hesitated for some time. Finally they leaped down and raced rompingly after the others.

Rocky Mountain bighorn sheep

    The massive horns of the rams, along with the audacious dives that sheep sometimes make on precipices, probably suggested the story that sheep jump off a cliff and effectively break the shock of the fall by landing on their horns at the bottom! John Charles Frémont appears to have started this story in print. Though sheep do not alight on their horns, this story is still in circulation and is too widely believed. Every one with whom I have talked who has seen sheep land after a leap says that the sheep land upon their feet. I have seen this performance a number of times, and on a few occasions there were several sheep; and each and all came down feet first. Incidentally I have seen two rams come down a precipice and strike on their horns; but they did not rise again! The small horns of the ewes would offer no shock-breaking resistance if alighted upon; yet the ewes rival the rams in making precipitous plunges.

    The sheep is the only animal that has circling horns. In rams these rise from the top of the head and grow upward, outward, and backward, then curve downward and forward. Commonly the circle is complete in four or five years. This

Wild Mountain Sheep

circular tendency varies with locality. In mature rams the horns are from twenty to forty inches long, measured round the curve, and have a basic circumference of twelve to eighteen inches. The largest horn I ever measured was at the base nineteen and a half inches in circumference. This was of the Colorado bighorn species, and at the time of measurement the owner had been dead about two months. The horns of the ewes are small, and extend upward, pointing slightly outward and backward.

The wildest leap I ever saw a sheep take was made in the Rocky Mountains a few miles northwest of Longs Peak. In climbing down a precipice I rounded a point near the bottom and came upon a ram at the end of the ledge I was following. Evidently he had been lying down, looking upon the scenes below. The ledge was narrow and it ended just behind the ram, who faced me only five or six feet away. He stamped angrily, struck an attitude of fight, and shook his head as if to say, "I've half a mind to butt you overboard!" He could have butted an ox overboard. My plan was to fling myself beneath a slight overhang of wall on the narrow ledge between us if he made a move.

While retreating backward along almost nothing of a ledge and considering the wisdom of keeping my eyes on the ram, he moved, and I flung myself beneath the few inches of projecting wall. The ram simply made a wild leap off the ledge.

This looked like a leap to death. He plunged down at an angle to the wall, head forward and a trifle lower than the rump, with feet drawn upward and thrust forward. I looked over the edge, hoping he was making a record jump. The first place he struck was more than twenty feet below me. When the fore feet struck, his shoulder blades jammed upward as though they would burst through the skin. A fraction of a second later his hind feet also struck and his back sagged violently; his belly must have scraped the slope. He bounded upward and outward like a heavy chunk of rubber. This contact had checked his deadly drop and his second striking-place was on a steeply inclined buttress; apparently in his momentary contact with this he altered his course with a kicking action of the feet.

There was lightning-like foot action, and from this striking-place he veered off and came down violently, feet first, upon a shelf of granite. With a splendid show of physical power, and with desperate effort, he got himself to a stand with stiff-legged, sliding bounds along the shelf. Here he paused for a second, then stepped out of sight behind a rock point. Feeling that he must be crippled, I hurriedly scrambled up and out on a promontory from which to look down upon him. He was trotting down a slope without even the sign of a limp!

Sheep do sometimes slip, misjudge a distance, and fall. Usually a bad bruise, a wrenched joint, or a split hoof is the worst injury, though now and then one receives broken legs or ribs, or even a broken neck. Most accidents appear to befall them while they are fleeing through territory with which they are unacquainted. In strange places they are likely to have trouble with loose stones, or they may be compelled to leap without knowing the nature of the landing-place.

A sheep, like a rabbit or a fox, does his greatest work in evading pursuers in territory with which he is intimately acquainted. If closely pursued in his own territory, he will flee at high speed up or down a precipice, perform seemingly impossible feats, and triumphantly escape. But no matter how skillful, if he goes his utmost in a new territory, he is as likely to come to grief as an orator who attempts to talk on a subject with which he is not well acquainted. It is probable that most of the accidents to these masters of the crags occur when they are making a desperate retreat through strange precipitous territory.

In the Elk Mountains a flock of sheep were driven far from their stamping-ground and while in a strange country were fired upon and pursued by hunters. They fled up a peak they had not before climbed. The leader leaped upon a rock that gave way. He tumbled off with the rock on top. He fell upon his back—to rise no more. A ewe missed her footing and in

Wild Mountain Sheep

her fall knocked two others over to their death, though she regained her footing and escaped.

One day a ram appeared on a near-by skyline and crossed along the top of a shattered knife-edge of granite. The gale had driven me to shelter, but along he went, unmindful of the gale that was ripping along the crags and knocking things right and left. Occasionally he made a long leap from point to point. Now and then he paused to look into the cañon far below. On the top of the highest pinnacle he stopped and became a splendid statue. Presently he rounded a spur within fifty feet of me and commenced climbing diagonally up a wall that appeared almost vertical and smooth. My glass showed that he was walking along a mere crack in the rock, where footholds existed mostly in imagination. On this place he would stop and scratch with one hind foot and then rub the end of a horn against the wall!

As he went on up, the appearance was like a stage effect, as though he were sustained by wires. At the end of the crack he reared, hooked his fore feet over a rough point, and drew himself up like an athlete, with utter indifference to the two hundred feet of drop beneath him. From this point he tacked back and forth until he had ascended to the bottom of a vertical gully, which he easily mastered with a series of zigzag jumps. In some of these he leaped several feet almost horizontally to gain a few inches vertically. Occasionally he leaped up and struck with his feet in a place where he could not stand, but from which he leaped to a place more roomy. His feet slipped as he landed from one high jump; instantly he pushed himself off backward and came down feet foremost on the narrow place from which he had just leaped. He tried again and succeeded.

The edges of sheep's hoofs are hard, while the back part of the bottom is a rubbery, gristly pad, which holds well on smooth, steep surfaces. Coöperating with these excellent feet are strong muscles, good eyes, and keen wits.

Wild sheep are much larger than tame ones. They are alert, resourceful, and full of energy. Among the Colorado bighorns the rams are from thirty-eight to forty-two inches high, and weigh from two hundred to three hundred and fifty pounds. The ewes are a third smaller. The common color is grayish brown, with under parts and inside of the legs white. In the north there is one pure-white species, while on neighboring ranges there is a black species. Though wild sheep usually follow a leader, each one is capable of independent action. Tame sheep are stupid and silly; wild sheep are wide-awake and courageous. Tame sheep are dirty and smelly, while wild sheep are as well-groomed and clean as the cliffs among which they live.

In discussing wild life many people fail to discriminate between the wild sheep and the wild goats. The goat has back-curving spike horns and a beard that makes the face every inch a goat's. Though of unshapely body and awkward gait, his ungainliness intensified by his long hair, the goat is a most skillful climber. The sheep excel him for speed, grace, and perhaps, alertness.

It is believed that the three or four species of sheep found in the wilds of America had their origin in Asia. In appearance and habits they bear a striking resemblance to the sheep which now inhabit the Asiatic mountains.

Wild sheep are found in Alaska, western Canada, and the United States west of the Plains, and extend a short distance down into Mexico. Most flocks in the Sierra and the Rocky Mountains live above the timber-line and at an altitude of twelve thousand feet. Winter quarters in these high stamping-grounds appear to be chosen in localities where the high winds prevent a deep accumulation of snow. This snow-removal decreases the danger of becoming snowbound and usually enables the sheep to obtain food.

Their warm, thick under covering of fine wool protects them from the coldest blasts. During storms the sheep commonly huddle together to the leeward of a cliff. Sometimes they stand thus for days and are completely drifted over. At the close of the storm the stronger ones lead and buck their way out through the snow. Occasionally a few weak ones perish, and occasionally, too, a mountain lion appears while the flock is almost helpless in the snow.

Excursions from their mountain-top homes are occasionally made into the lowlands. In the spring they go down early for green stuff, which comes first to the lowlands. They go to salt licks, for a ramble, for a change of food, and for the fun of it. The duration of these excursions may be a few hours or several days.

Most of the time the full-grown rams form one flock; the ewes and youngsters flock by themselves. Severe storms or harassing enemies may briefly unite these flocks. One hundred and forty is the largest flock I ever counted. This was in June, on Specimen Mountain, Colorado; and the sheep had apparently assembled for the purpose of licking salty, alkaline earth near the top of this mountain. Wild sheep appear to have an insatiable craving for salt and will travel a day's journey to obtain it. Occasionally they will cross a high, broken mountain-range and repeatedly expose themselves to danger, in order to visit a salt lick.

The young lambs, one or two at a birth, are usually born about the first of May in the alpine heights above timber-line. What a wildly royal and romantic birthplace! The strange world spreading far below and far away; crags, snowdrifts, brilliant flowers,—a hanging wild garden, with the ptarmigan and the rosy finches for companions! The mother has sole care of the young; for several weeks she must guard them from hungry foxes, eagles, and lions. Once I saw an eagle swoop and strike a lamb. Though the lamb was knocked heels over head, the blow was not fatal. The eagle wheeled to strike again, but the mother leaped up and shielded the wounded lamb. Eaglets are occasionally fed on young lambs, as skulls near eagle's nests in the cliffs bear evidence.

A number of ewes and lambs one day came close to my hiding-place. One mother had two children; four others had one each. An active lamb had a merry time with his mother, butting her from every angle, rearing up on his hind legs and striking with his head, and occasionally leaping entirely over her. While she lay in dreamy indifference, he practiced long jumps over her, occasionally stopping to have a fierce fight with an imaginary rival. Later he was joined by another lamb, and they proceeded to race and romp all over a cliff, while the mothers looked on with satisfaction. Presently they all lay down, and a number of magpies, apparently hunting insects, walked over them.

In one of the side cañons on the Colorado in Arizona, I was for a number of days close to a flock of wild sheep which evidently had never before seen man. On their first view of me they showed marked curiosity, which they satisfied by approaching closely, two or three touching me with their noses. Several times I walked among the flock with no excitement on their part. I was without either camera or gun. The day I broke camp and moved on, one of the ewes followed me for more than an hour.

They become intensely alert and wild when hunted; but in localities where they are not shot at they quickly become semi-domestic, often feeding near homes of friendly people. During the winter sheep frequently come from the heights to feed near my cabin. One day, after a number had licked salt with my pony, a ram which appeared as old as the hills walked boldly by my cabin within a few feet of it, headed proudly up. After long acquaintance and many attempts I took his photograph at five feet and finally was allowed to feel of his great horns!

A few years ago near my cabin a ram lost his life in a barbed-wire fence. He and a number of other rams had fed, then climbed to the top of a small crag by the roadside. While they were there, a man on horseback came along. Indifferently they watched him approach; but when he stopped to take a picture all but one fled in alarm, easily leaping a shoulder-high fence. After a minute the remaining ram became excited, dashed off to follow the others, and ran into the fence. He was hurled backward and one of his curved horns hooked over a wire. Finding himself caught, he surged desperately to tear himself free. In doing this a barb severed the jugular vein.

Wild Mountain Sheep

He fell and freed his horn from the wire in falling. Rising, he ran for the crag from which he had just fled, with his blood escaping in great gushes. As he was gaining the top of the crag he rolled over dead.

A flock which is often divided into two, one of ewes and one of rams, lives on the summit of Battle Mountain, at an altitude of twelve thousand feet, about four miles from my cabin. I have sometimes followed them when they were rambling. About the middle of one September this flock united and moved off to the south. I made haste to climb to the top of Mt. Meeker so as to command most of their movements. I had been watching for several hours without even a glimpse of them. Rising to move away, I surprised them as they lay at rest near-by, a little below the summit; and I also surprised a lion that evidently was sneaking up on them. This was close to the altitude of fourteen thousand feet. The mountain lion is the game-hog of the heights and is a persistent and insidious foe of sheep. He kills both old and young, and usually makes a capture by sneaking up on his victim. Sometimes for hours he lies in wait by a sheep trail.

The day following the surprise on Mt. Meeker, this flock appeared at timber-line about three miles to the southeast. Here some hunters fired on it. As it fled past me, I counted, and one of the twenty-eight was missing. The flock spent most of the next day about Chasm Lake, just under the northern crags of Meeker. Before night it was back at its old stamping-ground on Battle Mountain. Early the following morning the big ram led the way slowly to the west on the northern slope of Longs Peak, a little above timber-line.

During the morning a grizzly came lumbering up the slope, and as I thought he would probably intercept the sheep, I awaited the next scene with intense interest. The bear showed no interest in the sheep, which, in turn, were not alarmed by his approach. Within a few yards of the flock he concluded to dig out a fat woodchuck. The sheep, full of curiosity, crowded near to watch this performance,—evidently too near to suit Mr. Grizzly, who presently caused a lively scattering with a

Woof! and a charge. The bear returned to his digging, and the sheep proceeded quietly on their way.

The flock went down into Glacier Gorge, then out on the opposite side, climbing to the summit of the Continental Divide. The following day another flock united with it; and just at nightfall another, composed entirely of ewes and lambs, was seen approaching. At daylight the following morning the Battle Mountain flock was by itself and the other flocks nowhere in sight. During the day my flock traveled four or five miles to the north, then, doubling back, descended Flat-Top Mountain, and at sundown, after a day's trip of about twenty miles and a descent from twelve thousand feet to eight thousand, arrived at the Mary Lake salt lick in Estes Park. Before noon the following day this flock was on the Crags, about three miles south of the lake and at an altitude of eleven thousand feet.

Near the Crags I saw a fight between one of the rams of this flock and one that ranged about the Crags. The start of this was a lively pushing contest, head to head. At each break there was a quick attempt to strike each other with their horns, which was followed by goat-like rearing and sparring. As they reared and struck, or struck while on their hind legs, the aim was to hit the other's nose with head or horn. Both flocks paused, and most of the sheep intently watched the contest.

Suddenly the contestants broke away, and each rushed back a few yards, then wheeled with a fine cutting angle and came at the other full tilt. There was a smashing head-on collision, and each was thrown upward and almost back on his haunches by the force of the impact. Instantly they wheeled and came together in a flying butt. A number of times both walked back over the stretch over which they rushed together. It was a contest between battering rams on legs. Occasionally one was knocked to his knees or was flung headlong. The circular arena over which they fought was not more than twenty-five feet in diameter. In the final head-on butt the ram of the Crags was knocked end over end; then he arose and

Wild Mountain Sheep

trotted away down the slope, while the victor, erect and motionless as a statue, stared after him. Both were covered with blood and dirt. During the day the flock returned to Battle Mountain.

The following day this flock separated into two flocks, the youngsters and ewes in one and the old rams in the other. At mating-time, early in October, the flocks united, and the rams had it out among themselves. There were repeated fights; sometimes two contests were in progress at once. In the end a few rams were driven off without mates, while three or four rams each led off from one to five ewes.

Over the greater part of their range the wild mountain sheep are threatened with extermination. They are shot for sport and for their flesh, and are relentlessly hunted for their horns. But the mountain sheep are a valuable asset to our country. They are picturesque and an interesting part of the scenery, an inspiration to every one who sees them.

Says Mary Austin:

> But the wild sheep from the battered rocks,
> Sure foot and fleet of limb,
> Gets up to see the stars go by
> Along the mountain rim.

Fortunate is the locality that perpetuates its mountain sheep. These courageous climbers add much to the ancient mountains and snowy peaks; the arctic wild gardens and the crags would not be the same for us if these mountaineers were to vanish forever from the heights.

16.

Winter Mountaineering

AFTER A HEAVY SNOWFALL, one December morning, I started on skis for two weeks' camping in the Colorado Rockies. The fluffy snow lay smooth and unbroken over the broken mountains. Here and there black pine and spruce trees uplifted arrowheads and snow-cones of the white mantle. On the steep slope, half a mile from my cabin. I was knocked to one side by a barrel mass of snow dropping upon me from a tree, and one ski escaped. As if glad to be off on an adventure of its own, it sped down the mountainside like a shot. It bumped into a low stump, skied high into the air and over a tree-top, and then fell undamaged in the deep snow.

Recovering my runaway ski, I started for the summit of the range, a distance of about nine miles from my cabin. For an hour I followed a stream whose swift waters now and then splashed up through the broken, icy skylights. Then leaving the cañon and skirting the slope, I was on the plateau summit of the Continental Divide, twelve thousand feet above the sea.

This summit moor was deeply overlaid with undrifted snow. Southward it extended mile after mile, rising higher and higher into the sky in broken, snow-covered peaks. To the north the few small broken cliffs and low buttes emphasized the trackless solitude. This plateau or moorland was less than one mile wide and comparatively smooth. Its edges descended precipitously two thousand feet into cirques and cañons.

Southward I travelled along the nearly level expanse of undrifted snow. Looking back along the line of my ski tracks, I

Looking west from the summit of Longs Peak

saw a mountain lion leisurely cross from east to west. Apparently she had come up out of the woods for mad play and slaughter among the unfortunate snowbound folk of the summit. She stopped at my tracks for an interested look, turned her head, and glanced back along the way I had come. Then her eyes appeared to follow my tracks to the boulder pile from behind which I was then looking.

Playfully bouncing off the snow, she struck into my ski prints with one forepaw, lightly as a kitten. Then she dived into them, pretended to pick up something between her forepaws, reared, and with a swing tossed it into the air. Then her playful mood changed and she started on across the Divide. After several steps she stopped, looking back as if she had forgotten something but was a little too lazy to retrace her steps. But finally she came back. She walked along my ski tracks for a few steps, then began to romp, now and then making a great leap forward, and rolled and struck about with the pretence of worrying something she had captured. She repeated this pantomime a few times, and then, as if suddenly remembering her original plan of action, again walked westward. Arriving at the summit she hesitated, and when I saw her last she was calmly surveying the scenes far below. On the mountain skyline I crossed a white tundra, half expecting to see an Eskimo peer from a snow mound. Arctic plants buried in the snow and ptarmigan—"Eskimo chickens"—in their snow-white dress were the only signs of life. Later in the day I saw a white weasel slipping over the snow toward a number of the ptarmigan. Often on the summits the ptarmigan, in leggings and coats of pure white, watched me and allowed me to come and remain near. They, like the snowshoe rabbit, skimmed over the surface on home-grown snowshoes. Possibly from them the Eskimos got the idea for the webbed snowshoe, which they have used for ages. More than once, when weathering gales where the thick, insistent snow dust made me acquainted with the unpleasant sensations of strangulation, I have envied the rosy finch and other birds of the snow who have a well-developed screen to keep choking snow dust out of the nostrils. The Eskimos also have a slotted wooden shield to protect the eye from the burning glare of reflected sunlight.

I descended a few hundred feet into the upper edge of the woods to find shelter for the night. Clearing out the snow between a cliff and a rock about six feet from it, I had an excellent lodging place. I built a roaring fire and heated a number of stones. When this space was warmed I pushed the fire and the heated stones along the open space between the rock and the cliff. Then I started a fire against the base of the detached rock. Two huge sticks were placed at the bottom of this fire pile. Over these smaller ones were laid, and at the top still smaller ones. I set fire to this on the top so that it would burn slowly and not be at its hottest for an hour or two. Within the circle of warmth I placed my elkskin sleeping bag, crawled into it, and slept for nearly four hours. When the cold awakened me I renewed both fires, then had another short sleep. When I again awoke I was ready for another day's adventure.

I set off through a forested slope that tilted gently toward

Winter Mountaineering

the sun. Black shadows, long and straight, lay upon the forest floor. The crowded pines were slender and limbless except at the top. Across an opening these slender shadows were at their best, with the snow glistening in white lines between their deep black ones. After two hours I came out upon a white and treeless meadow, across which shadows were flying—moving cloud shadows rushed across, and the shadow of a soaring eagle appeared swiftly skating in circles over the snow.

I spent hours reading the news, observing the illustrations, and studying the hieroglyphics on the snow. Whether footprints in the mud or snow may have suggested printing cannot be told, but it is certain that the tracks, stains, and impressions in snow print the news and record the local animal doings. Here the rabbits played; there the grouse searched for dinner; while over yonder the long, lacy trail of a mouse ends significantly between the impressions of two wing feathers. One sees a trail made by a long-legged animal and another by a fellow with a long body and short legs— perhaps a weasel. At one place near the foot of an old tree a squirrel had abandoned a cone and run home. Near by was the trail of a porcupine who was well-fed, well-protected, and though dull-witted, not at all afraid. Apparently he hadn't any idea where he was going and did not care whom he should meet; for at one place he came face to face with a fox and the fox turned aside.

Footprints often reveal the excitement, hesitation, change of plan, and the preparation of two wild folks advancing and about to meet. Most animals, except the grizzly, though concerned with sight and scent, appear not to consider the impressions in the tell-tale snow.

I passed again through woods where the previous winter I had walked upon ten feet of snow. In that trip I had looked down upon a camp-bird cuddled in an old nest. I talked to her for a minute, and, as is common with her kind, she came close, seeking something to eat. Three eggs were in the nest, though it was February. Never before had I found a bird nesting in the famine month of the year. These eggs may not have hatched, but another time I saw a nest of this species in March with eggs that did hatch. April is the nesting time for this bird. Why a pair sometimes nest unusually early is their secret.

I found the crested jay, that flings forth its jarring note as harsh and cold as frosty steel, using these mountains for winter quarters. A few of this species remain for the summer, but the majority nest farther north. The water ouzel is a winter songster, and twice during this outing, in a snow-filled cañon, he sang to me cheerily. He may be seen and heard in any month of the year. This bird of quiet, cheering presence is an outdoor enthusiast. He was always delightfully busy, and indifferent to my close approach if I came quietly and slowly.

The scarlet berries and small, shining green leaves of the kinnikinnick gave colour and charm to many snowy places. Half buried in the snow, in the sun or shadow, in niches of crags, or as wreathlike coverings for the rocks, they were bright and cheerful everywhere.

I can imagine that the winter birds and animals worship the chinook wind. One evening I went to sleep shivering. I was awakened through being too warm, and leaped out of my sleeping bag thinking it must be on fire. Then I discovered that in the night a chinook had come. This warm, dry wind occasionally follows a blizzard, and often it appears to make a sudden and triumphant attack upon a cold period. During the short day or two that it dominates it is a blessing. It often raises the temperature thirty or more degrees in a few hours.

On another cold, windy night I had a poor camp and damp clothes. I had examined the ice around a beaver house to see if it was built by a spring. It was, and I had broken through the thin ice. That night as I shivered by a slow fire I wished that I might have occupied a woodpecker's house. I took comfort in the fact that at no time during the trip would I be annoyed by flies and mosquitoes.

From the sheltering edge of the woods I watched the high

Winter Mountaineering

wind stir and sweep the excited snow. The snowflakes had long since been reduced to powder and dust by colliding with cliffs and by being thrown violently against the earth. The wind was intermittent. A wave of snow dust swept along the snow-covered earth, filling the air; then a few seconds of sunshine played before the next wave followed. Occasionally everything cleared and stopped for an exhibit of the whirlwind. A towering white column of snow dust would spin across the scene. This commonly was followed by another and heavier spiral that was more like a confusion of white whirled clouds. All this time the sun was shining in a blue sky; and all this time, too, a sparkling pennant of diamond snow dust and powder a mile long was fluttering from the tip of a triangular peak.

With such scenes in mind—the trees abloom with flakes, the white and sparkling whirlwinds, the vast and scintillating snow-powder pennants—I could understand the poetic fancy of primitive people who happily named winter's gifts "snow-flowers" and who honoured the snow period with an outdoor celebration.

After all, winter is but a transient return of the ice age. With fresh falls on the heights above timberline, before the wind blows, the vast world appears overlaid with a permanent stratum of snow. Across white distances one looks for miles without seeing a tree or any living object, or even a shadow unless it be that of a passing cloud.

Though the high mountains have their snowstorms and their eternal snowfields, in most mountain ranges the snowfall on the middle slopes of the mountains is heavier than upon the high plateaus and summits. On the heights the wind has free play and sweeps most of the snow into enormous piles or drifts. These are one hundred or more feet deep and sometimes cover nearly a square mile. Owing to their depth, the low temperature of the heights, and the fact that they are so densely packed, these snow masses endure throughout the year. Wind is thus the chief factor in the making of snow topography. Small hills and plains, cañons, plateaus, and mountain ranges—all of snow—are a constant source of interest.

One morning I awoke with dense, white storm clouds all around me and the snow coming down. Wishing to camp that night at timberline, I travelled up the mountainside in the thickly falling snow and dense clouds. These clouds were drifting easily along the mountainside and, together with the feathery flakes which they were shedding, made it impossible to see distinctly even to the end of an extended arm. Suddenly I became aware of a diminished depth of snow underfoot. I stooped to measure it. It was less than three inches. On rising I thrust my head through the silver lining—the upper surface—of the cloud into the sunshine.

The altitude was about eleven thousand feet. Above and about me the peaks and plateaus stood in gray and brown. Not a flake of all this snow had fallen upon them. There was nothing to indicate that a storm had prevailed just below during the last two days and nights, or that only a step down the mountain snow was still falling.

Soundless and motionless the cloud sea lay below. Here and there an upthrusting pinnacle cast a shadow upon it. Unable to make myself believe that below me the flakes were falling thick and fast and that the ground was deeply covered with soft white snow, I plunged down into the cloud. After enjoying the novelty for a few minutes I climbed out of the snowstorm again and then once more descended into it. As the mountainside was comparatively unbroken I walked along the upper edge of the cloud for some distance. Two or three times this fluffy mass swelled and rose slightly above me and then settled easily back. In the head of a gulch cloud swells rose slightly higher than out in the main sea. I climbed down into them a short distance, thinking to cross the hidden cañon, but, finding it too steep-walled, climbed out again.

As I emerged from the gulch I saw, near by, a huge grizzly bear sunning himself on a cliff that rose a few feet out of the cloud into the sunshine. He, like myself, appeared greatly interested in the slow rise and fall and ragged outline of the storm cloud. He was all attention to every new movement near him. On scenting me he stared for a moment, as if thinking: "Where on earth did he come from?" Then he stepped overboard into the clouds.

I camped that night beside a clump of storm-battered trees that marked the upper limit of the forest. In the morning all was clear. The cloud sea of the day before had rolled silently away. Along the mountainside the ragged edge of snow stretched for miles. Above it barren, rocky peaks rose in a great mountain desert. Below, all was soft and white—a wonderful world of mountains made of snowflakes.

Near my camp was an ancient-looking tree clump. None of the trees was taller than my head, and though of almost normal form they were somewhat gnarled and appeared as old as the hills. Centuries they surely had seen. Trees on the forest outpost in high mountains endure severe trials. They are dwarfed, battered, and broken; huddled behind boulders, buried, or half buried in snow. The forest frontier is maintained by these brave tree people. Seen again and again, this region displays features of new interest as often as the visitor returns to it.

On the heights I frequently saw conies. One day I lingered to watch one that was less shy than the majority. He sat with his back against the sunny side of a boulder, looking serious and keeping a careful survey of his field of vision. Presently I discovered his haystack—his supply of winter food—a tiny heap of grass, sedge, and alpine plants. It was about two feet high and was sheltered beneath two half-arching stones.

Many were the ways in which I found animals spending the winter. In the course of this outing I saw several flocks of mountain sheep. All these were in the heights above the tree line. On the day following the snow-drifting one I crossed the heights and on the summit passed close to a flock. They were feeding in a space that the wind had swept bare of snow. Happy highlanders they were, well fed and contented, in their home twelve thousand feet above the tides.

One sunny, though cold, morning I came upon a large dead tree. In it were a number of woodpecker holes. Wondering if these houses had winter dwellers I struck the tree with my hatchet. Instantly a dozen or more chickadees came pouring out of one of the holes like so many merry children. From a hole in the opposite side of the tree flew one or more birds that I did not see. Out of one of the upper holes a downy woodpecker thrust his head. Glaring down at me with one eye—impatient, as late sleepers usually are when called—he appeared to be wanting to say: "Why am I disturbed? This is a cold morning. There are no early worms to be had in winter." From another hole flew another downy. I felt sure that none of these late sleepers had breakfasted. Seldom is an old woodpecker house without a tenant. Bluebirds, wrens, and numbers of weak-billed folk nest in them during summer, while birds of other species find them life-savers in the winter. A hummingbird's nest that I found brought to mind the fact that its builder, if alive, was then among the tropical flowers of Central America.

Later in the day I saw a flock of chickadees, one or two brown creepers, and a solitary woodpecker food hunting together. The chickadees kept up a cheering conversation and twice I thought I heard the woodpecker give a call. I wondered if these fellow food hunters also all lodged in one many-roomed apartment house.

Coming one day to a beaver pond I scraped off the snow and looked through the clear ice into the water. Two or three beavers were swimming. The water between the ice and the bottom of the pond was about two feet deep. Each autumn the beavers pile ample winter supplies in deep water close to the house. The pond may freeze over, but this ice covering is a protection. The house entrance is on the bottom of the pond beneath the ice, and the floor is above the level of the pond. The water in the lower part of the house does not freeze. The beaver residents were here having a comfortable time while deer in near-by woods were floundering in the snow. I have known deer to have a hard time of it in winter. Commonly

Winter Mountaineering

deer winter in lower altitudes, but sometimes they stay in the middle mountain region and worry through the snowy weeks by yarding—that is, a number remaining in one small area, where through daily trampling they keep on top of the snow and still find enough to eat.

A number of animals hibernate. Fat woodchucks live in a den five or six feet below the surface. Storms may come and go, but the woodchuck sleeps till the first flowers wake. The grizzly and black bear spend from three to five months in a heavy, hibernating sleep.

Plants, too, though anchored, have a variety of winter customs. Trees may be said to hibernate, even the firs and spruces that go to sleep in full dress. Beneath the snow are countless seeds that will live their life next year, and numbers of plants that have hauled down their towers and colours for the winter. You may seek them and walk over them, and Mother Nature will only say: "Trouble me not, for the door is now shut and my children are with me in bed."

Moss in midwinter is as fresh and charming as though knee-deep in June. It is dainty and striking in a white setting. Mosses and lichens are ever a part of the poetry associated with ferns and the golden sands of bubbling springs; they are sharers in the cheerful, ever-silent beauty of the wild. They never intrude, but are among the most subdued and harmonious decorations in all nature. Yet lichens carry all the colours of the rainbow. In dark woods, deep cañons, and on the pinnacles of high peaks they cling in leafy, maplike decorations of oxidized silver, hammered brass, pure copper, and stains of yellow, brown, scarlet, gray, and green. They are almost classical decorations and touch with soft colour and beauty the roughest bark and boulders. Until one knows that they are living things they seem only chemical colourings on the crags, and a part of the colour scheme in the bark of trees.

One day during this outing I had been walking in the shadow of a mountain, which, together with the darkness of the spruce woods, made the snow almost a gray expanse. As I climbed out of the shadow on to a plateau, just at sunset, how splendidly, dazzlingly white was the skyline of peaks! On this white and broken line the sunset-coloured clouds strangely rested. A sunset is never an old story, and a coloured sunset above the white west line of winter's silent earth renews the imagination of youth.

Though I crossed a number of alpine lakes they were not to be seen. They were gone from the landscape. A stratum of marble instead of snow could not better have concealed them. Lakes, flowers, and bears were asleep for the winter.

In snowless places the brooks had decorated their ways with beautiful ice structures—arches and arcades, spires and frozen splashes, and endless stretches and forms of silver streamside platings and boulder drapings; ice, crystal clear, frosted and opaque. Many rocks were overspread with ice sheets and icy drapery, and cliffs were decked with fretwork and stupendous icicles. Smaller streams froze to the bottom, overflowed and outbuilt. In places wide areas were covered to enormous depths. Looking upon these one might almost fancy the Ice Age returning. But three months later the ice was gone to the far-off sea, and the flowers that slept beneath were massing their brilliant blossoms in the sun.

An old Ute chief once told me that during the hardest winter he had ever known in his country the snow for weeks lay "six ponies deep." The average annual snowfall in the Rocky Mountains is less than twenty-five feet. This is less than the average for the Alps.

Meetings with other human beings were few. One day, while walking down a plateau, I saw a dark figure that stood waiting on the edge of a snowy mountain moor a mile distant. As I approached the man waved an arm to attract my attention and when I came near enough he said by way of greeting:

"I thought you had not seen me."

We were above the limits of tree growth and below and about us was a wild array of peaks and cañons.

"When I saw you come racing down that peak shoulder," said the man, "I fancied that you were an escaping Siberian

Winter Mountaineering

convict, sentenced for political aims. What is your sentence or your service?"

"They call me the Snow Man," I replied. "I am making winter experiments and gathering information along the summit of the Continental Divide." I had not as yet become official "Colorado Snow Observer."

In answer to a counter question of mine he said: "Oh, I'm a prospector, fifty-four, born in Ireland, raised in Australia and Siberia. Am after gold in Spruce Gulch. If I don't strike it by spring I'm off for Alaska. Stirring reports from there."

It was a good place to look around. Several towering peaks were strangely near. A number of summits reached up fourteen thousand feet into the blue sky. Colorado is crowded with a vast and wondrous array of mountains. Many of these are united by narrow plateaus that are savagely side-cut with deep cañons. Each time I gained a commanding height I looked again and again, awed by the immensity of it all, at peaks and cañons with their broken strata of snow.

This outing, as usual, was all too short. Ten of its fourteen days were sunny and calm. Through two days the wind roared. Two other days were filled with snowstorms. Each day I went to some new scene. I climbed one fourteen-thousand-foot peak. I occupied one camp three nights, but on each of the other nights I had a new camp. Most of the nights were filled with stars, and always there was the blazing camp-fire. On my way home I met a man who had heard of my winter camping habits. After questioning me concerning the objects of interest seen, he asked:

"Is this a good time of year for a vacation?"

I replied:

"A good time for a vacation is whenever you can spare the time, and the very best time for a vacation in the mountains is when you can stay the longest."

17.

Wind-Rapids on the Heights

TERRIFIC WINTER WINDS occasionally sweep through the high passes of the Continental Divide. Believing that their velocity was sometimes more than one hundred miles an hour, I planned to go up and measure the velocity of the next wind that appeared to be exceeding the speed limit. An air meter was placed in Granite Pass. This was on the Longs Peak trail, about one mile beyond the limits of tree growth and at an elevation of more than two miles above the level of the sea.

One February morning the rush and boom of the wind among the pines proclaimed that previous speed records were likely to be broken. I left my cabin and started up to the meter, which was about three thousand feet higher than my cabin and five miles from it.

In irregular succession the heavy waves of wind rolled down this slope into the forest. A splendid and stormy sea roared through the tree-tops. The first half mile was through a thicket growth of tall young pines. These young and pliant trees were bending, shaking, and streaming in the wind. I turned aside from the trail to see the behaviour of the tallest woods, a dense growth of Engelmann spruce, at the bottom of the steep slope of Battle Mountain.

I climbed into a tree-top one hundred feet high. Around me the tall and crowded trees were swaying and bowing through a dignified dance. Invisible wind breakers produced sudden dips and vigorous sweeps that my old tree thought he

Mount Meeker, Longs Peak, and windblown tree

enjoyed. Occasionally the tree-top swayed in one direction, then bowed in another. Once he nodded in succession toward all points of the compass, tracing a wavy circle perhaps twenty feet in diameter. Then he straightened up again to the perpendicular. The entire forest was suddenly tilted forward by a violent wind wave and without the least warning I was clinging to a leaning tower. Engelmann spruce wood is not celebrated for toughness so I quickly descended to earth.

In the shelter of the storm-battered trees at timberline I looked out into the yellow, sand-filled air upon a treeless Arctic moorland. The gale tore among the trees with ever-varying intensity. Sand and gravel pattered and rattled against the scarred and veteran pines. I climbed a low, stocky tree which the hardest wind waves struck. This tree was so rigid that it quivered and oscillated like a building in an earthquake.

At the altitude of 11,500 feet I emerged from the woods and faced the gale. It assailed me with a sand blast which bruised my hands and brought blood from my face, and speedily drove me back into the woods. Again I tried. This time I crawled forward between low, heathy growths. At the start these afforded a little protection but as I advanced the wind swept through more swiftly and violently. I was glad to crawl out into the open moorland. Here, after an advance of a few hundred yards, I paused to rest in the lee of a butte of granite. Thicker than hail the sand and gravel rained down upon me; a roll of my coat caught a handful. Much of this consisted of sand-bits the size of a pencil point, but there were a few pieces of gravel the size of hazel nuts; the remainder was rock dust crushed by colliding with the cliff.

It was a warm, dry, chinook wind. Its temperature was several degrees above the freezing point. There had been but little snow, and only a few small, icy drifts lay scattered upon the brown, bare moor. The sun shone in a cloudless sky, but the air was so filled with rock dust that objects more than one hundred feet away were out of focus in the hazy yellow air. The effect was that of a desert sand storm; the wind, however, was of greater velocity and carried less dust than in desert storms.

Leaving the shelter of the cliff, I again advanced by crawling. A brief stop was made behind a rock point about five feet high. Here the wind poured down upon me with such force that it could not be endured.

Thus far above the limits of the trees not a living thing had showed itself, but in crawling along the edge of an icy snow-drift I came upon a number of ptarmigan. Many were sitting in little nests just the size of their bodies, which they had made in the hard snow. A few were bravely feeding. Squatting low, they grabbed at weed seeds and other edible objects that came sifting down over the snow. Though in a sheltered place, one of them was occasionally bowled over by the wind. On regaining its feet, it struggled back into its nest. But not one risked opening its wings. Apparently they considered me as harmless as a mountain sheep. With curious eyes, they allowed me to crawl by within three feet.

The wind met me with violent dashes, with moderate movements, and with occasional intervals that were almost

Wind-Rapids on the Heights

calm. In many of its rushes the wind rolled forward like a stormy breaker, with invisible, unbroken wave front in a sustained roar. At other times, this great wave was broken into wild maelstroms, terrific spirals of various diameters and tilted at every angle. Sometimes a wave went forward with long, bouncing leaps, bounding entirely clear of the earth for long distances, then striking heavily to roll and break, like a breaker on the beach. Occasionally, over a small space, there was an explosive effect that sent dust and gravel flying. With slouch hat and mittened hands I protected my face as best I could. A few times a violent, narrow whirlwind cut unrestrained into unrelated air currents. Like the explosion of a cannon and by sheer speed and force, it smashed its way diagonally across and through other rushing winds.

Most of the time I crawled, but occasionally during a calm I rose up and ran forward a few hundred feet. Except during lulls it was perilous to stand erect. These winds could not be withstood by bracing. Main strength did not answer. Rarely did they strike straight forward; they struck on every side. Seldom was I blown over, but I was kicked into the air and I was sometimes knocked down or hurled to one side.

At last I gained the air meter. It was up at 12,000 feet and stood where the wind simply pounded through the pass. The meter cups were making a blurred wheel of speed; a few times they showed the wind at one hundred and seventy miles an hour.

Around me were high peaks and deep cañons, level plateaus and crag-torn slopes. These intercepted and deflected the wind waves and currents. Against these obstructions the powerful, invisible wind hurled itself more uproariously than storm-stirred sea against defying and moveless shore.

Ever from some quarter came an unending roar. Splendid were the deep sounds and thunderings, ponderously heavy and prolonged were the booms of the wind. These often mingled with terrific, crashing explosions which even the elastic air did not always soften. There were long, ripping sounds, as the diverted wind rolled up a slope or tore around a corner. Then, strange were the seconds of ominous, almost breathless, calm.

After reading the meter, I went higher. Carried away with the wild, elemental eloquence of the storm, I concluded to get effects from the high ledges and finally from the summit of Longs Peak.

Every step advanced, each new height somehow gained, was a fight. It took all my endurance and it stimulated utmost alertness. I simply crawled forward and upward. And I wrestled with an invisible, unresting contestant who occasionally tried to hurl me over a ledge or smash my bones against the rocks.

For a mile I made my way across a moraine with the wind beating against my right side. The scattered boulders made travelling difficult; many were large and had to be climbed over. Such activities often gave the wind the eagerly used opportunity of shooting me with icy pellets and of knocking me off my feet.

At the altitude of thirteen thousand feet, the trail was through a rocky opening called Keyhole. Here the wind rushed in an invisible but irresistible flood. To go against it was sheer madness, so I climbed down and around Keyhole. While doing this, as I lay flat on my face, I was caught by a rush of wind. It lifted me a foot or two, then jammed me back. After repeating this, it pitched me headlong!

The wind swept out of the west and came in contact with the Divide at right angles. On the east the wind blew everywhere; but strangely enough on the western side it struck the mountains from eleven thousand feet upward, below this was perfect calm. By watching the whirling snow and other wind-blown materials, I judged this wind current to be about two thousand feet thick. Above, approximately thirteen thousand feet, was an air current moving in nearly the opposite direction. In crossing the Divide this wind that was blowing high above the earth on the west side closely raked the earth on the eastern side. From points near the top of the Peak I looked

Wind-Rapids on the Heights

out over my home to the east. Two thousand feet above it the air was comparatively free from dust. To the east I saw a number of birds flying high and plainly in a calm stratum of air.

As I continued upward above thirteen thousand feet, the wind gushed and stormed through the narrow openings between pinnacles and around the large rocks in débris piles. I crawled through a number of these openings. There are rapids in rivers and rapids in air streams. Running a river rapid in a boat is exhilarating. Crawling through a wind rapid is even more intense. It lacks most of the exhilaration that goes with the river rapid, but exhilaration is not wholly absent. In bays and channels of the sea the restless waters wildly eddy; powerful, invisible undertows and whirlpools are present where wild, defiant winds are diverted.

Rock projections, behind which I hoped to find shelter, were more unfriendly places than the open. The wind appeared to round them with increased speed, and to batter the leeward more furiously than the stormward front. Around a number of rocky projections the wind revolved with swirling rapidity. It hurled me off with centrifugal motion each time I made close approach. Once I blundered by breaking into one of these whirls, and was roughly handled while in and while getting out of it.

Each time that I hugged the earth more closely than usual, the wind took a sheer delight in paying me personal attentions. While many of these calls were with evil intentions, the others were but the investigations of the curious. I was grabbed and then slammed back; I was trampled upon and several times was recklessly dragged over rough stones. I was occasionally raised gently upward, then laid gently down; rolled slowly over, then turned slowly back. Once I was picked carefully up by a current that carried me off as carefully as if to first aid; but from this I was rudely snatched by an angry wind, whose every effort was to put me in need of this aid.

The most difficult and dangerous place was at a point at

an altitude of about fourteen thousand feet. This was where a long, narrow gulch and a fan-like slope converged and ended on the summit of a narrow ridge, beyond which there was a narrow ledge, bounded by unbanistered space. Sweeping upward three thousand feet from the bottom of a cañon came the wind through converging channels that ended in this one narrow gorge. My struggles were intense in the last few feet of this channel. The gorge in which I climbed was extremely steep, yet so powerful was the wind current that all my strength was required to prevent being torn loose, shot upward, and thrown over the precipice. Icy fragments torn from the walls, twigs from a mile below, went hurtling and rattling by and shot far out over the precipice. Had I let go for even a second, I should have followed them. Not for an instant did the wind stop; it had the constant rush of rapids. I eased myself upward in the rushing wind, crawling close, holding with hands, and anchoring and holding rear down by hooking feet behind and beneath rocks. Trail conditions were favourable, and these together with my climbing experiences, endurance, and knowledge of the place were of advantage to me. All these were needed.

Just before reaching the top of the narrow ridge and the precipice, I felt the wind getting the better of me and feared that a slightly more violent rush or surge would tear my holds loose. So I concluded to reverse ends. Putting a shoulder against a rock point, I allowed the wind to push my legs around, then forward. I was then going up feet foremost instead of head foremost. The gulley was so extremely steep that I was almost standing or walking on my head. This reverse of ends enabled me to brace effectively with my feet, and also to hang on more securely with my hands. Little by little I eased myself upward. There was no climbing; the wind sucked, dragged, pushed, and floated me ever upward.

At last I safely crossed the ridge, rounded a point, and sat down for a long rest on the famous Narrows of the Longs Peak trail. The Narrows is a ledge with a precipice in front and a wall behind. This wall rises precipitously to the sum-

Wind-Rapids on the Heights

mit; the precipice makes a wild, step descent of two thousand feet. It is none too wide for a thoroughfare that has unbanistered space before it. Fortunately, it was sheltered from the wind, otherwise traversing it would not have been either safe or sane.

Why did I, in this perilous gale, in this wild wind, venture precipices and go up into the sky on a peak nearly three miles above the seven restless seas?

Irresistible is nature's call to play. This call comes in a thousand alluring forms. It comes at unexpected times and sends us to unheard-of places. We simply cannot tell what nature will have of us, or where next. But from near and far, ever calls her eloquent voice. In work and in dreams she shows a thousand ways, suggests the presence of wonderlands yet unseen. She pictures alluring scenes in which to rest and play; in mysterious ways she sends us eagerly forth for unscaled heights and fairylands. Of these she whispers, or of them she sounds her bugle song. She fascinatingly commands and charms us to other scenes. We rush to respond and fix our eyes on a happy horizon, toward which we hurry; but ere we reach it she calls elsewhere, and elsewhere, with highest hopes of a boy at play, we hasten. It was seriously splendid to play with these wild winds. There is no greater joy than wrestling naked handed with the elements.

My most uncertain work was a little below the summit. The ridge that had shielded my crawling came to an end. I was on the edge of a steep, short slope that ended at the top, but this slope was smooth and icy and at the bottom paid tribute to a precipice. It was too slippery to climb. Across it swept the deflected wind current. On the opposite side the current struck a ridge and with diminished force shot upward to the summit. Apparently this wind rushed as steadily as a mountain river. It was swift enough to sweep me across; but if it hesitated after I cast my lot in it, down the toboggan slope I would slide. Eagerly I pushed myself out into it and let go. Across it rushed me, sprawling, bumping me into the rocky ridge beyond. Here the interrupted current lifted me upward.

I had little else to do than guide myself. Rapidly it boosted me to the top. Standing on the edge of the summit I turned for a moment to look back down this icy slope which later I must somehow retrace.

The summit of Longs Peak is 14,255 feet above the sea and about four hundred feet in diameter. It is comparatively level though not smooth. Granite stones and slabs of various sizes cover the top.

In terrific, weighty rushes the wind splendidly thundered against the west wall of the summit. All this time the wind was continuously roaring round lower pinnacles and terrifically booming against the lower obstructions. The old Peak met these cyclonic rushes with strange impassiveness, without a tremble. Deflected by the west wall, the current shot upward for a hundred feet or so. The top of the Peak was thus left in comparative calm.

I ventured too close to the west edge, and my hat was torn off. It started skyward like a rocket, but less than one hundred feet above the Peak it fell out of the uprush and into the large, slowly rotating eddy that covered the space over the top. Slowly around in a large air whirlpool the hat was carried. I threw a number of stones, trying to bring it back to earth. Presently the forward current caught it. Then like a duck in a wind the hat shot forward, pointing straight at a lower and near-by lighting place.

A flock of rosy finches were feeding off the stuff that sifted down out of the wind. As I watched them, they were unmindful of the wind and had thought of no danger. But behind a near-by stone a beady-eyed weasel watched and waited.

Far down the range to the south quantities of snow were being explosively hurled into the air. This showed that there had been a recent snowfall and also that the wind had just reached that scene. The scattered snow was thrown high in the air into spirals and whirls and then seized and carried flying to the leeward. This powdered snow trimmed the Peak points with steamy whirls and gauzy banners and silky pennants through which the sunlight played. Northward for one hundred miles the gale was sweeping eastward, and a stratum of dust hid the Wyoming plains. The sky above was clear and strangely blue. The sun shone brightly. My shadow against a granite monolith stood out as if of a dark and sculptured figure cut from stone.

18.

Snow-Blinded on the Summit

As I climbed up out of the dwarfed woods at timberline in the Rocky Mountains, and started across the treeless white summit, the terrific sun glare on the snow warned me of the danger of snow-blindness. I had lost my snow glasses. But the wild attractions of the heights caused me to forget the care of my eyes and I lingered to look down into cañons and to examine magnificent snow cornices. A number of mountain sheep also interested me. Then for half an hour I circled a confiding flock of ptarmigan and took picture after picture.

Through the clear air the sunlight poured with burning intensity. I was 12,000 feet above the sea. Around me there was not a dark crag nor even a tree to absorb the excess of light. A wilderness of high, rugged peaks stood about — splendid sunlit mountains of snow. To east and west they faced winter's noonday sun with great shadow mantles flowing from their shoulders.

As I started to hurry on across the pass I began to experience the scorching pains that go with seared, sunburnt eyes — snow-blindness. Unfortunately, I had failed to take even the precaution of blackening my face, which would have dulled the glare. At the summit my eyes became so painful that I could endure the light only a few seconds at a time. Occasionally I sat down and closed them for a minute or two. Finally, while doing this, the lids adhered to the balls and the eyes swelled so that I could not open them.

Longs Peak from Chasm Lake

Blind on the summit of the Continental Divide! I made a grab for my useful staff which I had left standing beside me in the snow. In the fraction of a second that elapsed between thinking of the staff and finding it my brain woke up to the seriousness of the situation. To the nearest trees it was more than a mile, and the nearest house was many miles away across ridges of rough mountains. I had matches and a hatchet, but no provisions. Still, while well aware of my peril, I was only moderately excited, feeling no terror. Less startling incidents have shocked me more, narrow escapes from street automobiles have terrified me.

It had been a wondrous morning. The day cleared after a heavy fall of fluffy snow. I had snowshoed up the slope through a ragged, snow-carpeted spruce forest, whose shadows wrought splendid black-and-white effects upon the shining floor. There were thousands of towering, slender spruces, each brilliantly laden with snow flowers, standing soft, white, and motionless in the sunlight. While I was looking at one of these artistically decorated trees, a mass of snow dropped upon me from its top, throwing me headlong and causing me to lose my precious eye-protecting snow glasses. But now I was blind.

With staff in hand, I stood for a minute or two planning the best manner to get along without eyes. My faculties were intensely awake. Serious situations in the wilds had more than once before this stimulated them to do their best. Temporary blindness is a good stimulus for the imagination and the memory—in fact, is good educational training for all the senses. However perilous my predicament during a mountain trip, the possibility of a fatal ending never even occurred to me. Looking back now, I cannot but wonder at my matter-of-fact attitude concerning the perils in which that snow-blindness placed me.

I had planned to cross the pass and descend into a trail at timberline. The appearance of the slope down which I was to travel was distinctly in my mind from my impressions just before darkness settled over me.

Off I slowly started. I guided myself with information from feet and staff, feeling my way with the staff so as not to step off a cliff or walk overboard into a cañon. In imagination I pictured myself following the shadow of a staff-bearing and slouch-hatted form. Did mountain sheep, curious and slightly suspicious, linger on crags to watch my slow and hesitating advance? Across the snow did the shadow of a soaring eagle coast and circle?

I must have wandered far from the direct course to timberline. Again and again I swung my staff to right and left hoping to strike a tree. I had travelled more than twice as long as it should have taken to reach timberline before I stood face to face with a low-growing tree that bristled up through the deep snow. But had I come out at the point for which I aimed—at the trail? This was the vital question.

The deep snow buried all trail blazes. Making my way from tree to tree I thrust an arm deep into the snow and felt of the bark, searching for a trail blaze. At last I found a blaze and going on a few steps I dug down again in the snow and examined a tree which I felt should mark the trail. This, too, was blazed.

Feeling certain that I was on the trail I went down the mountain through the forest for some minutes without searching for another blaze. When I did examine a number of trees not another blaze could I find. The topography since entering the forest and the size and character of the trees were such that I felt I was on familiar ground. But going on a few steps I came out on the edge of an unknown rocky cliff. I was now lost as well as blind.

During the hours I had wandered in reaching timberline I had had a vague feeling that I might be travelling in a circle, and might return to trees on the western slope of the Divide up which I had climbed. When I walked out on the edge of the cliff the feeling that I had doubled to the western slope became insistent. If true, this was most serious. To reach the nearest house on the west side of the range would be extremely difficult, even though I should discover just where I was. But I believed I was somewhere on the eastern slope.

I tried to figure out the course I had taken. Had I, in descending from the heights, gone too far to the right or to the left? Though fairly well acquainted with the country along this timberline, I was unable to recall a rocky cliff at this point. My staff found no bottom and warned me that I was at a jumping-off place. Increasing coolness indicated that night was upon me. But darkness did not matter, my light had failed at noon. Going back along my trail a short distance I avoided the cliff and started on through the night down a rocky, forested, and snow-covered slope. I planned to get into the bottom of a cañon and follow downstream. Every few steps I shouted, hoping to attract the attention of a possible prospector, miner, or woodchopper. No voice answered. The many echoes, however, gave me an idea of the topography—of the mountain ridges and cañons before me. I listened intently after each shout and noticed the direction from which the reply came, its intensity, and the cross echoes, and concluded that I was going down into the head of a deep, forest-walled cañon, and, I hoped, travelling eastward.

For points of the compass I appealed to the trees, hoping through my knowledge of woodcraft to orient myself. In the study of tree distribution I had learned that the altitude might often be approximated and the points of the compass determined by noting the characteristic kinds of trees.

Cañons of east and west trend in this locality carried mostly limber pines on the wall that faces south and mostly Engelmann spruces on the wall that faces the north. Believing that I was travelling eastward I turned to my right, climbed out of the cañon, and examined a number of trees along the slope. Most of these were Engelmann spruces. The slope probably faced north. Turning about I descended this slope and ascended the opposite one. The trees on this were mostly limber pines. Hurrah! Limber pines are abundant only on southern slopes. With limber pines on my left and Engelmann spruces on my right, I was now satisfied that I was travelling eastward and must be on the eastern side of the range.

To put a final check upon this—for a blind or lost man sometimes manages to do exactly the opposite of what he thinks he is doing—I examined lichen growths on the rocks and moss growths on the trees. In the deep cañon I dug down into the snow and examined the faces of low-lying boulders. With the greatest care I felt the lichen growth on the rocks. These verified the information that I had from the trees—but none too well. Then I felt over the moss growth, both long and short, on the trunks and lower limbs of trees, but this testimony was not absolutely convincing. The moss growth was so nearly even all the way around the trunk that I concluded that the surrounding topography must be such as to admit the light freely from all quarters, and also that the wall or slope on my right must be either a gentle one or else a low one and somewhat broken. I climbed to make sure. In a few minutes I was on a terrace—as I expected. Possibly back on the right lay a basin that might be tributary to this cañon. The reports made by the echoes of my shoutings said that this was true. A few minutes of travel down the cañon and I came to the expected incoming stream, which made its swift presence heard beneath its cover of ice and snow.

A short distance farther down the cañon I examined a number of trees that stood in thick growth on the lower part of what I thought was the southern slope. Here the character of the moss and lichens and their abundant growth on the northerly sides of the trees verified the testimony of the tree distribution and of previous moss and lichen growths. I was satisfied as to the points of the compass. I was on the eastern side of the Continental Divide travelling eastward.

After three or four hours of slow descending I reached the bottom. Steep walls rose on both right and left. The enormous rock masses and the entanglements of fallen and leaning trees made progress difficult. Feeling that if I continued in the bottom of the cañon I might come to a precipitous place down which I would be unable to descend, I tried to walk along one of the side walls, and thus keep above the bottom. But the walls were too steep and I got into trouble.

Out on a narrow, snow-corniced ledge I walked. The snow gave way beneath me and down I went over the ledge. As I struck, feet foremost, one snowshoe sank deeply. I wondered, as I wiggled out, if I had landed on another ledge. I had. Not desiring to have more tumbles, I tried to climb back up on the ledge from which I had fallen, but I could not do it. The ledge was broad and short and there appeared to be no safe way off. As I explored again my staff encountered the top of a dead tree that leaned against the ledge. Breaking a number of dead limbs off I threw them overboard. Listening as they struck the snow below I concluded that it could not be more than thirty feet to the bottom.

I let go my staff and dropped it after the limbs. Then, without taking off snowshoes, I let myself down the limbless trunk. I could hear water running beneath the ice and snow. I recovered my staff and resumed the journey.

In time the cañon widened a little and travelling became easier. I had just paused to give a shout when a rumbling and crashing high up the righthand slope told me that a snowslide was plunging down. Whether it would land in the cañon before me or behind me or on top of me could not be guessed. The awful smashing and crashing and roar proclaimed it of enormous size and indicated that trees and rocky débris were being swept onward with it. During the few seconds that I stood awaiting my fate, thought after thought raced through my brain as I recorded the ever-varying crashes and thunders of the wild, irresistible slide.

With terrific crash and roar the snowslide swept into the cañon a short distance in front of me. I was knocked down by the outrush or concussion of air and for several minutes was nearly smothered with the whirling, settling snow-dust and rock powder which fell thickly all around. The air cleared and I went on.

I had gone only a dozen steps when I came upon the enormous wreckage brought down by the slide. Snow, earthy matter, rocks, and splintered trees were flung in fierce confusion together. For three or four hundred feet this accumulation filled the cañon from wall to wall and was fifty or sixty feet high. The slide wreckage smashed the ice and dammed the stream. As I started to climb across this snowy débris a shattered place in the ice beneath gave way and dropped me into the water, but my long staff caught and by clinging to it I saved myself from going in above my hips. My snowshoes caught in the shattered ice and while I tried to get my feet free a mass of snow fell upon me and nearly broke my hold. Shaking off the snow I put forth all my strength and finally pulled my feet free of the ice and crawled out upon the débris. This was a close call and at last I was thoroughly, briefly, frightened.

As the wreckage was a mixture of broken trees, stones, and compacted snow I could not use my snowshoes, so I took them off to carry them till over the débris. Once across I planned to pause and build a fire to dry my icy clothes.

With difficulty I worked my way up and across. Much of the snow was compressed almost to ice by the force of contact, and in this icy cement many kinds of wreckage were set in wild disorder. While descending a steep place in this mass, carrying snowshoes under one arm, the footing gave way and I fell. I suffered no injury but lost one of the snowshoes. For an hour or longer I searched, without finding it.

The night was intensely cold and in the search my feet became almost frozen. In order to rub them I was about to take off my shoes when I came upon something warm. It proved to be a dead mountain sheep with one horn smashed off. As I sat with my feet beneath its warm carcass and my hands upon it, I thought how but a few minutes before the animal had been alive on the heights with all its ever wide-awake senses vigilant for its preservation; yet I, wandering blindly, had escaped with my life when the snowslide swept into the cañon. The night was calm, but of zero temperature or lower. It probably was crystal clear. As I sat warming my hands and feet on the proud master of the crags I imagined the bright, clear sky crowded thick with stars. I pictured to myself the dark slope down which the slide had come. It appeared to reach up close to the frosty stars.

But the lost snowshoe must be found; wallowing through the deep mountain snow with only one snowshoe would be almost hopeless. I had vainly searched the surface and lower wreckage projections but made one more search. This proved successful. The shoe had slid for a short distance, struck an obstacle, bounced upward over smashed logs, and lay about four feet above the general surface. A few moments more and I was beyond the snowslide wreckage. Again on snowshoes, staff in hand, I continued feeling my way down the mountain. My ice-stiffened trousers and chilled limbs were not good travelling companions, and at the first cliff that I encountered I stopped to make a fire. I gathered two or three armfuls of dead limbs, with the aid of my hatchet, and soon had a lively blaze going. But the heat increased the pain in my eyes, so with clothes only partly dried, I went on. Repeatedly through the night I applied snow to my eyes trying to subdue the fiery torment.

From timberline I had travelled downward through a green forest mostly of Engelmann spruce with a scattering of fir and limber pine. I frequently felt of the tree trunks. But a short time after leaving my camp-fire I came to the edge of an extensive region that had been burned over. For more than an hour I travelled through dead standing trees, on many of which only the bark had been burned away; on others the fire had burned more deeply.

Pausing on the way down, I thrust my staff into the snow and leaned against a tree to hold snow against my burning eyes. While I was doing this two owls hooted happily to each other and I listened to their contented calls with satisfaction.

Hearing the pleasant, low call of a chickadee I listened. Apparently he was dreaming and talking in his sleep. The dream must have been a happy one, for every note was cheerful. Realizing that he probably was in an abandoned woodpecker nesting hole, I tapped on the dead tree against which I was leaning. This was followed by a chorus of lively, surprised chirpings, and one, two, three!—then several—chickadees flew out of a hole a few inches above my head. Sorry to have disturbed them I went on down the slope.

At last I felt the morning sun in my face. With increased

Snow-Blinded on the Summit

light my eyes became extremely painful. For a time I relaxed upon the snow, finding it difficult to believe that I had been travelling all night in complete darkness. While lying here I caught the scent of smoke. There was no mistaking it. It was the smoke of burning aspen, a wood much burned in the cook-stoves of mountain people. Eagerly I rose to find it. I shouted again and again but there was no response. Under favourable conditions, keen nostrils may detect aspen-wood smoke for a distance of two or three miles.

The compensation of this accident was an intense stimulus to my imagination—perhaps our most useful intellectual faculty. My eyes, always keen and swift, had ever supplied me with almost an excess of information. But with them suddenly closed my imagination became the guiding faculty. I did creative thinking. With pleasure I restored the views and scenes of the morning before. Any one seeking to develop the imagination would find a little excursion afield, with eyes voluntarily blindfolded, a most telling experience.

Down the mountainside I went, hour after hour. My ears caught the chirp of birds and the fall of icicles which ordinarily I would hardly have heard. My nose was constantly and keenly analyzing the air. With touch and clasp I kept in contact with the trees. Again my nostrils picked up aspen smoke. This time it was much stronger. Perhaps I was near a house! But the whirling air currents gave me no clue as to the direction from which the smoke came, and only echoes responded to my call.

All my senses worked willingly in seeking wireless news to substitute for the eyes. My nose readily detected odours and smoke. My ears were more vigilant and more sensitive than usual. My fingers, too, were responsive from the instant that my eyes failed. Delightfully eager they were, as I felt the snow-buried trees, hoping with touch to discover possible trail blazes. My feet also were quickly, steadily alert to translate the topography.

Occasionally a cloud shadow passed over. In imagination

I often pictured the appearance of these clouds against the blue sky and tried to estimate the size of each by the number of seconds its shadow took to drift across me.

Mid-afternoon, or later, my nose suddenly detected the odour of an ancient corral. This was a sign of civilization. A few minutes later my staff came in contact with the corner of a cabin. I shouted "Hello!" but heard no answer. I continued feeling until I came to the door and found that a board was nailed across it. The cabin was locked and deserted! I broke in the door.

In the cabin I found a stove and wood. As soon as I had a fire going I dropped snow upon the stove and steamed my painful eyes. After two hours or more of this steaming they became more comfortable. Two strenuous days and one toilsome night had made me extremely drowsy. Sitting down upon the floor near the stove I leaned against the wall and fell asleep. But the fire burned itself out. In the night I awoke nearly frozen and unable to rise. Fortunately, I had on my mittens, otherwise my fingers probably would have frozen. By rubbing my hands together, then rubbing my arms and legs, I finally managed to limber myself, and though unable to rise, I succeeded in starting a new fire. It was more than an hour before I ceased shivering; then, as the room began to warm, my legs came back to life and again I could walk.

I was hungry. This was my first thought of food since becoming blind. If there was anything to eat in the cabin, I failed to find it. Searching my pockets I found a dozen or more raisins and with these I broke my sixty-hour fast. Then I had another sleep, and it must have been near noon when I awakened. Again I steamed the eye pain into partial submission.

Going to the door I stood and listened. A campbird only a few feet away spoke gently and confidingly. Then a crested jay called impatiently. The camp-bird alighted on my shoulder. I tried to explain to the birds that there was nothing to eat. The prospector who had lived in this cabin evidently had been friendly with the bird neighbours. I wished that I might know him.

Snow-Blinded on the Summit

Again I could smell the smoke of aspen wood. Several shouts evoked echoes—nothing more. I stood listening and wondering whether to stay in the cabin or to venture forth and try to follow the snow-filled roadway that must lead down through the woods from the cabin. Wherever this open way led I could follow. But of course I must take care not to lose it.

In the nature of things I felt that I must be three or four miles to the south of the trail which I had planned to follow down the mountain. I wished I might see my long and crooked line of footmarks in the snow from the summit to timberline.

Hearing the open water in rapids close to the cabin, I went out to try for a drink. I advanced slowly, blind-man fashion, feeling the way with my long staff. As I neared the rapids, a water ouzel, which probably had lunched in the open water, sang with all his might. I stood still as he repeated his liquid, hopeful song. On the spot I shook off procrastination and decided to try to find a place where someone lived.

After writing a note explaining why I had smashed in the door and used so much wood, I readjusted my snowshoes and started down through the woods. I suppose it must have been late afternoon.

I found an open way that had been made into a road. The woods were thick and the open roadway readily guided me. Feeling and thrusting with my staff, I walked for some time at normal pace. Then I missed the way. I searched carefully, right, left, and before me for the utterly lost road. It had forked, and I had continued on the short stretch that came to an end in the woods by an abandoned prospect hole. As I approached close to this the snow caved in, nearly carrying me along with it. Confused by blinded eyes and the thought of oncoming night, perhaps, I had not used my wits. When at last I stopped to think I figured out the situation. Then I followed my snowshoe tracks back to the main road and turned into it.

For a short distance the road ran through dense woods.

Several times I paused to touch the trees each side with my hands. When I emerged from the woods, the pungent aspen smoke said that I must at last be near a human habitation. In fear of passing it I stopped to use my ears. As I stood listening, a little girl gently, curiously, asked:

"Are you going to stay here to-night?"

19.

Racing an Avalanche

I HAD GONE INTO the San Juan Mountains during the first week in March to learn something of the laws which govern snow slides, to get a fuller idea of their power and destructiveness, and also with the hope of seeing them in wild, magnificent action. Everywhere, except on wind-swept points, the winter's snows lay deep. Conditions for slide movement were so favorable it seemed probable that, during the next few days at least, one would "run" or chute down every gulch that led from the summit. I climbed on skis well to the top of the range. By waiting on spurs and ridges I saw several thrilling exhibitions.

It was an exciting experience, but at the close of one great day the clear weather that had prevailed came to an end. From the table-like summit I watched hundreds of splendid clouds slowly advance, take their places, mass, and form fluffy seas in valley and cañons just below my level. They submerged the low places in the plateau, and torn, silver-gray masses of mists surrounded crags and headlands. The sunset promised to be wonderful, but suddenly the mists came surging past my feet and threatened to shut out the view. Hurriedly climbing a promontory, I watched from it a many-colored sunset change and fade over mist-wreathed spires, and swelling, peak-torn seas. But the cloud-masses were rising, and suddenly points and peaks began to settle out of sight; then a dash of frosty mists, and my promontory sank into the sea. The light vanished from the heights, and I was caught in dense, frosty clouds and winter snows without a star.

I had left my skis at the foot of the promontory, and had climbed up by fingers and toes over the rocks without great difficulty. But on starting to return I could see only a few inches into the frosty, sheep's-wool clouds, and quickly found that trying to get down would be a perilous pastime. The side of the promontory stood over the steep walls of the plateau, and, not caring to be tumbled overboard by a slip, I concluded that sunrise from this point would probably be worth while.

It was not bitter cold, and I was comfortably dressed; however, it was necessary to do much dancing and arm-swinging to keep warm. Snow began to fall just after the clouds closed in, and it fell rapidly without a pause until near morning. Early in the evening I began a mental review of a number of subjects, mingling with these, from time to time, vigorous practice of gymnastics or calisthenics to help pass the night and to aid in keeping warm. The first subject I thought through was Arctic exploration; then I recalled all that my mind had retained of countless stories of mountain-climbing experiences; the contents of Tyndall's "Hours of Exercise in the Alps" was most clearly recalled. I was enjoying the poetry of Burns, when broken clouds and a glowing eastern sky claimed all attention until it was light enough to get off the promontory.

Planning to go down the west side, I crossed the table-like top, found, after many trials, a break in the enormous snow-cornice, and started down the steep slope. It was a dangerous descent, for the rock was steep and smooth as a wall, and was overladen with snow which might slip at any moment. I descended slowly and with great caution, so as not to start the snow, as well as to guard against slipping and losing control of myself. It was like descending a mile of steep, snow-covered barn roof,—nothing to lay hold of and omnipresent opportunity for slipping. A short distance below the summit the clouds again were around me and I could see only a short distance. I went sideways, with my long skis, which I had now regained, at right angles to the slope; slowly, a few inches at a time, I eased myself down, planting one ski firmly before I moved the other.

At last I reached a point where the wall was sufficiently tilted to be called a slope, though it was still too steep for safe coasting. The clouds lifted and were floating away, while the sun made the mountains of snow still whiter. I paused to look back and up, to where the wall ended in the blue sky, and could not understand how I had come safely down, even with the long tacks I had made, which showed clearly up to the snow-corniced, mist-shrouded crags at the summit. I had come down the side of a precipitous amphitheatre which rose a thousand feet or more above me. A short distance down the mountain, the slopes of this amphitheatre concentrated in a narrow gulch that extended two miles or more. Altogether it was like being in an enormous frying-pan lying face up. I was in the pan just above the place where the gulch handle joined.

It was a bad place to get out of, and thousands of tons of snow clinging to the steeps and sagging from corniced crests ready to slip, plunge down, and sweep the very spot on which I stood, showed most impressively that it was a perilous place to be in.

As I stood gazing upward and wondering how the snow ever could have held while I came down over it, there suddenly appeared on the upper steeps an upburst as from an explosion. Along several hundred feet of cornice, sprays and clouds of snow dashed and filled the air. An upward breeze curled and swept the top of this cloud over the crest in an inverted cascade.

All this showed for a few seconds until the snowy spray began to separate and vanish in the air. The snow-cloud settled downward and began to roll forward. Then monsters of massed snow appeared beneath the front of the cloud and plunged down the slopes. Wildly, grandly they dragged the entire snow-cloud in their wake. At the same instant the remainder of the snow-cornice was suddenly enveloped in another explosive snow-cloud effect.

A general slide had started. I whirled to escape, pointed my skis down the slope,—and went. In less than half a minute a tremendous snow avalanche, one hundred or perhaps two hundred feet deep and five or six hundred feet long, thundered over the spot where I had stood.

There was no chance to dodge, no time to climb out of the way. The only hope of escape lay in outrunning the magnificent monster. It came crashing and thundering after me as swift as a gale and more all-sweeping and destructive than an earthquake tidal wave.

I made a desperate start. Friction almost ceases to be a factor with skis on a snowy steep, and in less than a hundred yards I was going like the wind. For the first quarter of a mile, to the upper end of the gulch, was smooth coasting, and down this I shot, with the avalanche, comet-tailed with snow-dust, in close pursuit. A race for life was on.

The gulch down which I must go began with a rocky gorge and continued downward, an enormous U-shaped depression between high mountain-ridges. Here and there it expanded and then contracted, and it was broken with granite crags and ribs. It was piled and bristled with ten thousand fire-killed trees. To coast through all these snow-clad obstructions at breakneck speed would be taking the maximum number of life-and-death chances in the minimum amount of time. The worst of it all was that I had never been through the place. And bad enough, too, was the fact that a ridge thrust in from the left and completely hid the beginning of the gulch.

As I shot across the lower point of the ridge, about to plunge blindly into the gorge, I thought of the possibility of becoming entangled in the hedge-like thickets of dwarfed, gnarled timber-line trees. I also realized that I might dash against a cliff or plunge into a deep cañon. Of course I might strike an open way, but certain it was that I could not stop, nor see the beginning of the gorge, nor tell what I should strike when I shot over the ridge.

It was a second of most intense concern as I cleared the ridge blindly to go into what lay below and beyond. It was like leaping into the dark, and with the leap turning on the all-revealing light. As I cleared the ridge, there was just time to pull myself together for a forty-odd-foot leap across one arm of the horseshoe-shaped end of the gorge. In all my wild mountainside coasts on skis, never have I sped as swiftly as when I made this mad flight. As I shot through the air, I had a glimpse down into the pointed, snow-laden tops of a few tall fir trees that were firmly rooted among the rocks in the bottom of the gorge. Luckily I cleared the gorge and landed in a good place; but so narrowly did I miss the corner of a cliff that my shadow collided with it.

There was no time to bid farewell to fears when the slide started, nor to entertain them while running away from it. Instinct put me to flight; the situation set my wits working at their best, and, once started, I could neither stop nor look back; and so thick and fast did obstructions and dangers rise before me that only dimly and incidentally did I think of the oncoming danger behind.

I came down on the farther side of the gorge, to glance forward like an arrow. There was only an instant to shape my course and direct my flight across the second arm of the gorge, over which I leaped from a high place, sailing far above the snow-mantled trees and boulders in the bottom. My senses were keenly alert, and I remember noticing the shadows of the fir trees on the white snow and hearing while still in the air the brave, cheery notes of a chickadee; then the snowslide on my trail, less than an eighth of a mile behind, plunged into the gorge with a thundering crash. I came back to the snow on the lower side, and went skimming down the slope with the slide only a few seconds behind.

Fortunately most of the fallen masses of trees were buried, though a few broken limbs peeped through the snow to snag or trip me. How I ever dodged my way through the thickly standing tree growths is one feature of the experience that was too swift for recollection. Numerous factors presented themselves which should have done much to dispel mental procrastination and develop decision. There were scores of progressive propositions to decide within a few seconds; should I dodge that tree on the left side and duck under low limbs just beyond, or dodge to the right and scrape that pike of rocks? These, with my speed, required instant decision and action.

With almost uncontrollable rapidity I shot out into a small, nearly level glacier meadow, and had a brief rest from swift decisions and oncoming dangers. How relieved my weary brain felt, with nothing to decide about dodging! As though starved for thought material, I wondered if there were willows buried beneath the snow. Sharp pains in my left hand compelled attention, and showed my left arm drawn tightly against my breast, with fingers and thumb spread to the fullest, and all their muscles tense.

The lower edge of the meadow was almost blockaded with a dense growth of fire-killed trees. Fortunately the easy slope here had so checked my speed that I was able to dodge safely through, but the heavy slide swept across the meadow after me with undiminished speed, and came crashing into the dead trees so close to me that broken limbs were flung flying past as I shot down off a steep moraine less than one hundred feet ahead.

All the way down I had hoped to find a side cañon into which I might dodge. I was going too rapidly to enter the one I had seen. As I coasted the moraine it flashed through my mind that I had once heard a prospector say it was only a quarter of a mile from Aspen Gulch up to the meadows. Aspen Gulch came in on the right, as the now slightly widening track seemed to indicate.

At the bottom of the moraine I was forced between two trees that stood close together, and a broken limb of one pierced my open coat just beneath the left armhole, and slit

Racing an Avalanche

the coat to the bottom. My momentum and the resistance of the strong material gave me such a shock that I was flung off my balance, and my left ski smashed against a tree. Two feet of the heel was broken off and the remainder split. I managed to avoid falling, but had to check my speed with my staff for fear of a worse accident.

Battling breakers with a broken oar or racing with a broken ski are struggles of short duration. The slide did not slow down, and so closely did it crowd me that, through the crashing of trees as it struck them down, I could hear the rocks and splintered timbers in its mass grinding together and thudding against obstructions over which it swept. These sounds, and flying, broken limbs cried to me "Faster!" and as I started to descend another steep moraine, I threw away my staff and "let go." I simply flashed down the slope, dodged and rounded a cliff, turned awkwardly into Aspen Gulch, and tumbled heels over head—into safety.

Then I picked myself up, to see the slide go by within twenty feet, with great broken trees sticking out of its side, and a snow-cloud dragging above.

A Short Chronology: Events in the Life of Enos Mills

1870	•	born in Kansas
1884	•	travels by rail to Estes Park
1885	•	begins work on homestead cabin
1886	•	helps construct Longs Peak trail
	•	completes cabin
1887	•	climbs Longs Peak solo for the first time
	•	begins mining career in Butte, Montana
1889	•	guides his first party to summit of Longs Peak
	•	meets John Muir in San Francisco
1890	•	visits the natural wonders of California
	•	attends business college in San Francisco
1891	•	works with U.S. Geological Survey in Yellowstone
1892	•	travels to Alaska
1893	•	tours the World's Columbian Exposition in Chicago
1894	•	revisits Alaska and treks alone more than two hundred miles
1896	•	begins covering news of Estes Park for Denver newspapers
1898	•	completes first nature writing
1900	•	travels widely in Europe with Elkanah Lamb
1901	•	purchases 160 acres in Tahosa Valley
1901	•	ends mining career

1902	•	purchases Longs Peak House from Lamb
	•	publishes his first major magazine article in *Outdoor Life*
1903	•	works first of two winters as Colorado State Snow Observer
	•	becomes first to climb Longs Peak in winter
1904	•	establishes Longs Peak Inn
1905	•	self-publishes his first book, *The Story of Estes Park and a Guide Book*
	•	lectures in the eastern U.S.
1906	•	guides thirty-two ascents of Longs Peak in his last season as guide
1907	•	appointed Government Lecturer on Forestry by Theodore Roosevelt
1908	•	lectures widely throughout the U.S.
1909	•	first major book, *Wild Life on the Rockies,* is published by Houghton Mifflin
	•	resigns government position
	•	begins extended campaign to create a national park on the front range
1915	•	presides at dedication of Rocky Mountain National Park
1918	•	marries Esther Burnell at the homestead cabin
1918	•	establishes trail school
1919	•	daughter, Enda, born
	•	begins embittered battle with the National Park Service
1922	•	injured in subway collision in New York City
	•	dies on September 22 at age fifty-two

A Selected Bibliography of the Writings of Enos Mills

Books

The Story of Estes Park and a Guide Book (self-published, 1905).
Wild Life on the Rockies (Houghton Mifflin, 1909; University of Nebraska Press, 1988).
The Spell of the Rockies (Houghton Mifflin, 1911; University of Nebraska Press, 1989).
In Beaver World (Houghton Mifflin, 1913; University of Nebraska Press, 1990).
The Story of a Thousand-Year Pine (Houghton Mifflin, 1914).
Rocky Mountain Wonderland (Houghton Mifflin, 1915; University of Nebraska Press, 1991).
The Story of Scotch (Houghton Mifflin, 1916).
Your National Parks (Houghton Mifflin, 1917).
Being Good to Bears (Houghton Mifflin, 1919).
The Grizzly: Our Greatest Wild Animal (Houghton Mifflin, 1919; Comstock, 1976).
The Adventures of a Nature Guide (Doubleday-Page, 1920; New Past Press, 1991).
Waiting in the Wilderness (Doubleday, Page, 1921).
Watched by Wild Animals (Doubleday, Page, 1922).
Wild Animal Homesteads (Doubleday, Page, 1923).

Rocky Mountain National Park (Doubleday, Page, 1924).
Romance of Geology (Doubleday, Page, 1926).
Bird Memories of the Rockies (Houghton Mifflin, 1931).

Selected Articles

"Dangers of Snow Slides," *Harper's Weekly*, December 24, 1904.

"At the Stream's Source," *Country Life in America*, September, 1910.

"Racing an Avalanche," *Country Life in America*, November, 1910.

"The Story of Scotch," *Country Life in America*, May, 1912.

"Beautiful America," *Country Life in America*, August, 1912.

"Touring in Our National Parks," *Country Life in America*, January, 1913.

"The Forest Fire," *Country Life in America*, January, 1915.

"The Battle Along the Timberline," *Country Life in America*, December, 1916.

"Twisted Trees," *Country Life in America*, January, 1920.

"A Home of Forest Fire Logs," *Sunset Magazine*, May 1921.

About Enos Mills

Enos Mills, "Who's Who—and Why: Enos A. Mills Himself, By Himself," *The Saturday Evening Post*, September, 1917.

Arthur Chapman, "Enos A. Mills, Nature Guide," *Country Life in America*, May, 1920.

Hildegarde Hawthorne and Esther Burnell Mills, *Enos Mills of the Rockies* (Houghton Mifflin, 1935).

Peter Wild, *Enos Mills* (Boise State University, Western Writers Series, 1979).